Authors In Depth

. . . .

THE AMERICAN EXPERIENCE

PRENTICE HALL
Upper Saddle River, New Jersey
Glenview, Illinois
Needham, Massachusetts

ISBN 0-13-050404-1

1 2 3 4 5 6 7 8 9 10   03 02 01 00 99

PRENTICE HALL

Acknowledgments

Grateful acknowledgment is made to the following for permission to reprint copyrighted material:

Susan Bergholz Literary Services
"Papi Working" from *The Other Side*/El Otro Lado. Copyright © 1995 by Julia Alvarez. Published by Dutton, a division of Penguin USA. "Storm Windows" from *Homecoming*. Copyright © 1984, 1996 by Julia Alvarez. Published by Plume, an imprint of Dutton Signet, a division of Penguin USA; originally published by Grove Press. "Snow" and "Writing Matters," copyright 1982, 1998 by Julia Alvarez. Published in *Something to Declare*, Algonquin Books of Chapel Hill, 1998. Both first appeared in a different version in *The Writer*, September 1998. "Snow" from *How the Garcia Girls Lost Their Accents*. Copyright © 1991 by Julia Alvarez. Published by Plume, an imprint of Dutton Signet, a division of Penguin USA, Inc., and originally in hardcover by Algonquin Books of Chapel Hill. Reprinted by permission of Susan Bergholz Literary Services, New York. All rights reserved.

Joan Chatfield-Taylor
Excerpts from "Cosmo Talks to Amy Tan" by Joan Chatfield-Taylor, from *Cosmopolitan*, November 1989.

Estate of Robert Frost
On "Choose Something Like a Star" by Robert Frost from *Richardson*, 320.

Harvard University Press
"Eldorado" from *Collected Works of Edgar Allan Poe, Volume I: Poems*, edited by Thomas Ollive Mabbott, Cambridge, Mass.: The Belknap Press of Harvard University Press. Copyright © 1969 by The President and Fellows of Harvard College. Reprinted by permission of the publisher. No. 4, 9, 10, 25, 43 and 47 of "Meditations Divine and Moral," "Here Follows Some Verses Upon The Burning Of Our House July 10th, 1666. Copied Out Of A Loose Paper," "Before The Birth Of One Of Her Children," and "A Letter To Her Husband, Absent Upon Public Employment" from *The Works of Anne Bradstreet*, edited by Jeannine Hensley. Copyright 1967 by the President and Fellows of Harvard College. All rights reserved.

Acknowledgments continue on page 206

ontents

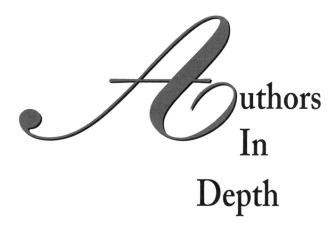

Authors
In
Depth

· · · ·

THE AMERICAN EXPERIENCE

*A*nne Bradstreet In Depth

"To have written poems, the first good poems in America, while rearing eight children, lying frequently sick, keeping house at the edge of wilderness, was to have managed a poet's range and extension within confines as severe as any American poet has confronted."

—Adrienne Rich

ANNE BRADSTREET'S poems are of significant importance in the history of American literature. Her poems are the first book of poems published by an American poet and the first book published by an American woman. Her place in literary history, however, doesn't explain why we enjoy reading her today. Something in the experience of one strong Puritan woman still speaks to the modern reader.

A Puritan Child Born in 1612 in Northampton, England, Anne Bradstreet never went to a school. Her father, a learned Puritan named Thomas Dudley, taught her himself and hired tutors for her.

Anne learned the Puritan view of life, that God was always present to watch what she did. Her obligation was always to learn to do what God would want. Later in her life, Bradstreet wrote a memoir for the benefit of her children. She told them that she learned by the age of seven that lying and disobeying her parents was sinful. She found that if she did something wrong, "I could not be at rest 'till by prayer I had confessed it unto God."

Marriage and Migration In the 1620's the Puritans feared imprisonment by the English government, and felt threatened that they might be unable to maintain their beliefs. One solution was to set up their own colony in the New World.

Anne was married at sixteen to Simon Bradstreet, the son of a Puritan minister. He was a twenty-five-year-old graduate of Cambridge University who worked for her father. Bradstreet traveled with her husband and parents to the Massachusetts Bay Colony in 1630. Conditions were very difficult on the long sea voyage. In the colony, there was sickness and hunger among the settlers.

A Hard Life Bradstreet's father and husband both served as officials of the new colony. Her father became governor while Anne lived, and her husband would become governor after her death. For most of her life, Anne Bradstreet coped with the problems of running a household, rearing her four boys and four girls, and supporting her husband in his work.

Early Poems Bradstreet's father had brought his books to the new colony. She continued to study and began writing verses based on what she read. She stayed active as a scholar and writer. As the daughter and wife of important officials, Bradstreet did not question the authority of leaders or ministers. In a style that imitated the poetry she had read, she presented the learning that they would think important, in poems designed to help a reader—and the writer—live a moral life.

It was not unusual at that time for people to write poems, but they wrote them for their friends or family members. They would not have intended them for publication. In the early years of the Massachusetts colony, there was only one printing press. It was used for printing psalms and other religious writings. Also, women were not encouraged as writers.

Publication Bradstreet's brother-in-law, John Woodbridge, didn't ask her, but he took a copy of her poems with him when he went to England. He found a publisher for them. In 1650, *The Tenth Muse Lately Sprung Up in America* was published. Bradstreet is not identified by name, but as "a Gentlewoman in those parts" [that is, America].

The book received a good deal of attention in England because readers were curious about life in the American wilderness, especially since the writer was a woman. When Bradstreet received a copy of her book, she wrote modestly about her reaction in a poem called "The Author to Her Book":

> At thy return my blushing was
>   not small,
>
> My rambling brat (in print)
>   should mother call.

Later Life Much of what we know about Bradstreet's last years comes from the details in the poems she wrote after her book was published. Many of them were collected after she died in 1672 and published in Boston in 1678. In the new collection she is still identified only as "a Gentlewoman in New-England."

The 1678 collection includes corrections and revisions that Bradstreet made in the poems from the 1650 book. The newer poems are more personal, presenting her own thoughts about religion, her husband, her children, and her daily life. She tries in her writing to balance her love for her life and her family with her duty to God's will.

Bradstreet's poems still appeal to the modern reader, because of their natural sense of being. These later poems are of her personal experiences and struggles.

◆ The Puritans

The Puritans wanted to return their religious practice to the simple ways of the early Christian church, as they understood it from the Bible. They wanted to rid themselves of elaborate rituals. They also rejected the leadership of bishops. These actions put them in conflict with the official Church of England, whose head was the ruling King or Queen.

A person's goal was heaven—his or her reward after death—while life was a series of tests by God of one's goodness and faith. Living simply was one way to demonstrate concentration on important matters. Many forms of entertainment, including the theater, were discouraged.

Cut off from their friends and relatives in England, life was especially hard for the New England Puritans. Strict obedience to community standards was required—anyone expressing doubts could be punished, and even banished from the community.

◆ Literary Works

Early Poems Written with the expectation that poetry should be useful, Bradstreet's collection of poems, *The Tenth Muse Lately Sprung Up in America*, was published in 1650. The poems demonstrate Bradstreet's knowledge of earlier poetry and her studies in religion, history, and science.

Later Poems After Bradstreet's death, a volume of her work was published with the title *Several Poems Compiled with Great Variety of Wit and Learning, Full of Delight*. They describe her feelings about her home, her family, her illnesses, and her personal search to accept God's will and to live a good, simple life. It was nearly two centuries later, in 1867, that her remaining works were published by John Harvard Ellis.

TIMELINE

Bradstreet's Life	World Events
1612 Anne Dudley is born in Northampton, England	**1603** Elizabeth I dies; James I becomes king; *Hamlet* is performed
1628 Suffers smallpox; marries Simon Bradstreet	**1605** *Don Quixote* is published
1630 Voyage to Massachusetts Bay Colony with parents and husband	**1607** English settle Jamestown, Virginia
1630–72 Moves from Salem to homes in Charlestown, Cambridge, Ipswich, and Andover	**1611** King James translation of Bible is published
1632–50 Writes several poems, sharing them with her family	**1618–48** Thirty Years' War in Europe
1633–52 Four sons and four daughters are born	**1619** First African slaves brought to North America
1634–35 First term as governor for her father, Thomas Dudley; he also serves 1640–41, 1645–46, and 1650–51	**1620** Pilgrims land at Plymouth, Massachusetts
1650 *The Tenth Muse Lately Sprung Up in America,* her book of poems, published in England	**1630** Migration of Puritans to Massachusetts begins
1650–72 Writes many of the poems that are now widely read	**1632** Building of Taj Mahal in India is begun
1661 Simon Bradstreet travels to England to work on new charter for the Bay Colony	**1633** John Donne's *Poems* published
	1642 Rembrandt paints *The Night Watch*
1664 Dedicates "Meditations Divine and Moral" to her son Simon	**1642–46** English Civil War
1672 Bradstreet dies, September 16	**1644** Manchus found Ch'ing Dynasty in China
1678 *The Tenth Muse* published in Boston, with new poems and revisions of old poems	**1649** King Charles I is executed
	1649–58 England ruled by Commonwealth and by Cromwell as Lord Protector
1679–86 Simon Bradstreet is governor of Massachusetts Bay Colony; also serves 1689–92	**1652** Sor Juana Ines de la Cruz, Mexican poet, is born
	1660 King Charles II restored to English throne
	1665 Great Plague in London; 70,000 die
	1667 Milton's *Paradise Lost* published
	1678 Bunyan *Pilgrim's Progress* published

Anne Bradstreet

Before the Birth of One of Her Children

All things within this fading world hath end,
Adversity doth still our joys attend;
No ties so strong, no friends so dear and sweet,
But with death's parting blow is sure to meet.
5   The sentence past is most irrevocable,
A common thing, yet oh, inevitable.
How soon, my Dear, death may my steps attend,
How soon't may be thy lot to lose thy friend,
We both are ignorant, yet love bids me
10   These farewell lines to recommend to thee,
That when that knot's untied that made us one,
I may seem thine, who in effect am none.
And if I see not half my days that's due,
What nature would, God grant to yours and you;
15   The many faults that well you know I have
Let be interred in my oblivious grave;
If any worth or virtue were in me,
Let that live freshly in thy memory
And when thou feel'st no grief, as I no harms,
20   Yet love thy dead, who long lay in thine arms.
And when thy loss shall be repaid with gains
Look to my little babes, my dear remains.
And if thou love thyself, or loved'st me,
These O protect from step-dame's[1] injury.
25   And if chance to thine eyes shall bring this verse,
With some sad sighs honor my absent hearse;
And kiss this paper for thy love's dear sake,
Who with salt tears this last farewell did take.

---

1. step-dame's: Stepmother's

Anne Bradstreet

A Letter to Her Husband, Absent Upon Public Employment

My head, my heart, mine eyes, my life, nay, more,
My joy, my magazine[1] of earthly store,
If two be one, as surely thou and I,
How stayest thou there, whilst I at Ipswich[2] lie?
5   So many steps, head from the heart to sever,
If but a neck, soon should we be together.
I, like the Earth this season, mourn in black,
My Sun is gone so far in's zodiac,
Whom whilst I 'joyed, nor storms, nor frost I felt,
10 His warmth such frigid colds did cause to melt.
My chilled limbs now numbed lie forlorn;
Return, return, sweet Sol, from Capricorn;[3]
In this dead time, alas, what can I more
Than view those fruits which through thy heat I bore?
15 Which sweet contentment yield me for a space,
True living pictures of their father's face.
O strange effect! now thou art southward gone,
I weary grow the tedious day so long;
But when thou northward to me shalt return,
20 I wish my Sun may never set, but burn
Within the Cancer[4] of my glowing breast,
The welcome house of him my dearest guest.
Where ever, ever stay, and go not thence,
Till nature's sad decree shall call thee hence;
25 Flesh of thy flesh, bone of thy bone,
I here, thou there, yet both but one.

---

1. **magazine** (mag′ ə zēn′) *n.*: Storage place.
2. **Ipswich:** City north of Boston.
3. **Capricorn** (Kap′ ri kôrn′) *n.*: Tenth sign of the zodiac, representing winter, beginning about December 22.
4. **Cancer** (Kan′ sər) *n.*: Fourth sign of the zodiac, representing summer, entered by the sun about June 21.

Upon the Burning of Our House July 10TH, 1666

In silent night when rest I took
For sorrow near I did not look
I wakened was with thund'ring noise
And piteous shrieks of dreadful voice.
5   That fearful sound of "Fire!" and "Fire!"
Let no man know is my desire.
I, starting up, the light did spy,
And to my God my heart did cry
To strengthen me in my distress
10   And not to leave me succorless.
Then, coming out, beheld a space
The flame consume my dwelling place.
And when I could no longer look,
I blest His name that gave and took,
15   That laid my goods now in the dust.
Yea, so it was, and so 'twas just.
It was His own, it was not mine,
Far be it that I should repine;
He might of all justly bereft
20   But yet sufficient for us left.
When by the ruins oft I past
My sorrowing eyes aside did cast,
And here and there the places spy
Where oft I sat and long did lie:
25   Here stood that trunk, and there that chest,
There lay that store I counted best.
My pleasant things in ashes lie,
And them behold no more shall I.
Under thy roof no guest shall sit,
30   Nor at thy table eat a bit.
No pleasant tale shall e'er be told,
Nor things recounted done of old.
No candle e'er shall shine in thee,
Nor bridegroom's voice e'er heard shall be.

35   In silence ever shall thou lie,
        Adieu, Adieu,[1] all's vanity.
        Then straight I 'gin my heart to chide,
        And did thy wealth on earth abide?
        Didst fix thy hope on mold'ring dust?
40   The arm of flesh didst make thy trust?
        Raise up thy thoughts above the sky
        That dunghill mists away may fly.
        Thou hast an house on high erect,
        Framed by that mighty Architect,
45   With glory richly furnished,
        Stands permanent though this be fled.
        It's purchased and paid for too
        By Him who hath enough to do.
        A price so vast as is unknown
50   Yet by His gift is made thine own;
        There's wealth enough, I need no more,
        Farewell, my pelf,[2] farewell my store.
        The world no longer let me love,
        My hope and treasure lies above.

---

1. Adieu (ə dyoo´): Farewell (French).
2. pelf *n*.: Money or wealth regarded with contempt.

☑ Check Your Comprehension

1. (a) Assuming the speaker of "Before the Birth of One of Her Children" is Anne Bradstreet, to whom is it addressed? (b) What fear about childbirth is the reason for the poem?

2. Name three things that the speaker of "Before the Birth of One of Her Children" requests of her "Dear" in the event of her death.

3. (a) In "A Letter to Her Husband," what are the "fruits" that the speaker bore (line 14)? (b) What is the "Cancer" that she refers to in line 21? Why is it important to her?

4. Why does the speaker of "Upon the Burning of Our House" say God was just in laying "my goods now in the dust" (lines 19–20)?

5. Why does the speaker "'gin my heart to chide" (line 41) in "Upon the Burning of Our House"? (b) What better house is she looking forward to?

◆ Critical Thinking

1. The likelihood of death in childbirth is much less today than it was in Bradstreet's time. How might the focus of the poem "Before the Birth of One of Her Children" be written today? **[Modify]**

2. In what ways does the speaker of "A Letter to Her Husband" suggest she resembles the earth and her husband the sun? **[Analyze]**

3. How do you think people's attitudes differ from Bradstreet's time and what she expresses in "Upon the Burning of Our House"? Explain your answer. **[Relate]**

COMPARE LITERARY WORKS

4. Both "Before the Birth of One of Her Children" and "Upon the Burning of Our House" deal with what will happen after the speaker's death. Which description seems more personal and emotional? **[Distinguish]**

Anne Bradstreet

from Meditations Divine and Mor

4

A ship that bears much sail and little or no ballast is easily
overset, and that man whose head hath great abilities and his
heart little or no grace is in danger of foundering.

9

Sweet words are like honey: a little may refresh, but too much
gluts the stomach.

10

Diverse children have their different natures: some are like
flesh which nothing but salt will keep from putrefaction, some
again like tender fruits that are best preserved with sugar.
Those parents are wise that can fit their nurture according to
their nature

19

Corn, till it have passed through the mill and been ground to
powder, is not fit for bread. God so deals with his servants: he
grinds them with grief and pain till they turn to dust, and
then are they fit manchet for his mansion.

25

An aching head requires a soft pillow, and a drooping heart a strong support.

43

Fire hath its force abated by water, not by wind, and anger must be allayed by cold words and not by blustering threats.

47

A shadow in the parching sun and a shelter in a blustering storm are of all seasons the most welcome; so a faithful friend in time of adversity is of all other most comfortable.

☑ Check Your Comprehension

1. In Meditation 9, what two things would the speaker consider excessive?
2. In Meditation 10, what kinds of nurture by parents would be like "salt" and "sugar"?
3. (a) Who are the "servants" referred to in Meditation 19? (b) Does the speaker suggest it is a good thing to be ground "with grief and pain till they turn to dust"? Why or why not?

◆ Critical Thinking

1. Many of the "Meditations" use an example from daily life or nature to point out a conclusion about people's spiritual or mental life. Find two of the "Meditations" in which this is true. Explain how, in each one, the example from real life resembles an aspect of a person's spiritual life. **[Support]**
2. In Mediation 25, what are some possibilities of what "a drooping heart" could represent? **[Infer]**
3. Choose one of the "Meditations" and explain how an event in your own life—or an incident you know about—could serve as an illustration of Bradstreet's point. **[Relate]**

Comparing and Connecting the Author's Works

◆ **Literary Focus: Paradox**

In her poems Bradstreet often makes use of a paradox. A **paradox** is a statement that seems to be contradictory, but that actually presents something true. Because a paradox is surprising, it draws the reader's attention to whatever is being expressed.

For example, lines 3–4 of "A Letter to Her Husband" ask, "If two be one"— as the speaker and her husband are— "How stayest thou there, whilst I at Ipswich lie?" In one sense, a husband and wife can be said to be "one," since they are united in marriage and love. In all other senses, of course, they are separate people. The speaker can be in the town of Ipswich while her husband is somewhere else. The paradox calls attention to some aspects of the union of husband and wife.

1. Find another statement of the same paradox in "A Letter to My Husband."

2. Describe the paradox in lines 18–19 of "Upon the Burning of Our House."

3. What is the paradox in lines 53–54 of "Upon the Burning of Our House"?

◆ **Drawing Conclusions About Bradstreet's Work**

Bradstreet often writes about the contrast between the enjoyment of life on the one hand and the realities of loss or death on the other. Below is a chart showing a few of these contrasts in "Before the Birth of One of Her Children." Draw a similar chart in which you show the contrasts in one of the other poems. Write a paragraph about the importance of the contrasts to the meaning of the poem.

Earthly Pleasures	Realities of Loss or Death
Friends are "dear and sweet."	They are sure to meet with "death's parting blow."
There is a "knot ... that made us one ...."	Death may untie it.
He might "kiss this paper for thy love's dear sake ...."	She "with salt tears this last farewell did take."

◆ **Idea Bank**

Writing

1. **Letter** "Before the Birth of One of Her Children" expresses the speaker's feelings about her husband. She fears that childbirth could cause her death, and has written a letter of farewell. Imagine moving to a distant state or country. Write a letter to someone you know, assuming you may not see each other again.

2. **Fiction** Choose one of the "Meditations Divine and Moral." Decide what point it makes about life. Write a story or dramatic scene that illustrates the point made in the "Meditation."

3. **Poem** Write a poem in Anne Bradstreet's style. Choose a subject about which you can make an interesting point. Note that Bradstreet usually writes in rhyming iambic pentameter (lines of five "feet," each consisting of an unstressed syllable followed by a stressed syllable) or iambic tetrameter (four "feet"). Draw a chart like the one below and fill in three lines from Bradstreet that show how the words fit the iambic pentameter pattern. When writing your

own iambic verse, it's okay to sometimes vary the pattern of accents or to add an extra syllable or use one syllable less.

⌣ ⁄ ⌣ ⁄ ⌣ ⁄ ⌣ ⁄ ⌣ ⁄
And when thy loss shall be repaid with gains

Speaking and Listening

4. **Dramatic Presentation** Working with a small group, choose one of Bradstreet's poems. Decide how to present the poem as a performance piece. Divide the lines between two or more speakers. Find appropriate music to play in the background, either live or from recordings. Decide whether to use costumes or props. **[Group Activity; Performing Arts Link]**

Researching and Representing

5. **Report** In the library, research the history of the Puritans in England and New England. Find one aspect of their history that provides background for Anne Bradstreet's life or writing. Write a short report of what you find. **[History Link]**

6. **Artists** While Bradstreet lived (1612–78), other artists were active. The Puritans discouraged the visual arts, but visual artists created many important works. (a) Find reproductions of Rembrandt's paintings. Write down your impressions. Do the people in his portraits resemble the people you imagine in Bradstreet's world? Why or why not? (b) Compare the simplicity of Puritan life with the extravagance of the Taj Mahal, which was built in India during Bradstreet's lifetime. Tell which you prefer. **[Art Link]**

◆ Further Reading, Listening, and Viewing

The Works of Anne Bradstreet (Belknap Press, Harvard University, 1981)

John Demos: *A Little Commonwealth; Family Life in Plymouth Colony* (Oxford University Press, 1971)

Anne Bradstreet: A Reference Guide (Macmillan, 1990)

Richard Middleton: *Colonial America; A History 1585–1776* (Blackwell 1996)

Simple Gifts: Shaker Chants and Spirituals (Erato, 1995). The Boston Camerata, directed by Joel Cohen. Audio CD

Tom Shachtman: *The Most Beautiful Villages of New England* (Thames and Hudson, 1997)

On the Web:

http://www.phschool.com/atschool/literature
Go to the student edition of *The American Experience*. Proceed to Unit 1. Then, click Hot Links to find Web sites featuring Anne Bradstreet.

$\mathcal{E}$dward Taylor In Depth

> "... had the poetry of Edward Taylor been published during his lifetime, he would long since have taken a place among the major figures of colonial American literature."
> —*Thomas H. Johnson*

EDWARD TAYLOR'S poems provide the modern reader with little that seems familiar. His world can seem as distant or strange as another galaxy. Its setting is the wilderness of 300 years ago; its subject is religious salvation.

The Unknown Poet

Considered the best poet of colonial America, Taylor was unknown in his own time and for almost two hundred years thereafter.

Some people write to clarify their own thoughts. This need probably motivated Taylor's best work, *Preparatory Meditations*. These poems were written as part of his religious practice as a minister.

Religion and Study

Religion was part of all the important events of Taylor's life. He was born into a Puritan family in England in 1642. By the time he was a schoolteacher in the 1660's, it was difficult for Puritans to teach, preach, or practice their religion in England. Taylor's refusal to sign the 1662 Act of Uniformity most likely kept him from a teaching or clerical career. Taylor ultimately exiled himself and sailed to the Massachusetts Bay Colony in 1668.

After arriving in Boston, he enrolled at Harvard College. A Harvard education, designed to prepare ministers, included Latin, Greek, Hebrew, logic, philosophy, and astronomy. Soon after his graduation, he met with some men from a farming village at the western edge of the Bay Colony. These men from Westfield were looking for a minister for their town. Taylor accepted their offer and stayed in Westfield until his death fifty-eight years later.

Minister of Westfield

The villagers built Taylor a log house. The next year they built a church, strong enough to be useful if Westfield were attacked by hostile Native Americans.

Taylor married Elizabeth Fitch, the well-educated daughter of a minister, in 1674. Their union produced eight children, but five died before their first birthdays. Elizabeth Fitch Taylor died at age thirty-nine. Marrying again when he was forty-seven, Taylor and his second wife, Ruth Wyllys, had six children.

Taylor had a long career as minister and distinguished citizen of Westfield. He tended his own farm and served as physician for the town. His grandson later wrote that he was "A man of small stature but firm: of quick Passions—yet serious and grave."

Taylor had an impressive library for his time—220 books. Many of these he copied by hand from borrowed volumes, as books were rare in the colonies. The only book of English poetry in his library was Anne Bradstreet's *The Tenth Muse*.

Taylor's Poems

From the 1670's until his death in 1729, Taylor wrote the poems for which he is now esteemed and remembered. They were meant to be inspirational. The speaker is directly involved in the struggle of faith. In the tradition of the English poets he studied, Taylor often uses striking comparisons in unusual language. He combines religious ideas with images of the daily life of New England or the English countryside of his youth.

The only publication in his lifetime was two stanzas from one poem, quoted in another minister's sermon, which was then published in England. Late in his life, Taylor bound 400 pages of his poems in a leather binding. The volume was passed on to his descendants. A great-grandson donated the volume to the Yale University library, where it was rediscovered in the 1930's.

◆ The Puritans and the Native Americans

When the English first came to North America, they brought with them many diseases to which Native Americans had no natural immunity. Smallpox could wipe out as much as 75 percent of a native settlement's people in weeks.

Beginning in the 1630's, thousands of Puritans came to the Massachusetts Bay Colony to establish what they envisioned as God's kingdom on earth. The decimated native population seemed to reinforce the Puritans' belief that New England was God's intended homeland for true believers. Efforts were made to bring the natives under the laws of the colony and to convert them to Christianity.

In 1675, after pressure from the English in Plymouth Colony to give up their land and pay taxes, a Wampanoag Indian chief known as King Philip attacked English settlements in Plymouth and the Bay Colony. Other tribes joined both sides, and King Philip's War began.

For a while it appeared that the Native Americans might drive the colonists from New England, but Philip's forces were seriously outnumbered. Fierce fighting by the colonists, and the capture and killing of Philip in 1676, ended the war. Many on both sides lost their lives, making this the bloodiest war, relative to the population, in American history.

◆ Literary Works

Taylor's large output of work, including some miscellaneous short poems, like "Upon a Spider Catching a Fly," was organized by his own hand in manuscript form. Publication began only in the 1930's.

God's Determinations touching the Elect was probably finished in the early 1680's. It is a collection of short poems about a Christian's relationship with God, and may have been intended to instruct his parishioners.

From 1682 to 1725, Taylor worked on his most important poems, the *Preparatory Meditations.* Each of these 221 poems was written to bring him to the right state of mind for preaching a sermon and offering communion to his congregation. In the *Preparatory Meditations* we see the drama of a person's private thoughts as he works to perfect his relationship with his God.

TIMELINE

Taylor's Life

1642	Edward Taylor is born in Leicestershire, England
1657	Taylor's mother dies
1658	Taylor's father dies
1662	Taylor refuses to sign the Act of Uniformity (against Puritanism); loses teaching job
1668	Sails to Massachusetts Bay Colony; enters Harvard College
1671	Graduates from Harvard; goes to Westfield to be minister
1673	Church built in Westfield
1674	Marries Elizabeth Fitch
1675–88	Eight children born to Taylor and his wife
1679	Ordained as minister of Westfield
1680's	Completes writing of *God's Determinations*
1682–1725	Writes *Preparatory Meditations*
1689	Marries Ruth Wyllys
1693–1708	Six children born
1720	Harvard honors him with a master's degree
1729	Dies; buried in Westfield

World Events

1643	New England Confederation unites Massachusetts Bay, Plymouth, and Connecticut colonies
1648	End of Thirty Years' War in Europe
1652	Cape Town, South Africa, settled by Dutch
1656	Bible translated into a Native American dialect
1664	English capture New Amsterdam and name it New York; Ottoman Turks occupy Hungary
1666	Isaac Newton invents calculus
1675–76	King Philip's War
1680's	Asante kingdom prospers in West Africa
1681	Pennsylvania founded by William Penn, a Quaker
1685–88	James II is king of England
1688	Revolution in England; William of Orange becomes king
1690	Calcutta, India, founded by English
1707	England and Scotland unite as Great Britain
1719	Defoe publishes *Robinson Crusoe*
1721	Bach writes Brandenburg Concertos
1727	Swift's *Gulliver's Travels* published

Edward Taylor

Prologue

from Preparatory Meditations

Lord, can a crumb of dust the earth outweigh,
    Outmatch all mountains, nay the crystal sky?
Embosom in't designs that shall display
    And trace into the boundless deity?
5   Yea hand a pen whose moisture doth gild o'er
    Eternal glory with a glorious glore.[1]

If it its pen had of an angel's quill,
    And sharpened on a precious stone ground tight,
And dipped in liquid gold, and moved by skill
10   In crystal leaves should golden letters write
    It would but blot and blur yea jag, and jar
    Unless thou mak'st the pen, and scrivener.[2]

I am this crumb of dust which is designed
    To make my pen unto Thy praise alone,
15 And my dull fancy[3] I would gladly grind
    Unto an edge on Zion's[4] precious stone.
    And write in liquid gold upon thy name
    My letters till Thy glory forth doth flame.

Let not th'attempts break down my dust I pray
20   Nor laugh thou them to scorn but pardon give.
Inspire this crumb of dust till it display
    Thy glory throughout: and then thy dust shall live.
    Its failings then thou'lt overlook I trust,
    They being slips slipped from Thy crumb of dust.

25 Thy crumb of dust breathes two words from its breast,
    That Thou wilt guide its pen to write aright
To prove Thou art, and that Thou are the best
    And show Thy properties to shine most bright.
    And then Thy works will shine as flowers on stems
30   Or as in jewelry shops, do gems.

---

1. **glore:** Glow, shine, glitter.
2. **scrivener** (skriv′ ən ər) *n.*: Scribe; clerk.
3. **fancy:** Imagination.
4. **Zion** (zi ən) *n.*: Hill in Jerusalem on which the Jews built their temple.

Edward Taylor

The Preface

from God's Determinations

Infinity, when all things it beheld
In nothing, and of nothing all did build,
Upon what base was fixed the lathe, wherein
He turned this Globe, and riggalled[1] it so trim?
5   Who blew the bellows of his furnace vast
Or held the mould wherein the world was cast?
Who laid its corner stone[2]? Or whose command?
Where stand the pillars upon which it stands?
Who laced and filletted[3] the earth so fine,
10   With rivers like green ribbons smaragdine?[4]
Who made the seas its selveage, and it locks
Like a quilt ball within a silver box?
Who spread its canopy? Or curtains spun?
Who in this bowling alley bowled the sun?
15   Who made it always when it rises set
To go at once both down, and up to get?
Who the curtain rods made for this tapestry?
Who hung the twinkling lanterns in the sky?
Who? Who did this? Or who is he? Why, know
20   It's only Might Almighty this did do.
His hand hath made this noble work which stands
His glorious handiwork not made by hands.
Who spake all things from nothing; and with ease
Can speak all things to nothing, if He please.
25   Whose little finger at His pleasure can
Out mete[5] ten thousand worlds with half a span;
Whose might almighty can by half a looks
Root up the rocks and rock the hills by the roots.
Can take this mighty world up in His hand,
30   And shake it like a squitchen[6] or a wand.

---

1. **riggalled:** Grooved.
2. **corner stone:** Foundation.
3. **filletted:** Bound and decorated with ornamental lines.
4. **smaragdine**, later **smeragdite** (smə rag′ dīt) *n.*: Bright green.
5. **mete** (mēt) *n.*: Measure.
6. **Squitchen:** Shield.

Whose single frown will make the heavens shake
Like as an aspen leaf the wind makes quake.
Oh! What a might is this whose single frown
Doth shake the world as it would shake it down?
35 Which all from nothing fetched, from nothing, all:
Hath all on nothing set, lets nothing fall.
Gave all to nothing man indeed, whereby
Through nothing man all might him glorify.
In nothing then embossed the brightest gem
40 More precious than all preciousness in them.
By nothing man did throw down all by sin:
And darkened that lightsome gem in him.
That now his brightest diamond is grown
Darker by far than any coalpit stone.

*E*dward Taylor

Upon a Spider Catching a Fly

Thou sorrow, venom elf.
   Is this thy play,
To spin a web out of thyself
   To catch a fly?
5   For why?

I saw a pettish[1] wasp
   Fall foul therein.
Whom yet thy whorl pins did not clasp
   Lest he should fling
10   His sting.

But as afraid, remote
   Didst stand hereat
And with thy little fingers stroke
   And gently tap
15   His back.

Thus gently him didst treat
   Lest he should pet,
And in a froppish,[2] waspish heat
   Should greatly fret
20   Thy net.

Whereas the silly fly,
   Caught by its leg
Thou by the throat tookst hastily
   And behind the head
25   Bite dead.

This goes to pot, that not
   Nature doth call.
Strive not above what strength hath got
   Lest in the brawl
30   Thou fall.

---

1. **pettish** *adj.*: Peevish, ill-humored.
2. **froppish** *adj.*: Fretful.

This fray seems thus to us.
    Hell's spider gets
His entrails spun to whip cords thus
    And wove to nets
35   And sets.

To tangle Adam's race
    In his stratagems
To their destruction, spoiled, made base
    By venom things
40   Damned sins.

But mighty, gracious Lord
    Communicate
Thy grace to break the cord, afford
    Us glory's gate
45   And state.

We'll nightingale sing like
    When perched on high
In glory's cage, Thy glory, bright,
    And thankfully,
50   For joy.

☑ Check Your Comprehension

1. In the "Prologue," why does the speaker describe himself as a "crumb of dust"?
2. In the final stanza of the "Prologue," what three things does the speaker want God to help him write about?
3. In "The Preface," what is shown by such actions as turning the earth on a lathe (lines 3-4), using the sun as a bowling ball (line 14), or speaking all things from nothing (line 23)?
4. Even though God, in "The Preface," "gave all to nothing man" (line 37), what did man do in return?
5. In "Upon a Spider Catching a Fly," in what ways does God overcome the Devil ("Hell's spider," line 32)?

◆ Critical Thinking

INTERPRET
1. In the second stanza of "Prologue," if a man uses a quill from an angel's wing for a pen, sharpens it on a precious stone, uses liquid gold for ink, and writes on crystal leaves, what else is needed to prevent blotting, blurring, jagging, and jarring of his writing? **[Interpret]**

APPLY
2. What would the examples of God's power in "The Preface," suggest to a reader about the actions of "nothing man" at the end of the poem? **[Speculate]**

INTERPRET
3. In "Upon a Spider Catching a Fly," what do the actions of spider, fly, and wasp have to do with God, "Hell's Spider," and "Adam's race"? **[Connect]**

COMPARE LITERARY WORKS
4. How do the "gems" in line 30 of "Prologue" compare with the "gem" in line 42 of "The Preface"? **[Compare and Contrast]**

Edward Taylor
Comparing and Connecting the Author's Works

◆ Literary Focus: Similes and Metaphors

Modern readers are often impressed by the vivid images in Taylor's poems. The comparisons he implies can be unusual. For instance, in "The Preface," God "bowled the sun" in the "bowling alley" of the heavens. The sun and a bowling ball are both round, of course. But the sun is vastly larger; only God, Taylor implies, would have the power to bowl with it. In the same poem, God's "single form will make the heavens shake/Like as an aspen leaf the wind makes quake." For the heavens to shake like a leaf in the wind, enormous power would be needed.

When a comparison between two unlike objects is expressed with the word *like* or *as,* the figure of speech is a **simile**, as in the second example. In a **metaphor**, one object is spoken of as if it were another, without the word *like* or *as.* In another metaphor in "The Preface," God "held the mold wherein the world was cast," comparing the creation of the earth with the molding of metal by a craftsman.

1. Find an example of one simile and one metaphor in Taylor's works. For each one, write a statement of the two objects, qualities, or beings that are being compared. What do they have in common? What differences are there between them?
2. Sit beside a window. Write a paragraph or poem to describe what you can see outside. Use at least two similes and two metaphors in your description.

◆ Drawing Conclusions About Taylor's Work

Most of Taylor's poems deal with the relations between people and God.

Sometimes a lesson is taught about God's power or mercy. Sometimes the speaker describes his own struggle with the difficulties of leading a life that honors God.

"Prologue," "The Preface," and "Upon a Spider Catching a Fly" all include examples of the power of God in relation to humanity. The chart below shows some examples from "Upon a Spider Catching a Fly." Make a similar chart for either "Prologue" or "The Preface."

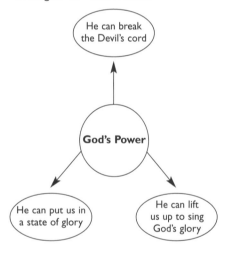

◆ Idea Bank

Writing

1. **Letter** Imagine being Edward Taylor, living in the small village of Westfield in the 1600's. Imagine what your activities would be like. Write a letter to a friend from your college days who now lives in Boston. Describe what your life is like.
2. **Poem** Write a poem that includes an unusual metaphor. Start by thinking of a striking comparison, such as "My room is a swamp." Use a diagram like the following to jot down features that are the same or different:

My Room

in a house
I could get it organized
created by a person

You can get lost in it
confusing
wild mixture of things

natural
many living things
open to weather

Swamp

Write a short poem based on your metaphor and the details you listed.

3. **Meditation** Many of Taylor's poems are meditations about human life and religion. Choose a topic that you are interested in. Jot down things you know about the topic, as well as fantasies and ideas about it that come to mind. Write your meditation as a poem or paragraphs that imitate your thinking about the topic. Try to reach a conclusion by the end of your meditation.

Speaking and Listening

4. **Sermon** Many sermons of the Puritan era have been published, including some of Edward Taylor's. Find one in the library or on the Internet. Prepare 3–5 minutes of it as an oral presentation to other students. Try to suggest the effectiveness of the message and wording to a Puritan congregation. **[Performing Arts Link]**

Researching and Representing

5. **Native American Culture** Like many of his contemporaries, Edward Taylor did not seem to pay much attention to the culture of the Native Americans of New England. The native population, however, had a rich culture of arts, foods, beliefs, and storytelling. Find out what you can about the Native Americans of seventeenth-century New England and share it with your class. **[Art and Social Studies Link]**

6. **Debate** Prepare a debate between groups representing Native Americans and Puritans in the Massachusetts of the 1670's. In the library, find out about issues of land ownership, living under Colonial laws, and religious conversion. Learn what each group said about the other. Form two teams to argue for and against the proposition: All Native Americans must obey all the laws of the Massachusetts Bay Colony. **[Social Studies Link; Group Activity]**

◆ Further Reading, Listening, and Viewing

- *Poems Of Edward Taylor*, Donald Stanford, ed.: Univ. of North Carolina, 1989
- *Tayloring Shop: Essays on the Poetry of Edward Taylor in Honor of Thomas M. and Virginia L. Davis*, University of Delaware Press, 1997
- James Collier: *Pilgrims And Puritans*, Marshall Cavendish Corporation, 1997
- *Trav'ling Home: American Spirituals 1770–1870*, The Boston Camerata, directed by Joel Cohen, audio CD, Erato 1996
- *The Crucible*, Repertory Theatre of Lincoln Center, 2 audiocassettes

On the Web:

http://www.phschool.com/atschool/literature
Go to the student edition of *The American Experience*. Proceed to Unit 1. Then, click Hot Links to find Web sites featuring Edward Taylor.

Benjamin Franklin In Depth

> "He that can compose himself, is wiser than he that composes books."
>
> —*Benjamin Franklin*

BEN FRANKLIN'S distinguished career as a diplomat was only one facet of a remarkable and varied life. Printer, scientist, inventor, and politician, Franklin was also an important and quintessentially American writer. His famous *Autobiography* brings to life the exciting and tumultuous era that led to the American Revolution.

Puritan Origins Benjamin Franklin's father, Josiah, came to New England seeking the freedom to practice his religion. He, his wife, and their three young children settled in Boston, where Benjamin was born in 1706. Franklin left school after only two years to work first in his father's candlemaking shop, then, at age twelve, in his older brother's printing shop.

What Franklin lacked in formal schooling, he made up through voracious reading. In addition to John Locke and other philosophers, he studied the essays of Joseph Addison and Richard Steele, as well as books on navigation, arithmetic, and Greek philosophy. By age sixteen, Franklin was publishing essays in his brother's weekly newspaper under the pseudonym "Silence Dogood." One of his essays contained this plea for freedom of speech:

"Without freedom of thought, there can be no such thing as wisdom; and no such thing as publick liberty, without freedom of speech; which is the right of every man, as far as by it, he does not hurt and control the right of another: and this is the only check it ought to suffer, and the only bounds it ought to know."

To Philadelphia Benjamin worked for his brother's paper from 1718 to 1723, during which time he mastered the printing trade and honed his writing skills.

Franklin left his apprenticeship and ran away to Philadelphia, where he found work as a printer.

By 1729, Franklin was publishing and writing for his own newspaper, the *Pennsylvania Gazette*. It became the most popular newspaper in the colonies.

In 1730, he entered into a common-law marriage with Deborah Read. Their relationship lasted forty-four years, until she died. She and Franklin had three children.

Important Citizen In 1732, Franklin began publishing *Poor Richard's Almanack*, which introduced readers to the fictional homespun philosopher Poor Richard. The almanac was published annually, until 1757. In addition to facts about tides and phases of the moon, it included such practical proverbs as "Early to bed and early to rise, makes a man healthy, wealthy, and wise."

Franklin's interest in social and political matters found voice in his publications. In pamphlets and articles, he argued for a public library, a voluntary fire company, and increased communication among scientists throughout the colonies. He often reported on his own scientific experiments and inventions, including his fascination (shared by many in the eighteenth century) with electricity. In his widely translated book *Experiments and Observations on Electricity* (1751), he proposed an experiment similar to his later attempt to fly a kite in a thunderstorm. For this book, he was awarded honorary doctorates from British universities, and as his fame spread throughout Europe, he became known as "Doctor Franklin."

Diplomat Between the years 1757 and 1764, Franklin made two diplomatic missions to England. He disputed unjust policies, such as the unpopular Stamp Act, imposed by the King and Parliament to further their control of the colonies. In London, he befriended many writers, scientists, and politicians.

He also published numerous articles on political issues. His writings reflect his skepticism about possible reconciliation between the British government and the American colonies.

Revolution Franklin left England in 1775, just before the outbreak of the Revolutionary War. He immediately joined the Continental Congress and helped draft the Declaration of Independence. Franklin was the oldest signer of the document.

In 1776, Congress sent Franklin to France to seek economic and military aid. Franklin was successful. His years in France were marked by great diplomatic success and popularity, especially among fashionable French society. When the Revolutionary War ended in 1783, Franklin was one of the signers of the peace treaty between Britain and the United States.

Last Years Franklin returned to the United States in 1785, as one of its most highly regarded citizens. He helped write the Constitution and joined the campaign to abolish slavery. He also worked on his *Autobiography*, chronicling his life up to 1757. At his death in 1790, he was widely eulogized as a great American.

◆ **The Enlightenment**

After centuries of disagreements about religion and warfare, a new spirit emerged in Europe during the 1700's. Called the Enlightenment or the Age of Reason, it was a period when scientists and philosophers began to investigate nature, human life, and society free from the restrictions of religious belief, and outdated governments and laws. Enlightenment philosophers argued that it was the individual's right to decide how to live and that progress would be achieved through education and increasing reliance on scientific reasoning.

In America, Benjamin Franklin, a devoted scientist and practical philosopher, helped to spread Enlightenment ideas through his writings. Franklin and others incorporated many of these ideas into the Declaration of Independence and the United States Constitution.

◆ **Literary Works**

Short Works From an early age, Franklin wrote articles and essays on his life and times. His letters to friends and public figures reveal his wit and clarity and speak to us of everyday life in the eighteenth century.

The Dogood Papers (1722); (articles written for the New-England Courant)
Articles and proposals written in Philadelphia (1729–55)
Articles and essays written in London (1757–75)
Essays and letters written in Paris (1776–85)
Speeches given in Philadelphia (1785–90)

Longer Works Franklin's longer works are also his best known. Like his essays and articles, they fall into the category of non-fiction prose. Franklin wrote annual volumes of *Poor Richard's Almanack* from 1732–57. He began writing his *Autobiography* in 1771, worked on it again in 1784, 1788, and just before his death in 1790. The uncompleted work was published after his death.

Poor Richard (1732–57)
Autobiography (published in complete form in 1874)

T I M E L I N E

Franklin's Life		World Events	
1706	Born in Boston, Massachusetts	1715	Japan's leading playwright, Chikamatsu Monzaemon, writes *The Battles of Coxinga*
1718	Apprenticed in his brother's printing shop	1718	Death of William Penn, founder of Pennsylvania
1722	Publishes "Silence Dogood" essays	1726	Swift's *Gulliver's Travels* published
1723	Runs away to Philadelphia	1735	Trial of Peter Zenger in New York helps establish freedom of the press
1724	Works in London as printer		
1726	Returns to Philadelphia		
1728	Starts his printing business		
1730	Marries Deborah Read	1739	Hume's *Treatise on Human Nature* published
1731	Founds the Philadelphia Library		
1732	Begins publishing *Poor Richard's Almanack*	1742	Handel's *Messiah* first performed
		1754–63	French and Indian War
1748	Sells his printing business and retires from business	1759	Voltaire's *Candide* published
		1762	Rousseau's *Social Contract* published
1751	Publishes *Experiments and Observations on Electricity*		
1752	Flies a kite in a storm, proving that lightning is a form of electricity	1765	Stamp Act provokes resistance in British colonies
1757	Travels to London as a diplomat for the Pennsylvania Assembly	1769	James Watt designs and patents a steam engine with a separate condenser
1762	Returns to Philadelphia	1772–75	Captain James Cook explores the Pacific Ocean
1764	Travels to London as a diplomat for Pennsylvania and three other colonies	1773	Boston Tea Party
		1774	Joseph Priestley discovers oxygen
1774	His wife, Deborah Franklin, dies	1776	Declaration of Independence
1775	Returns to Philadelphia and joins the Continental Congress	1781	Cornwallis surrenders to Washington
1776	Signs the Declaration of Independence; travels to France to arrange an alliance	1783	First flight in a hot-air balloon
		1789	French Revolution begins; George Washington elected first President
1785	Returns to Philadelphia		
1787	Sent by Pennsylvania as a delegate to the Constitutional Convention	1792	Denmark becomes the first country to ban the slave trade; Mary Wollstonecraft publishes *A Vindication of the Rights of Women*; Thomas Paine publishes *The Rights of Man*
1790	Dies in Philadelphia		

Benjamin Franklin

Autobiography

At the age of seventeen, Benjamin Franklin left Boston and traveled to Philadelphia, where he hoped to establish his own printing business. The following excerpt relates events that occurred when he arrived in Philadelphia.

When about sixteen years of age I happened to meet with a book, written by one Tryon, recommending a vegetable diet. I determined to go into it. My brother, being yet unmarried, did not keep house, but boarded himself and his apprentices in another family. My refusing to eat flesh occasioned an inconveniency, and I was frequently chided for my singularity. I made myself acquainted with Tryon's manner of preparing some of his dishes, such as boiling potatoes or rice, making hasty pudding, and a few others, and then proposed to my brother, that if he would give me, weekly, half the money he paid for my board, I would board myself. He instantly agreed to it, and I presently found that I could save half what he paid me. This was an additional fund for buying books. But I had another advantage in it. My brother and the rest going from the printing-house to their meals, I remained there alone, and, despatching presently my light repast, which often was no more than a bisket or a slice of bread, a handful of raisins or a tart from the pastry-cook's, and a glass of water, had the rest of the time till their return for study, in which I made the greater progress, from that greater clearness of head and quicker apprehension which usually attend temperance in eating and drinking.

And now it was that, being on some occasion made asham'd of my ignorance in figures, which I had twice failed in learning when at school, I took Cocker's book of Arithmetic, and went through the whole by myself with great ease. I also read Seller's and Shermy's books of Navigation, and became acquainted with the little geometry they contain; but never proceeded far in that science.

Walking in the evening by the side of the river, a boat came by, which I found was going towards Philadelphia, with several people in her. They took me in, and, as there was no wind, we rowed all the way; and about midnight, not having yet seen the city, some of the company were confident we must have passed it, and would row no farther; the others knew not where we were;

so we put toward the shore, got into a creek, landed near an old fence, with the rails of which we made a fire, the night being cold, in October, and there we remained till daylight. Then one of the company knew the place to be Cooper's Creek, a little above Philadelphia, which we saw as soon as we got out of the creek, and arrived there about eight or nine o'clock on the Sunday morning, and landed at the Market Street Wharf.

I have been the more particular in this description of my journey, and, shall be so of my first entry into that city, that you may in your mind compare such unlikely beginnings with the figure I have since made there. I was in my working dress, my best clothes being to come round by sea. I was dirty from my journey; my pockets were stuffed out with shirts and stockings, and I knew no soul nor where to look for lodging. I was fatigued with travelling, rowing and want of rest, I was very hungry; and my whole stock of cash consisted of a Dutch dollar, and about a shilling in copper. The latter I gave the people of the boat for my passage, who at first refused it, on account of my rowing; but I insisted on their taking it. A man being sometimes more generous when he has but a little money than when he has plenty, perhaps through fear of being thought to have but little.

Then I walked up the street, gazing about till near the market-house I met a boy with bread. I had made many a meal on bread, and, inquiring where he got it, I went immediately to the baker's he directed me to, in Second Street, and asked for bisket, intending such as we had in Boston; but they, it seems, were not made in Philadelphia. Then I asked for a three-penny loaf, and was told they had none such. So not considering or knowing the difference of money, and the greater cheapness nor the names of his bread, I bade him give me three-penny worth of any sort. He gave me, accordingly, three great puffy rolls. I was surprised at the quantity, but took it, and, having no room in my pockets, walked off with a roll under each arm, and eating the other. Thus I went up Market Street as far as Fourth Street, passing by the door of Mr. Read, my future wife's father; when she, standing at the door, saw me, and thought I made, as I certainly did, a most awkward, ridiculous appearance. Then I turned and went down Chestnut Street and part of Walnut Street, eating my roll all the way, and, coming round, found myself again at Market Street Wharf, near the boat I came in, to which I went for a draught of the river water; and, being filled with one of my rolls, gave the other two to a woman and her child that came down the river in the boat with us, and were waiting to go farther.

Thus refreshed, I walked again up the street, which by this

time had many clean-dressed people in it, who were all walking the same way. I joined them, and thereby was led into the great meetinghouse of the Quakers near the market. I sat down among them, and, after looking round awhile and hearing nothing said, being very drowsy through labor and want of rest the preceding night, I fell fast asleep, and continued so till the meeting broke up, when one was kind enough to rouse me. This was, therefore, the first house I was in, or slept in, in Philadelphia.

Walking down again toward the river, and, looking in the faces of people, I met a young, Quaker man, whose countenance I liked, and, accosting him, requested he would tell me where a stranger could get lodging. We were then near the sign of the Three Mariners. "Here," says he, "is one place that entertains strangers, but it is not a reputable house; if thee wilt walk with me, I'll show thee a better." He brought me to the Crooked Billet in Waterstreet. Here I got a dinner; and, while I was eating it, several sly questions were asked me, as it seemed to be suspected from my youth and appearance, that I might be some runaway.

After dinner, my sleepiness returned, and being shown to a bed, I lay down without undressing, and slept till six in the evening, was called to supper, went to bed again very early, and slept soundly till next morning. Then I made myself as tidy as I could, and went to Andrew Bradford the printer. I found in the shop the old man his father, whom I had seen at New York, and who, traveling on horseback, had got to Philadelphia before me. He introduced me to his son, who received me civilly, gave me a breakfast, but told me he did not at present want a hand, being lately supplied with one; but there was another printer in town, lately set up, one Keimer, who, perhaps, might employ me; if not, I should be welcome to lodge at his house, and he would give me a little work to do now and then till fuller business should offer.

The old gentleman said he would go with me to the new printer; and when we found him, "Neighbor," says Bradford, "I have brought to see you a young man of your business; perhaps you may want such a one." He asked me a few questions, put a composing stick in my hand to see how I worked, and then said he would employ me soon, though he had just then nothing for me to do; and, taking old Bradford, whom he had never seen before, to be one of the town's people that had a good will for him, entered into a conversation on his present undertaking and prospects; while Bradford, not discovering that he was the other printer's father, on Keimer's saying he expected soon to get the greatest part of the business into his own hands, drew him on by artful questions, and starting little doubts, to explain all his views, what interest he relied on, and in what manner he intended to proceed. I, who stood by and heard all, saw immediately that one of them was a crafty old sophister,[1] and the other a mere novice. Bradford left me with Keimer, who was greatly surprised when I told him who the old man was.

---

1. **sophister** (säf´ ist ər) *n.:* Clever person, using seemingly logical reasoning.

☑ Check Your Comprehension

1. Why did Franklin study an arithmetic book?
2. In what ways does the young Franklin show that he is generous?
3. Why does the printer's father seem to be "crafty"?

◆ Critical Thinking

INTERPRET

1. According to Franklin, what were the advantages of the vegetable diet that he put himself on? What disadvantages could there be? **[Connect]**
2. In what ways does Franklin show that, as a teenager, he could take care of himself? **[Draw Conclusions]**

APPLY

3. Franklin was only seventeen when he came to Philadelphia. Would a teenager today, needing work and a place to live, be able to do what Franklin did? **[Speculate]**

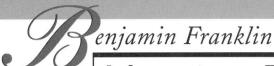

Benjamin Franklin

Information to Those Who Would Remove to America

Many persons in Europe having directly or by letters expressed to the writer of this, who is well acquainted with North America, their desire of transporting and establishing themselves in that country; but who appear to him to have formed through ignorance, mistaken ideas and expectations of what is to be obtained there; he thinks it may be useful and prevent inconvenient, expensive and fruitless removals and voyages of improper persons, if he gives some clearer and truer notions of that part of the world than appear to have hitherto prevailed.

The truth is, that though there are in that country few people so miserable as the poor of Europe, there are also very few that in Europe would be called rich: it is rather a general happy mediocrity that prevails. There are few great proprietors of the soil, and few tenants; most people cultivate their own lands, or follow some handicraft or merchandise; very few rich enough to live idly upon their rents or incomes; or to pay the high prices given in Europe, for paintings, statues, architecture, and the other works of art that are more curious than useful. Hence the natural geniuses that have arisen in America, with such talents, have uniformly quitted that country for Europe, where they can be more suitably rewarded. It is true that letters and mathematical knowledge are in esteem there, but they are at the same time more common than apprehended; there being already existing nine colleges or universities, viz. four in New England, and one in each of, the provinces of New York, New Jersey, Pensilvania, Maryland, and Virginia, all furnished with learned professors; besides a number of smaller academies. These educate many of their youth in the languages and those sciences that qualify men for the professions of divinity, law or physics. Strangers indeed are by no means excluded from exercising those professions, and the quick increase of inhabitants every where gives them a chance of employ, which they have in common with the natives. Of civil offices or employments there are few; no superfluous ones as in Europe; and it is a rule established in some of the states, that no office should be so profitable as to make it desirable. The 36 Article of the Constitution of Pennsylvania runs expressly in these words: *As every freeman, to preserve his independence, (if he has not a sufficient estate) ought to have some profession, calling, trade or farm, whereby he may honestly sub-*

sist, there can be no necessity for, nor use in, establishing offices of profit; the usual effects of which are dependence and servility, unbecoming freemen, in the possessors and expectants; faction, contention, corruption, and disorder among the people. Wherefore whenever an office, through increase of fees or otherwise, becomes so profitable as to occasion many to apply for it, the profits ought to be lessened by the legislature.

These ideas prevailing more or less in all the United States, it cannot be worth any man's while, who has a means of living at home, to expatriate himself in hopes of obtaining a profitable civil office in America; and as to military offices, they are at an end with the war; the armies being disbanded. Much less is it adviseable for a person to go thither who has no other quality to recommend him but his birth. In Europe it has indeed its value, but it is a commodity that cannot be carried to a worse market than to that of America, where people do not enquire concerning a stranger, *What is he?* but *What can he do?* If he has any useful art, he is welcome; and if he exercises it and behaves well, he will be respected by all that know him; but a mere man of quality, who on that account wants to live upon the public, by some office or salary, will be despised and disregarded.

enjamin Franklin

Speech in the Convention on the Subject of Salaries

Sir,

It is with reluctance that I rise to express a disapprobation of any one article of the plan, for which we are so much obliged to the honourable gentleman who laid it before us. From its first reading, I have borne a good will to it, and, in general, wished it success. In this particular of salaries to the executive branch, I happen to differ; and, as my opinion may appear new and chimerical,[1] it is only from a persuasion that it is right, and from a sense of duty, that I hazard it. The committee will judge of my reasons when they have heard them, and their judgment may possibly change mine. I think I see inconveniences in the appointment of salaries; I see none in refusing them, but on the contrary great advantages.

Sir, there are two passions which have a powerful influence in the affairs of men. These are *ambition* and *avarice;* the love of power and the love of money. Separately, each of these has great force in prompting men to action; but when united in view of the same object, they, have in many minds the most violent effects. Place before the eyes of such men a post of honor, that shall at the same time be a place of *profit* and they will move heaven and earth to obtain it. The vast number of such places it is that renders the British government so tempestuous. The struggles for them are the true source of all those factions which are perpetually dividing the nation, distracting its councils, hurrying it sometimes into fruitless and mischievous wars, and often compelling I submissions to dishonourable terms of peace.

And of what kind are the men that will strive for this profitable preeminence through all the bustle of cabal,[2] the heat of contention, the infinite mutual abuse of parties, tearing to pieces the best of characters? It will not be the wise and moderate, the lovers of peace and good order, the men fittest for the trust. It will be the bold and the violent, the men of strong passions and indefatigable activity in their selfish pursuits. These will thrust themselves into your government, and be your rulers. And these, too, will be mistaken in the expected happiness of their situation; for their vanquished competitors, of the same spirit, and from the same motives, will perpetually be endeavouring to distress their administration, thwart their measures, and render them odious to the people.

1. **chimerical** (kǐ′ mer′ i kəl) *adj.:* Unreal; absurd.
2. **cabal** (kə bal′) *n.:* Political intrigue.

Besides these evils, Sir, though we may set out in the beginning with moderate salaries, we shall find, that such will not be of long continuance. Reasons will never be wanting for proposed augmentations; and there will always be a party for giving more to the rulers, that the rulers may be able in return to give more to them. Hence, as all history informs us, there has been in every state and kingdom a constant kind of warfare between the governing and the governed; the one striving to obtain more for its support, and the other to pay less. And this has alone occasioned great convulsions, actual civil wars, ending either in dethroning of the princes or enslaving of the people. Generally, indeed, the ruling power carries its point, and we see the revenues of princes constantly increasing, and we see that they are never satisfied, but always in want of more. The more the people are discontented with the oppression of taxes, the greater need the prince has of money to distribute among his partisans, and pay the troops that are to suppress all resistance and enable him to plunder at pleasure. There is scarce a king in a hundred, who would not, if he could, follow the example of pharaoh, —get first all the people's money, then all their lands, and then make them and their children servants forever. It will be said, that we do not propose to establish kings. I know it. But there is a natural inclination in mankind to kingly government. It sometimes relieves them from aristocratic domination. They had rather have one tyrant than 500. It gives more of the appearance of equality among citizens; and that they like. I am apprehensive, therefore—perhaps too apprehensive—that the government of these states may in future times end in a monarchy. But this catastrophe, I think, may be long delayed, if in our proposed system we do not sow the seeds of contention, faction, and tumult, by making our posts of honour places of profit.

It may be imagined by some, that this is a utopian idea, and that we can never find men to serve us in the executive department, without paying them well for their services. I conceive this to be a mistake. Some existing facts present themselves to me, which incline me to contrary opinion. The high sheriff of a county in England is an honourable office, but it is not a profitable one. It is rather expensive, and therefore not sought for. But yet it is executed, and well executed, and usually by some of the principal gentlemen of the county.

To bring the matter nearer home, have we not seen the greatest and most important of our offices, that of general of our armies, executed for eight years together, without the smallest salary, by a patriot whom I will not now offend by any other praise; and this, through fatigues and distresses, in common with the other brave men, his military friends and companions, and the constant anxieties peculiar to his station? And shall we doubt finding three or four men in all the United States, with public spirit enough to bear sitting in peaceful council, for perhaps an equal term merely to preside over our civil concerns, and see that our laws are duly executed?

Sir, I have a better opinion of our country. I think we shall never be without a sufficient number of wise and good men to undertake, and execute well and faithfully, the office in question. Sir, the saving of the salaries, that may at first be proposed, is not an object with me. The subsequent mischiefs of proposing them are what I apprehend. And therefore it is that I move the amendment. If it is not seconded or accepted, I must be contented with the satisfaction of having delivered my opinion frankly, and done my duty.

☑ Check Your Comprehension

1. In "Information to Those Who Would Remove to America," why does Franklin recommend that a person with no talent or quality except his noble birth decide against coming to the United States?
2. In his "Speech . . . on the Subject of Salaries," what example does Franklin give to answer the objection that officials need to be paid?
3. Who is the "patriot" Franklin refers to in the next-to-last paragraph of his speech?

◆ Critical Thinking

INTERPRET

1. Although "Information to Those Who Would Remove to America" seems to be a set of helpful hints about America, is there another, satirical purpose to the essay? **[Distinguish]**

APPLY

2. How would modern-day politics work if government officials were not paid, as Franklin proposed in "Speech . . . on the Subject of Salaries"? **[Hypothesize]**

COMPARE LITERARY WORKS

3. Both the essay and the speech refer to problems related to paying government officials. Do you think Franklin would have wanted the Pennsylvania Article 36 adopted for the United States Constitution? Explain. **[Synthesize]**

Comparing and Connecting the Author's Works

◆ Literary Focus: Autobiography

Benjamin Franklin's *Autobiography* is one of the best-known examples of autobiography. Unlike a biography, in which a person's life is described by someone else, an **autobiography** is written by the subject himself or herself.

Autobiographies may consist of factual, objective descriptions of the writer's life, or they may be confessional, emphasizing self-examination and analysis. Benjamin Franklin's autobiography contains elements of objective description and of analysis.

Main Features of Autobiography

• Uses first person

• Describes the author's life, usually arranging events chronologically

• May be written as a journal or letter

1. Why would a reader be curious about the private life and thoughts of a writer like Benjamin Franklin?

2. Does Franklin describe himself objectively, without trying to appear better than he is? Explain.

3. Which is more likely to relate the facts of someone's entire life, an autobiography or a biography? Explain.

◆ Drawing Conclusions About Franklin's Work

One scholar of Benjamin Franklin's writing, Richard E. Amacher, wrote this description of Franklin's importance as a citizen and writer:

Benjamin Franklin holds forever a firm place in the hearts and minds of Americans . . . who honor good humor, common sense, and wisdom—traits in his writing for which he is best known.

The following chart includes one instance of each of these traits from the three works of Franklin that you have read. Draw a similar chart and write in another example of each trait.

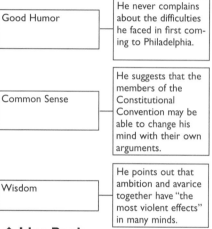

Good Humor	He never complains about the difficulties he faced in first coming to Philadelphia.
Common Sense	He suggests that the members of the Constitutional Convention may be able to change his mind with their own arguments.
Wisdom	He points out that ambition and avarice together have "the most violent effects" in many minds.

◆ Idea Bank

Writing

1. **Letter** Many of Franklin's articles and letters were written to persuade his readers to agree with his point of view about an issue. Write an argument taking a position on a controversial issue in your school or community. Then rewrite your argument in the form of a letter you might send to the editor of a newspaper.

2. **Autobiographical Incident** Good autobiographies include clear retellings of incidents in the writer's life. Choose an incident from your life and write a detailed, interesting account.

3. **Political Cartoon** Franklin wrote and published the first political cartoon in America. He satirized the reluctance of some colonies to join in a planned union of the American

colonies by drawing a snake cut into pieces. Each piece was labeled with the name of one of the colonies. The caption was "Join, or Die." Think of something that you have an opinion about in your school or community. Draw a political cartoon about it. Include whatever caption is needed to make the meaning clear. **[Art Link; Social Studies Link]**

Speaking and Listening

4. **Delivering a Speech** When Franklin delivered a speech, as in his "Speech in the Convention on the Subject of Salaries," he had a specific audience in mind. Choose part of one of his speeches from a collection of his writings. Practice speaking it aloud, trying to find the places he might have paused, spoken louder or softer, or emphasized particular points. Then deliver the speech to other students. **[Performing Arts Link]**

5. **Glass Harmonica** Among his other inventions, Franklin worked to improve a musical instrument called the glass harmonica (sometimes spelled "armonica"). Unlike the instrument we call "harmonica" today, the glass harmonica consisted of a series of moistened glasses "played" by rubbing the finger around the moistened glass rims. You can produce the same effect by rubbing a wet finger around the rim of a water glass or wineglass. Create your own glass harmonica of three to five glasses. Vary the sounds by using different water levels and glass sizes. Develop a musical song—practice—and perform it for your classmates, or make a recording of your song and play it for them. **[Music Link]**

Researching and Representing

6. **Inventions** Franklin invented or proposed a number of practical devices or institutions that we take for granted today, including bifocals, the Franklin stove, the lightning rod, the public library, Daylight Savings Time, the fire department, and fire insurance. Research the early history of one of these inventions or institutions, focusing on Franklin's involvement in its development. Write a brief essay describing the findings. **[Science; Social Studies Links]**

7. **Debate** Many of Franklin's speeches, articles, essays, and letters concern controversial issues of his day. With other students, choose one of his writings and present a debate on the two sides of the issue. **[Social Studies Link; Group Activity Link]**

◆ Further Reading, Listening, and Viewing

• Ronald W. Clark: *Benjamin Franklin* (1983). A popular biography

• I. Benjamin Cohen: *Benjamin Franklin's Science* (1990). Discusses Franklin's many inventions and contributions to science

• Arthur Bernon Tourtellot: *Benjamin Franklin: The Shaping of Genius: The Boston Years* (1977). Examines Franklin's heritage and youth

On the Web:

http://www.phschool.com/atschool/literature
Go to the student edition of *The American Tradition.* Proceed to Unit 2. Then, click Hot Links to find Web sites featuring Benjamin Franklin.

$\mathcal{P}$hillis Wheatley In Depth

"They dressed you in light but you dreamed with the night.
From Africa singing of justice and grace,
Your early verse sweetens the fame of our Race."

—*June Jordan*

PHILLIS WHEATLEY was the first African American writer of lasting importance in America. She was considered an intellectual phenomenon in the Boston of her day and in London. While she is best known for her Christian writings, she also wrote poems about American patriotism, imagination, slavery, and ancient culture. It was highly unusual for a slave to be an accomplished scholar and, indeed, for any woman in Colonial times to read Latin was noteworthy. Wheatley was not only well-educated, but a gifted poet. Her volume of poetry, published in London in 1773, was most likely the first book published by an African American.

Sold in Boston

There are no accurate records of when Phillis Wheatley was born; however, it is generally agreed that she was seven years old when she was brought from West Africa on a slave ship and then sold to the well-to-do family of John Wheatley in 1761. John Wheatley, a successful businessman in the busy seaport, described buying "a slender, frail female child ... for a trifle."

Wheatley's wife, Susanna, soon recognized the child's intelligence and under her guidance taught the child English, Greek, Latin, the Bible, history, and literature. Four years after her arrival, Phillis Wheatley was well on her way to becoming a writer.

Young Poet

In 1767, when Phillis Wheatley was about thirteen or fourteen, one of her poems was published in a Newport, Rhode Island, newspaper. Three years later, she wrote a poem, "On the Death of the Reverend Mr. George Whitefield," a famous evangelist in England and the Colonies, where the poem was widely published. Wheatley sent her poem to the Countess of Huntingdon, Selina Hastings (1702–1791), an English abolitionist who had known Whitefield. The countess later became Phillis Wheatley's advocate and patron.

When Wheatley sought a publisher, her literary accomplishments were so astonishing that some doubted their authenticity. In 1772, called before a group of illustrious Bostonians, Wheatley had to prove her authorship. The examiners at the Boston courthouse included Thomas Hutchinson, governor of the colony, John Hancock, who later signed the Declaration of Independence, and Samuel Mather, Congregational Minister and son of Cotton Mather. In all, eighteen members wrote a letter attesting to the truth of Phillis Wheatley's claim.

We whose Names are under-written, do assure the World, that the Poems ... were (as we verily believe) written by Phillis, a young Negro Girl, who was but a few Years since, brought ... from Africa, and has ever since been, and now is, under the Disadvantage of serving as a Slave in a Family in this Town.

A Notable Book

With the committee's letter attesting to her authorship, new publishing opportunities arose.

In 1773, Phillis Wheatley's most significant work was published in London, due largely to the help of the Countess of Huntingdon and Susanna Wheatley. It was called *Poems on Various Subjects, Religious and Moral, By Phillis Wheatley, Negro Servant to Mr. John Wheatley of Boston.* Unlike modern poetry, which often deals with daily life or the poet's feelings, eighteenth-century poetry tended to present ideas or moral lessons to the reader. Wheatley's poems often resemble essays or lectures.

Phillis Wheatley's book was well regarded in England and at home, especially by those who saw her work as an argument for the unfairness of slavery. To dispel any doubts the publisher included the statement signed by the group of well-respected Bostonians. The book also contained the letter of proof written by John Wheatley and displayed an engraved portrait of the poet on the cover.

Last Years Freed just before the American Revolution broke out, and without the support of the Wheatleys after their deaths, Phillis Wheatley had a hard time financially. Her marriage, in 1778, to a free black man named John Peters, did not improve conditions for her. Wheatley tried unsuccessfully to raise money to publish another book of poems. In addition, the war made earning a living difficult. Wheatley worked as a servant some of the time, until her death in 1784.

Her Enduring Work Wheatley's reputation continues to endure and grow as modern readers learn to appreciate how keenly aware Wheatley was of being caught up in the numerous social and intellectual forces of the societies in which she lived. Wheatley's writing remains one of the best available mirrors of the American colonial consciousness.

◆ Slavery in Massachusetts

Although slavery was not as widespread in New England as in the South, it was still part of the life of the northern colonies. New England ship owners and businessmen were involved in the slave trade during the 1600's. The right to keep slaves was made part of Massachusetts law in 1641. Most New Englanders who owned slaves had one or two. The slaves frequently lived and worked alongside the family members. The owners might educate the slaves and bring them to church, but the slaves were still considered the property of their owners.

Courts in Massachusetts ruled in 1781 and 1783, that having slaves was illegal. The other New England states abolished slavery by the early 1800's.

◆ Literary Works

Poems During her short lifetime, Wheatley is known to have published at least forty-six poems, of which twenty-eight were included in *Poems on Various Subjects, Religious and Moral* (published in London in 1773).

"On the Death of the Rev. Mr. George Whitefield"

"On the Death of a Young Gentleman"

"On Imagination"

"To the Right Honourable William, Earl of Dartmouth"

"To S. M. a Young African Painter, on Seeing His Works"

"A Farewell to America. To Mrs. S. W."

Some of her other poems were published in newspapers and magazines.

"On Messrs Hussey and Coffin" (her first published poem, 1767)

"To His Excellency General Washington"

"An Elegy on Leaving"

Letters Twenty-two letters by Wheatley have been collected and published providing a strong sense of her personality and life.

TIMELINE

Wheatley's Life		World Events	
1753	Approximate date of Phillis Wheatley's birth in West Africa	1700	First publication in the colonies of a protest against slavery
1761	Kidnapped and sold into slavery from the South Market, Boston	1712–74	Slave rebellions in New York and other colonies
1765	Begins to write, four years after arriving in Boston	1754–63	French and Indian War
1767	First work published in *The Newport Mercury*	1755	Earthquake in Lisbon, Portugal, kills 60,000
1770	"On the Death of the Rev. Mr. George Whitefield" published	1759	British defeat French in Battle of Quebec; take over Canada in 1763
1771	Becomes member of Old South Meeting House church, Boston	1760–	
1773	Trip to London; meets Benjamin Franklin and the Earl of Dartmouth; *Poems on Various Subjects, Religious and Moral* is published in London; freed from slavery	1820	George III is King of England
		1765	Stamp Act is protested in colonies
		1770	Crispus Attacks (of African and Native American descent) is killed in Boston Massacre
1774	Death of Mrs. Wheatley; writes her anti-slavery letter to Reverend Samson Occom about the hypocrisy of Christian slaveholders	1771	*Encyclopedia Britannica* is published
		1773	Boston Tea Party protest against British taxes
		1775–83	American Revolution
1775	Writes to George Washington, enclosing a poem about him	1776	Continental Congress allows blacks to fight on colonists' side; Edward Gibbon's *The History of the Decline and Fall of the Roman Empire* is published
1776	Visits George Washington		
1778	John Wheatley dies; Phillis Wheatley marries John Peters (3 children are later born)		
		1778	Slavery becomes illegal in British Isles
1779	Wheatley advertises in newspaper for subscribers for a book of her poems	1783	Courts in Massachusetts declare slavery abolished
1784	Dies in Boston	1787	United States Constitution written, permitting slavery; Sierra Leone, West Africa, settled by former slaves
1786	Wheatley's *Poems on Various Subjects* is published in Philadelphia		
1830's	Wheatley's poems are rediscovered when abolitionists reprint them	1789	French Revolution begins; William Blake publishes *Songs of Innocence*; George Washington becomes first President

Phillis Wheatley

To the Right Honorable William, Earl of Dartmouth, His Majesty's Principal Secretary of State for North America

Hail, happy day, when, smiling like the morn,
Fair Freedom rose New England to adorn:
The northern clime[1] beneath her genial ray,
Dartmouth, congratulates thy blissful sway:
5   Elate with hope her race no longer mourns,
Each soul expands, each grateful bosom burns,
While in thine hand with pleasure we behold
The silken reins, and Freedom's charms unfold.
Long lost to realms beneath the northern skies

10 She shines supreme, while hated faction dies:
Soon as appeared the Goddess long desired,
Sick at the view, she languished and expired;
Thus from the splendors of the morning light
The owl in sadness seeks the caves of night.

15   No more, America, in mournful strain
Of wrongs, and grievance unredressed complain,
No longer shalt thou dread the iron chain,
Which wanton Tyranny with lawless hand
Had made, and with it meant to enslave the land.

20   Should you, my lord, while you peruse my song,
Wonder from whence my love of Freedom sprung,
Whence flow these wishes for the common good,
By feeling hearts alone best understood,
I, young in life, by seeming cruel fate
25 Was snatched from Africa's fancied happy seat:[2]
What pangs excruciating must molest,
What sorrows labor in my parent's breast?
Steeled was that soul and by no misery moved
That from a father seized his babe beloved:

---

1. **clime:** Region.
2. **fancied happy seat:** Imagined home

30   Such, such my case. And can I then but pray
        Others may never feel tyrannic sway?

            For favors past, great Sir, our thanks are due,
        And thee we ask thy favors to renew,
        Since in thy power, as in thy will before,
35   To soothe the griefs, which thou didst once deplore.
        May heavenly grace the sacred sanction give
        To all thy works, and thou for ever live
        Not only on the wings of fleeting Fame,
        Though praise immortal crowns the patriot's name,
40   But to conduct to heaven's refulgent fane,[3]
        May fiery coursers[4] sweep the ethereal plain,
        And bear thee upwards to that blest abode,
        Where, like the prophet, thou shalt find thy God.

---

3. fane: Temple.
4. coursers: Horses.

Phillis Wheatley

To S. M., a Young African Painter, on Seeing His Works

To show the laboring bosom's deep intent,
And thought in living characters to paint,
When first thy pencil did those beauties give,
And breathing figures learned from thee to live,
5   How did those prospects give my soul delight,
A new creation rushing on my sight?
Still, wondrous youth! each noble path pursue,
On deathless glories fix thine ardent view:
Still may the painter's and the poet's fire
10   To aid thy pencil, and thy verse conspire!
And may the charms of each seraphic[1] theme
Conduct thy footsteps to immortal fame!
High to the blissful wonders of the skies
Elate thy soul, and raise thy wishful eyes.
15   Thrice happy, when exalted to survey
That splendid city, crowned with endless day,
Whose twice six gates on radiant hinges ring:
Celestial Salem[2] blooms in endless spring.

Calm and serene thy moments glide along,
20   And may the muse inspire each future song!
Still, with the sweets of contemplation blessed,
May peace with balmy wings your soul invest!
But when these shades of time are chased away,
And darkness ends in everlasting day,
25   On what seraphic pinions shall we move,
And view the landscapes in the realms above?
There shall thy tongue in heavenly murmurs flow,
And there my muse with heavenly transport glow:
No more to tell of Damon's[2] tender sighs,
30   Or rising radiance of Aurora's[3] eyes,
For nobler themes demand a nobler strain,
And purer language on the ethereal plain.
Cease, gentle muse! the solemn gloom of night
Now seals the fair creation from my sight.

---

1. **seraphic** (sē raf' ik) *adj.:* Angelic.
2. **Salem:** Jerusalem.
3. **Damon:** Mythical Greek god.
4. **Aurora:** Roman goddess of dawn.

Phillis Wheatley

On Imagination

Thy various works, imperial queen, we see,
How bright their forms! how decked with pomp by
thee! Thy wondrous acts in beauteous order stand,
And all attest how potent is thine hand.

5   From Helicon's[1] refulgent heights attend,
Ye sacred choir, and my attempts befriend:
To tell her glories with a faithful tongue,
Ye blooming graces, triumph in my song.

Now here, now there, the roving Fancy[2] flies,
10   Till some loved object strikes her wandering eyes,
Whose silken fetters all the senses bind,
And soft captivity involves the mind.

Imagination! who can sing thy force?
Or who describe the swiftness of thy course?
15   Soaring through air to find the bright abode,
The empyreal[3] palace of the thundering God,
We on thy pinions can surpass the wind,
And leave the rolling universe behind:
From star to star the mental optics rove,
20   Measure the skies, and range the realms above.
There in one view we grasp the mighty whole,
Or with new worlds amaze the unbounded soul.

Though Winter frowns to Fancy's raptured eyes
The fields may flourish, and gay scenes arise;
25   The frozen deeps may break their iron bands,
And bid their waters murmur over the sands.
Fair Flora[4] may resume her fragrant reign,
And with her flowery riches deck the plain;
Sylvanus[5] may diffuse his honors round,
30   And all the forest may with leaves be crowned:
Showers may descend, and dews their gems disclose,
And nectar sparkle on the blooming rose.

---

1. Helicon: Mount Helicon in Greece, mythical home of the nine muses.
2. Fancy: Imagination.
3. empyreal: Heavenly.
4. Flora: Roman goddess of fertility.
5. Sylvanus: Roman goddess of the forest.

Such is thy power, nor are thine orders vain,
O thou the leader of the mental train:
35   In full perfection all thy works are wrought,
And thine the scepter over the realms of thought.
Before thy throne the subject-passions bow,
Of subject-passions sovereign ruler Thou;
At thy command joy rushes on the heart,
40   And through the glowing veins the spirits dart.

Fancy might now her silken pinions try
To rise from earth, and sweep the expanse on high;
From Tithon's[6] bed now might Aurora[7] rise,
Her cheeks all glowing with celestial dyes,
45   While a pure stream of light overflows the skies.
The monarch of the day I might behold,
And all the mountains tipped with radiant gold,
But I reluctant leave the pleasing views,
Which Fancy dresses to delight the Muse:
50   Winter austere forbids me to aspire,
And northern tempests damp the rising fire;
They chill the tides of Fancy's flowing sea,
Cease then, my song, cease the unequal lay.

6. **Tithon:** A mortal from the city of Troy in ancient Greece.
7. **Aurora:** The Roman goddess of dawn.

John Wheatley

Letter

The following is a copy of a letter sent by Phillis Wheatley's owner to the publisher.

Phillis was brought from Africa to America, in the Year 1761, between Seven and Eight Years of Age. Without any Assistance from School Education, and by only what she was taught in the Family, she, in sixteen Months Time from her Arrival, attained the English Language, to which she was an Utter Stranger before, to such a Degree, as to read any, the most difficult Parts of the Sacred Writings, to the great Astonishment of all who heard her.

As to her Writing, her own Curiosity led her to it; and this she learnt in so short a Time that in the year 1765 she wrote a Letter to the Rev. Mr. Occom, the Indian Minister, while in England.

She has a great Inclination to learn the Latin Tongue, and has made some Progress in it. This Relation is given by her Master who bought her, and with whom she now lives.

John Wheatley

Boston, Nov.14, 1772

☑ Check Your Comprehension

1. What two kinds of freedom are valued by the speaker of "To the . . . Earl of Dartmouth"?

2. In "To S. M., a Young African Painter," what does the speaker say she enjoyed in S. M.'s work?

3. What special sights does the speaker wish to share with S. M.?

4. What other name does the speaker of "On Imagination" use for imagination?

5. What is Fancy able to see when it is winter?

6. What would the reader of Phillis Wheatley's book of poems conclude about the poet from John Wheatley's letter?

◆ Critical Thinking

1. "To the . . . Earl of Dartmouth" compares the freedom lost by a slave to the colonists' fear of the English government's tyranny. Is this a fair comparison? **[Social Studies Link]**

EVALUATE

2. Do you get a specific, detailed sense of S. M.'s paintings in "To S. M., a Young African Painter"? Do you think the writer had a different purpose in mind? **[Criticize]**

EXTEND

3. Why do you think the publisher included John Wheatley's letter in the book of Phillis Wheatley's poems? **[Analyze]**

COMPARE LITERARY WORKS

4. If Phillis Wheatley were writing today, she might include more details in her poems about her personal experiences and feelings. What details might she add to each of the three poems in this unit? **[Synthesize]**

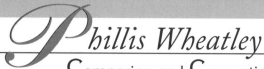

Phillis Wheatley

Comparing and Connecting the Author's Works

◆ Literary Focus: Apostrophe

In **apostrophe,** the writer addresses a person who is not actually present—or an object, a god or goddess, an animal, or an abstract quality.

Writers like Wheatley might use apostrophe to bring a sense of drama to a poem or other piece of writing. The situation is clear: the speaker is addressing someone or something, and the reader overhears the address taking place. The sense of a formal speech may add an impression of importance to the poem.

1. Wheatley actually may have known "S. M." Do you get the feeling in her poem that she really is speaking with him?
2. In her poem addressed to the Earl of Dartmouth, does the speaker seem to know him?
3. Why is "On Imagination" an example of the use of apostrophe?
4. Find other examples of apostrophe in Wheatley's poems.

◆ Drawing Conclusions About Wheatley's Work

One characteristic of eighteenth-century English poetry that Wheatley absorbed from her reading is a frequent use of **allusions,** references that the writer assumes the reader will recognize from his or her previous reading or study. They often refer to figures or incidents from history, mythology, literature, or the Bible. For example, at the end of her poem to the "Earl of Dartmouth," Wheatley expresses hope that "fiery coursers" will bear him to heaven "like the prophet." This is an allusion to the prophet Elijah in the Bible, who was

borne to heaven by "a chariot of fire, and horses of fire."

In the chart below, two allusions from Wheatley's poems are analyzed. Also noted are the qualities of the figures alluded to that are meaningful to Wheatley's topics. Find three other allusions and analyze them in a chart like the following one.

Allusion	Meaning	Symbolism
flora	goddess of flowers	flowers growing in fields
seraphic pinions	angel's feathers	ability to fly to heaven

◆ Idea Bank

Writing

1. **Obituary** Write an obituary for Phillis Wheatley that might have appeared in a newspaper at the time she died. Briefly describe her life and her works. Also compose a quotation that might have been said by someone who knew her.
2. **Letter or Diary Entry** Wheatley's writing does not provide us with insight into her own feelings about being a writer or a slave in colonial America. Imagine what Wheatley's feelings might be, considering her status as a slave and her dependence. Write a letter from her to a close friend or an entry for her diary, as she expresses her thoughts about her life.
3. **Allusions** Write a short poem of about ten lines in the style of Wheatley's poems. The lines should

have a rhyme scheme, and rhythm (a pattern of beats). You should also include at least two allusions.

Speaking and Listening

4. **Speech** Pretend you are an abolitionist of the pre–Civil War era of the 1800's. Prepare and deliver a speech against slavery, using specific details from Phillis Wheatley's life and poems as evidence that slavery is wrong. **[Social Studies Link]**

5. **Poetry Reading** Phillis Wheatley was one of the earliest African American poets. Some later poets have said that her example inspired them. Look for other poems by African Americans in the library. Find one that you like. Read it several times to be sure you understand it well, looking up the definitions of unfamiliar words. Read the poem aloud to other students. **[Literature; Performing Arts Links]**

Researching and Representing

6. **History of Slavery** Research two differences in slavery in the colonial era between the southern colonies and the northern colonies. You might concentrate on such things as numbers of slaves, how they were employed, relationships between slaves and owners, or laws about freedom. Summarize your findings in an essay and read it to your class. **[Social Studies Link]**

7. **Music** Cultured families of Boston in Wheatley's time would play music in their homes. They often played harpsi-

chord or piano music or music for the violin or a string quartet. They enjoyed music by European composers like Franz Joseph Haydn (1732–1809) and Wolfgang Amadeus Mozart (1756–1791). The music of the time emphasized elegance, directness, and melody. Listen to one composition by Haydn or Mozart and consider whether there is a relationship to eighteenth-century poetry. Write about any similarities or differences you may hear. **[Music Link]**

◆ **Further Reading, Listening, and Viewing**

• Henry Louis Gates and Nellie Y. McKay, editors: *The Norton Anthology of African American Literature,* W. W. Norton And Company, 1997

• Deirdre Mullane, editor: *Crossing the Danger Water: 300 Years of African American Writing,* Anchor Books, 1993

• Deborah Willis, editor: *Picturing US: African American Identity in Photography,* New Press, 1994

• Harold Courlander, editor: *A Treasury of Afro-American Folklore,* Marlowe and Co., 1996

• Video: *Liberty! The American Revolution* PBS Home Video, 1997

On the Web:

http://www.phschool.com/atschool/literature
Go to the student edition of *The American Experience.* Proceed to Unit 2. Then, click Hot Links to find Web sites featuring Phillis Wheatley.

Edgar Allan Poe In Depth

> "To award or deny him greatness seems almost irrelevant when the small body of his finest work has struck so strong a chord in the imaginations of generations of readers in so many countries."
>
> —*Julian Symons*

EDGAR ALLAN POE's literary legacy is sometimes overshadowed by his personal life. After he died, his enemies published unflattering reports about him concerning the reckless way in which he lived his life. Poe's other, and more important, legacy is the poems, essays, and stories that have influenced writers and other artists throughout the decades. Much of his work is still read and studied today.

Early Tragedy Edgar Allan Poe was born in 1809; his parents were actors. Poe's father deserted the family in 1810. In 1811, his mother died in Richmond, Virginia, at the age of twenty-four. Poe went to live with a guardian.

Poe's guardian was John Allan, a tobacco exporter. Although he never adopted Poe legally, Allan gave him the name Edgar Allan. At schools in Virginia and Great Britain, Poe was considered a scholar and athlete.

Studies and Problems Poe studied at the University of Virginia until, deep in debt, he was forced to leave the university. He ran off to Boston, where he paid to have his first book of poems published. To earn a living, he joined the Army.

When Mrs. Allan died in 1829, Poe and John Allan resumed relations. Poe's next plan was to apply to the U. S. Military Academy at West Point. He entered in 1830, after publishing another collection of his poems. At West Point, he again got into trouble with debt and was court-martialed and expelled for disobeying orders. He then published a third collection of poems, which included "To Helen."

Magazine Work In 1831, Poe worked part-time for newspapers and wrote stories for literary magazines. When John Allan died in 1834, Poe was left out of his will. He moved to Richmond in 1835 to work as an editor of a new magazine, the *Southern Literary Messenger*.

The book reviews that Poe wrote for the magazine attracted attention and subscribers. He was often harsh in his criticism, but always interesting. He challenged the New England writers who were the literary establishment of his day. In 1836, Poe married Virginia Clemm. By then he had begun writing the stories that he is known for today, but the magazine's owner complained about his depressed moods and fired Poe at the end of 1836.

Fame After a year in New York and the publication of a short novel which did not sell well, Poe moved with his wife to Philadelphia. He held editing jobs there while publishing many of his best-known stories. Some of Poe's work reflected the popular taste of the time for Gothic art, architecture, and literature, with its dark mysteries, ruined castles, horror, and the supernatural. Like other Americans of his era, Poe was interested in the classical ideals of order, light, and rationality, exemplified in the ancient Greeks and Romans.

By 1844, Poe was becoming recognized for his writing, especially when his poem "The Raven" was published in dozens of magazines and newspapers. He began to give public lectures on poetry.

In addition, a volume of his stories called, *The Raven and Other Poems,* was published in 1845.

At the height of his success and fame, Poe also experienced several difficult years as well. No one is certain what caused his troubles. Many observers wrote about Poe's excesses. Recent scholarship, however, suggests too much emphasis may have been placed on Poe's behavior. It may be that Poe's macabre way of writing had more to do with the popular interests of the time than with his personal life.

Nightmare's End Poe's best known characters are fascinating because they seem driven by terrible forces. It would be a mistake, however, to view the author as one of his own creations, because Poe functioned relatively well in his life and was a productive writer. In his later years, however, Poe grieved over Virginia's death, often making him morose.

On a lecture tour in 1849, he was found unconscious on a street in Baltimore. After treatment in a hospital, he fell into a coma and died. The doctor, limited by the medical knowledge of the times, called Poe's condition "congestion of the brain." We will probably never know exactly what caused Poe's death, and it is indeed ironic that one of America's foremost creators of the detective story died in a mysterious way.

◆ Poe's Invention, the Detective Story

While watching detective characters on television or in a movie, we probably do not realize they are frequently offshoots of Edgar Allan Poe's work.

Poe most likely based C. Auguste Dupin, the detective in three of his stories, on the memoirs of a French detective named Vidocq. Many features found in detective stories today are claimed to be inventions of Poe's, including the super-intelligent detective, the police who are stumped by a crime, and the detective's friend who narrates the story. "Sherlock Holmes," the famous detective story, by Sir Arthur Conan Doyle, shares all of these characteristics, as do many others.

A fitting recognition of Poe's literary contribution is the name of the awards given each year by the Mystery Writers of America: the Edgar Awards.

◆ Literary Works

Poetry
"Sonnet—To Science" (1829); **"To Helen"** (1831); **"The Raven"** (1845); **"Ulalume"** (1847); **"The Bells"** (1848); **"For Annie"; "Eldorado"** (1849).

Short Stories Poe's short stories were written between (1829–1849).

"MS. Found in a Bottle" (1832); **"Hans Phaall"** (1836); **"The Fall of the House of Usher"** (1839); **"The Murders in the Rue Morgue"** (1841); **"The Pit and the Pendulum"** (1842); **"The Mystery of Marie Roget"; "The Gold-Bug"; "The Tell-Tale Heart"** (1843); **"The Purloined Letter"** (1845); **"Hop-Frog"** (1849).

Criticism Poe published essays providing perspective on his stories and poems, and on writing in general.

"How to Write a Blackwood Article" (1838); **"The Philosophy of Composition"** (1846); **"The Poetic Principle"** (1850).

TIMELINE

Poe's Life

1809	Edgar Allan Poe is born in Boston
1811	His mother dies; the Allans provide a home for Edgar and his sister
1815–20	The Allans live in Scotland and England
1826	Enters and leaves the University of Virginia
1827	Moves to Boston and enlists in Army
1829	Mrs. Allen dies; Poe leaves army
1830	At West Point
1831	Expelled from West Point; lives with relatives in Baltimore
1831–34	Begins publishing stories
1835–36	Works for *Southern Literary Messenger*
1836	Marries Virginia Clemm; fired from *Messenger*
1837–44	Magazine and newspaper work in New York and Philadelphia; publishes many of best-known stories
1845	Publishes "The Raven" and becomes famous; lectures on literature
1847	Virginia dies
1849	After sickness, depression, and irrational episodes, Poe dies in Baltimore and is buried there

World Events

1804–15	Napoleon is Emperor of France
1808	Beethoven writes Fifth and Sixth Symphonies; Goethe publishes Part One of *Faust*
1812	Grimms' *Fairy Tales* published
1812–15	U. S. at war with Great Britain
1817–25	Thomas Jefferson founds University of Virginia and designs its buildings in Classical style
1818	*Frankenstein* published
1821	Mexican independence
1822	Liberia founded in West Africa as homeland for freed slaves
1827	Photography is invented
1833	Slavery abolished in British Empire
1837	Accession of Queen Victoria, rules Great Britain and the British Empire until her death in 1901
1838	Telegraph is invented
1839	Dickens's *Oliver Twist* published
1846	Potato famine in Ireland
1846–48	War between U. S. and Mexico
1847	*Jane Eyre* and *Wuthering Heights* are published
1848	Revolutions in Europe; meeting for women's rights in Seneca Falls, New York
1848–49	California Gold Rush

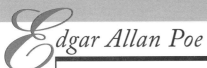

The Purloined Letter

AT PARIS, just after dark one gusty evening in the autumn of 18–, I was enjoying the twofold luxury of meditation and a meerschaum, in company with my friend C. Auguste Dupin, in his little back library, or book-closet, *au troisème, No. 33, Rue Dunôt, Faubourg St. Germain.* For one hour at least we had maintained a profound silence; while each, to any casual observer, might have seemed intently and exclusively occupied with the curling eddies of smoke that oppressed the atmosphere of the chamber. For myself, however, I was mentally discussing certain topics which had formed matter for conversation between us at an earlier period of the evening; I mean the affair of the Rue Morgue, and the mystery attending the murder of Marie Rogêt. I looked upon it, therefore, as something of a coincidence, when the door of our apartment was thrown open and admitted our old acquaintance, Monsieur G——, the Prefect of the Parisian police.

We gave him a hearty welcome; for there was nearly half as much of the entertaining as of the contemptible about the man, and we had not seen him for several years. We had been sitting in the dark, and Dupin now arose for the purpose of lighting a lamp, but sat down again, without doing so, upon G——'s saying that he had called to consult us, or rather to ask the opinion of my friend, about some official business which had occasioned a great deal of trouble.

"If it is any point requiring reflection," observed Dupin, as he forbore to enkindle the wick, "we shall examine it to better purpose in the dark."

"That is another of your odd notions," said the Prefect, who had a fashion of calling everything "odd" that was beyond his comprehension, and thus lived amid an absolute legion of "oddities."

"Very true," said Dupin, as he supplied his visitor with a pipe, and rolled towards him a comfortable chair.

"And what is the difficulty now?" I asked. "Nothing more in the assassination way, I hope?"

"Oh no; nothing of that nature. The fact is, the business is *very* simple indeed, and I make no doubt that we can manage it sufficiently well ourselves; but then I thought Dupin would like to hear the details of it, because it is so excessively *odd.*"

"Simple and odd," said Dupin.

"Why, yes; and not exactly that, either. The fact is, we have all been a good deal puzzled because the affair *is* so simple, and yet baffles us altogether."

"Perhaps it is the very simplicity of the thing which puts you at fault," said my friend.

"What nonsense you *do* talk!" replied the Prefect, laughing heartily.

"Perhaps the mystery is a little *too* plain," said Dupin.

"Oh, good heavens! who ever heard of such an idea?"

"A little *too* self-evident."

"Ha! ha! ha!—ha! ha! ha!—ho! ho! ho!"—roared our visitor, profoundly amused, "oh, Dupin, you will be the death of me yet!"

"And what, after all, *is* the matter on hand?" I asked.

"Why, I will tell you," replied the Prefect, as he gave a long, steady, and contemplative puff, and settled himself in his chair. "I will tell you in a few words; but, before I begin, let me caution you that this is an affair demanding the greatest secrecy, and that I should most probably lose the position I now hold, were it known that I confided it to any one."

"Proceed," said I.

"Or not," said Dupin.

"Well, then; I have received personal information, from a very high quarter, that a certain document of the last importance, has been purloined[1] from the royal apartments. The individual who purloined it is known; this beyond a doubt; he was seen to take it. It is known, also, that it still remains in his possession."

"How is this known?" asked Dupin.

"It is clearly inferred," replied the Prefect, "from the nature of the document, and from the non-appearance of certain results which would at once arise from its passing *out* of the robber's possession;—that is to say, from his employing it as he must design in the end to employ it."

"Be a little more explicit," I said.

"Well, I may venture so far as to say that the paper gives its holder a certain power in a certain quarter where such power is immensely valuable." The Prefect was fond of the cant[2] of diplomacy.

"Still I do not quite understand," said Dupin.

"No? Well; the disclosure of the document to a third person, who shall be nameless, would bring in question the honor of a personage of most exalted station; and this fact gives the holder of the document an ascendancy over the illustrious personage whose honor and peace are so jeopardized."

"But this ascendancy," I interposed, "would depend upon the

---

1. **purloined** (pər loind´) *adj.*: Stolen.
2. **cant** (kant) *n.*: Special vocabulary.

robber's knowledge of the loser's knowledge of the robber. Who would dare—"

"The thief," said G——, "is the Minister D——, who dares all things, those unbecoming as well as those becoming a man. The method of the theft was not less ingenious than bold. The document in question—a letter, to be frank—had been received by the personage robbed while alone in the royal *boudoir*.[3] During it's perusal she was suddenly interrupted by the entrance of the other exalted personage from whom especially it was her wish to conceal it. After a hurried and vain endeavor to thrust it in a drawer, she was forced to place it, open as it was, upon a table. The address, however, was uppermost, and, the contents thus unexposed, the letter escaped notice. At this juncture enters the Minister D——. His lynx eye immediately perceives the paper, recognizes the handwriting of the address, observes the confusion of the personage addressed, and fathoms her secret. After some business transactions, hurried through in his ordinary manner, he produces a letter somewhat similar to the one in question, opens it, pretends to read it, and then places it in close juxtaposition to the other. Again he converses, for some fifteen minutes, upon the public affairs. At length, in taking leave, he takes also from the table the letter to which he had no claim. Its rightful owner saw, but, of course, dared not call attention to the act, in the presence of the third personage who stood at her elbow. The minister decamped; leaving his own letter—one of no importance—upon the table."

"Here, then," said Dupin to me, "you have precisely what you demand to make the ascendancy complete—the robber's knowledge of the loser's knowledge of the robber."

"Yes," replied the Prefect; "and the power thus attained has, for some months past, been wielded, for political purposes, to a very dangerous extent. The personage robbed is more thoroughly convinced, every day, of the necessity of reclaiming her letter. But this, of course, cannot be done openly. In fine, driven to despair, she has committed the matter to me."

"Than whom," said Dupin, amid a perfect whirlwind of smoke, "no more sagacious agent could, I suppose, be desired, or even imagined."

"'You flatter me," replied the Prefect; "but it is possible that some such opinion may have been entertained."

"It is clear," said I, "as you observe, that the letter is still in possession of the minister; since it is this possession, and not any employment of the letter, which bestows the power. With the employment the power departs."

"True," said G——; "and upon this conviction I proceeded. My

---

3. **boudoir:** Woman's sitting room.

first care was to make thorough search of the minister's hotel; and here my chief embarrassment lay in the necessity of searching without his knowledge. Beyond all things, I have been warned of the danger which would result from giving him reason to suspect our design."

"But," said I, "you are quite *au fait*[4] in these investigations. The Parisian police have done this thing often before."

"Oh yes; and for this reason I did not despair. The habits of the minister gave me, too, a great advantage. He is, frequently absent from home all night. His servants are by no means numerous. They sleep at a distance from their master's apartment, and, being chiefly Neapolitans, are readily made drunk. I have keys, as you know, with which I can open any chamber or cabinet in Paris. For three months a night has not passed, during the greater part of which I have not been engaged, personally, in ransacking the D——Hôtel. My honor is interested, and, to mention a great secret, the reward is enormous. So I did not abandon the search until I had become fully satisfied that the thief is a more astute man than myself. I fancy that I have investigated every nook and corner of the premises in which it is possible that the paper can be concealed."

"But is it not possible," I suggested, "that although the letter may be in possession of the minister, as it unquestionably is, he may have concealed it elsewhere than upon his own premises?"

"This is barely possible," said Dupin. "The present peculiar condition of affairs at court, and especially of those intrigues in which D——is known to be involved, would render the instant availability of the document—its susceptibility of being produced at a moment's notice—a point of nearly equal importance with its possession."

"Its susceptibility of being produced?" said I.

"That is to say, of being *destroyed*," said Dupin.

"True," I observed; "the paper is clearly then upon the premises. As for its being upon the person of the minister, we may consider that as out of the question."

"Entirely," said the Prefect. "He has been twice waylaid, as if by footpads, and his person rigorously searched under my own inspection."

"You might have spared yourself this trouble," said Dupin. "D——, I presume, is not altogether a fool, and, if not, must have anticipated these waylayings, as a matter of course."

"Not *altogether* a fool," said G——, "but then he's a poet, which I take to be only one remove from a fool."

"True," said Dupin, after a long and thoughtful whiff from his

---

4. *au fait:* Meticulous.

meerschaum,[5] "although I have been guilty of certain doggerel myself."

"Suppose you detail," said I, "the particulars of your search."

"Why the fact is, we took our time, and we searched *everywhere*. I have had long experience in these affairs. I took the entire building, room by room; devoting the nights of a whole week to each. We examined, first, the furniture of each apartment. We opened every possible drawer; and I presume you know that, to a properly trained police agent, such a thing as a *secret* drawer is impossible. Any man is a dolt who permits a 'secret' drawer to escape him in a search of this kind. The thing is *so* plain. There is a certain amount of bulk—of space—to be accounted for in every cabinet. Then we have accurate rules. The fiftieth part of a line could not escape us. After the cabinets we took the chairs. The cushions we probed with the fine long needles you have seen me employ. From the tables we removed the tops."

"Why so?"

"Sometimes the top of a table, or other similarly arranged piece of furniture, is removed by the person wishing to conceal an article; then the leg is excavated, the article deposited within the cavity, and the top replaced. The bottoms and tops of bed-posts are employed in the same way."

"But could not the cavity be detected by sounding?" I asked.

"By no means, if, when the article is deposited, a sufficient wadding of cotton be placed around it. Besides, in our case, we were obliged to proceed without noise."

"But you could not have removed—you could not have taken to pieces *all* articles of furniture in which it would have been possible to make a deposit in the manner you mention. A letter may be compressed into a thin spiral roll, not differing much in shape or bulk from a large knitting-needle, and in this form it might be inserted into the rung of a chair, for example. You did not take to pieces all the chairs?"

"Certainly not; but we did better—we examined the rungs of every chair in the hotel, and, indeed, the jointings of every description of furniture, by the aid of a most powerful micro-scope.[6] Had there been any traces of recent disturbance we should not have failed to detect it instantly. A single grain of gim-let-dust, for example, would have been as obvious as an apple. Any disorder in the gluing—any unusual gaping in the joints—would have sufficed to insure detection."

"I presume you looked to the mirrors, between the boards and the plates, and you probed the beds and the bed-clothes, as well as the curtains and carpets."

---

5. **meerschaum** (mir´ shəm) *n.*: Pipe.
6. **microscope:** Magnifying glass.

"That of course; and when we had absolutely completed every particle of the furniture in this way, then we examined the house itself. We divided its entire surface into compartments, which we numbered, so that none might be missed; then we scrutinized each individual square inch throughout the premises, including the two houses immediately adjoining, with the microscope, as before."

"The two houses adjoining!" I exclaimed; "you must have had a great deal of trouble."

"We had; but the reward offered is prodigious."

"You include the *grounds* about the houses?"

"All the grounds are paved with brick. They gave us comparatively little trouble. We examined the moss between the bricks, and found it undisturbed."

"You looked among D——'s papers, of course, and into the books of the library?"

"Certainly; we opened every package and parcel; we not only opened every book, but we turned over every leaf in each volume, not contenting ourselves with a mere shake, according to the fashion of some of our police officers. We also measured the thickness of every book-*cover,* with the most accurate admeasurement, and applied to each the most jealous scrutiny of the microscope. Had any of the bindings been recently meddled with, it would have been utterly impossible that the fact should have escaped observation. Some five or six volumes, just from the hands of the binder, we carefully probed, longitudinally, with the needles."

"You explored the floors beneath the carpets?"

"Beyond doubt. We removed every carpet, and examined the boards with the microscope."

"And the paper on the walls?"

"Yes."

"You looked into the cellars?"

"We did."

"Then," I said, "you have been making a miscalculation, and the letter is *not* upon the premises, as you suppose."

"I fear you are right there," said the Prefect. "And now, Dupin, what would you advise me to do?"

"To make a thorough re-search of the premises."

"That is absolutely needless," replied G——. "I am not more sure that I breathe than I am that the letter is not at the Hotel."

"I have no better advice to give you," said Dupin. "You have, of course, an accurate description of the letter?"

"Oh yes!"—And here the Prefect, producing a memorandum-book, proceeded to read aloud a minute account of the internal, and especially of the external appearance of the missing document. Soon after finishing the perusal of this description, he took his departure, more entirely depressed in spirits than I had ever known the good gentleman before.

In about a month afterwards he paid us another visit, and found us occupied very nearly as before. He took a pipe and a chair and entered into some ordinary conversation. At length I said,—

"Well, but G——, what of the purloined letter? I presume you have at last made up your mind that there is no such thing as overreaching the minister?"

"Confound him, say I—yes; I made the reexamination, however, as Dupin suggested—but it was all labor lost, as I knew it would be."

"How much was the reward offered, did you say?" asked Dupin.

"Why, a very great deal—a *very* liberal reward—I don't like to say how much, precisely; but one thing I *will* say, that I wouldn't mind giving my individual check for fifty thousand francs to any one who could obtain me that letter. The fact is, it is becoming of more and more importance every day; and the reward has been lately doubled. If it were trebled, however, I could do no more than I have done."

"Why, yes," said Dupin, drawlingly, between the whiffs of his meerschaum, "I really—think, G——, you have not exerted yourself—to the utmost in this matter. You might—do a little more, I think, eh?"

"How?—in what way?"

"Why—puff, puff—you might—puff, puff—employ counsel in the matter, eh?—puff, puff, puff. Do you remember the story they tell of Abernethy?"

"No; hang Abernethy!"

"'To be sure! hang him and welcome. But, once upon a time, a certain rich miser conceived the design of spunging upon this Abernethy for a medical opinion. Getting up, for this purpose, an ordinary conversation in a private company, he insinuated his case to the physician, as that of an imaginary individual. 'We will suppose', said the miser, 'that his symptoms are such and such; now, doctor, what would *you* have directed him to take?'"

"'Take!' said Abernethy, 'why, take *advice*, to be sure.'"

"But," said the Prefect, a little discomposed, "I am *perfectly* willing to take advice, and to pay for it. I would *really* give fifty thousand francs to any one who would aid me in the matter."

"In that case," replied Dupin, opening a drawer, and producing a check-book, "you may as well fill me up a check for the amount mentioned. When you have signed it, I will hand you the letter."

I was astounded. The Prefect appeared absolutely thunderstricken. For some minutes he remained speechless and motionless, looking incredulously at my friend with open mouth, and eyes that seemed starting from their sockets; then, apparently recovering himself in some measure, he seized a pen, and after several pauses and vacant stares, finally filled up and signed a check for fifty thousand francs, and handed it across the table to Dupin. The latter examined it carefully and deposited it in his pocket-book; then, unlocking an *escritoire*,[7] took thence a letter and gave it to the Prefect. This functionary grasped it in a perfect agony of joy, opened it with a trembling hand, cast a rapid glance at its contents, and then, scrambling and struggling to the door, rushed at length unceremoniously from the room and from the house, without having uttered a syllable since Dupin had requested him to fill up the check.

When he had gone, my friend entered into some explanations.

"The Parisian police," he said, "are exceedingly able in their way. They are persevering, ingenious, cunning, and thoroughly versed in the knowledge which their duties seem chiefly to demand. Thus, when G—— detailed to us his mode of searching the premises at the Hôtel D——, I felt entire confidence in his having made a satisfactory investigation—so far as his labors extended."

"So far as his labors extended?" said I.

"Yes" said Dupin. "The measures adopted were not only the best of their kind, but carried out to absolute perfection. Had the letter been deposited within the range of their search, these fellows would, beyond a question, have found it."

I merely laughed—but he seemed quite serious in all that he said.

"The measures, then," he continued, "were good in their kind, and well executed; their defect lay in their being inapplicable to the case, and to the man. A certain set of highly ingenious resources are, with the Prefect, a sort of Procrustean[8] bed, to which he forcibly adapts his designs. But he perpetually errs by being too deep or too shallow, for the matter in hand; and many a schoolboy is a better reasoner than he. I knew one about eight years of age, whose success at guessing in the game of 'even and odd' attracted universal admiration. This game is simple, and is played with marbles. One player holds in his hand a number of these toys, and demands of another whether that number is even or odd. If the guess is right, the guesser wins one; if wrong, he

---

7. *escritoire:* Writing desk.
8. **Procrustean:** In Greek legend, Procrustes was a thief who made every one of his victims fit a particular bed by stretching them if too short or cutting off their legs if too tall.

loses one. The boy to whom I allude won all the marbles of the school. Of course he had some principle of guessing; and this lay in mere observation and admeasurement of the astuteness of his opponents. For example, an arrant simpleton is his opponent, and, holding up his closed hand, asks, 'Are they even or odd?' Our schoolboy replies, 'odd'—and loses; but upon the second trial he wins, for he then says to himself, 'the simpleton had them even upon the first trial, and his amount of cunning is just sufficient to make him have them odd upon the second; I will therefore guess odd,—he guesses odd, and wins. Now, with a simpleton a degree above the first, he would have reasoned thus: 'This fellow finds that in the first instance I guessed odd, and, in the second, he will propose to himself upon the first impulse, a simple variation from even to odd, as did the first simpleton; but then a second thought will suggest that this is too simple a variation, and finally he will decide upon putting it even as before. I will therefore guess even;'—he guesses even, and wins. Now this mode of reasoning in the schoolboy, whom his fellows termed 'lucky,'—what, in its last analysis, is it?"

"It is merely," I said, "an identification of the reasoner's intellect with that of his opponent."

"It is," said Dupin; "and, upon inquiring of the boy by what means he effected the *thorough* identification in which his success consisted, I received answer as follows: 'When I wish to find out how wise, or how stupid, or how good, or how wicked is any one, or what are his thoughts at the moment, I fashion the expression of my face, as accurately as possible, in accordance with the expression of his, and then wait to see what thoughts or sentiments arise in my mind or heart, as if to match or correspond with the expression.' This response of the schoolboy lies at the bottom of all the spurious profundity which has been attributed to Rochefoucauld,[9] to La[10] to Machiavelli,[11] and to Campanella."[12]

"And the identification," I said, "of the reasoner's intellect with that of his opponent, depends, if I understand you aright, upon the accuracy with which the opponent's intellect is admeasured."

"For its practical value it depends upon this," replied Dupin; "and the Prefect and his cohort fail so frequently, first, by default of this identification, and, secondly, by ill-admeasurement, or rather through non-admeasurement, of the intellect with which they are engaged. They consider only their *own* ideas of ingenuity; and, in searching for anything hidden, advert only to the

---

9. Rochefoucauld: French writer known for his maxims and observations.
10. La Bougive: A printer's mistake for La Bruyère, another French writer of maxims.
11. Machiavelli: Italian writer on politics.
12. Campanella: Italian philosopher.

modes in which *they* would have hidden it. They are right in this much—that their own ingenuity is a faithful representative of that of *the mass*; but when the cunning of the individual felon is diverse in character from their own, the felon foils them, of course. This always happens when it is above their own, and very usually when it is below. They have no variation of principle in their investigations; at best, when urged by some unusual emergency—some extraordinary reward—they extend or exaggerate their old modes of practice, without touching their principles. What, for example, in this case of D——, has been done to vary the principle of action? What is all this boring, and probing, and sounding, and scrutinizing with the microscope, and dividing the surface of the building into registered square inches—what is it all but an exaggeration *of the application* of the one principle or set of principles of search, which are based upon the one set of notions regarding human ingenuity, to which the Prefect, in the long routine of his duty, has been accustomed? Do you not see he has taken it for granted that *all* men proceed to conceal a letter—not exactly in a gimlet-hole bored in a chair-leg—but, at least, in *some* out-of-the-way hole or corner suggested by the same tenor of thought which would urge a man to secrete a letter in a gimlet-hole bored in a chair-leg? And do you not see also, that such *recherchés*[13] nooks for concealment are adapted only for ordinary occasions, and would be adopted only by ordinary intellects; for, in all cases of concealment, a disposal of the article concealed—a disposal of it in this *recherché* manner,—is, in the very first instance, presumable and presumed; and thus its discovery depends, not at all upon the acumen, but altogether upon the mere care, patience, and determination of the seekers; and where the case is of importance—or, what amounts to the same thing in the policial eyes, when the reward is of magnitude,—the qualities in question have *never* been known to fail. You will now understand what I meant in suggesting that, had the purloined letter been hidden anywhere within the limits of the Prefect's examination—in other words, had the principle of its concealment been comprehended within the principles of the Prefect—its discovery would have been a matter altogether beyond question. This functionary, however, has been thoroughly mystified; and the remote source of his defeat lies in the supposition that the Minister is a fool, because he has acquired renown as a poet. All fools are poets; this the Prefect *feels*; and he is merely guilty of a *non distributio medii*[14] in thence inferring that all poets are fools."

"But is this really the poet?" I asked. "There are two brothers,

---

13. *recherchés:* Rare and unusual.
14. *non distributio medii:* Error in logic.

I know; and both have attained reputation in letters. The Minister I believe has written learnedly on the Differential Calculus. He is a mathematician, and no poet."

"You are mistaken; I know him well; he is both. As poet *and* mathematician, he would reason well; as mere mathematician, he could not have reasoned at all, and thus would have been at the mercy of the Prefect."

"You surprise me," I said, "by these opinions, which have been contradicted by the voice of the world. You do not mean to set at naught the well-digested idea of centuries. The mathematical reason has long been regarded as *the* reason *par excellence.*"

"*'Il y a `a parier,'*" "replied Dupin, quoting from Chamfort, "'*que toute idée publique, toute convention reçue, est une sottise, car elle a convenu an plus grand nombre.*'[15] The mathematicians, I grant you, have done their best to promulgate the popular error to which you allude, and which is none the less an error for its promulgation as truth. With an art worthy a better cause, for example, they have insinuated the term 'analysis' into application to algebra. The French are the originators of this particular deception; but if a term is of any importance—if words derive any value from applicability—then 'analysis' conveys 'algebra' about as much as, in Latin, '*ambitus*' implies 'ambition,' '*religio*' 'religion,' or '*homines honesti,*' a set of *honorable* men."

"You have a quarrel on hand, I see," said I, "with some of the algebraists of Paris; but proceed."

"I dispute the availability, and thus the value, of that reason which is cultivated in any especial form other than the abstractly logical. I dispute, in particular, the reason educed by mathematical study. The mathematics are the science of form and quantity; mathematical reasoning is merely logic applied to observation upon form and quantity. The great error lies in supposing that even the truths of what is called *pure* algebra, are abstract or general truths. And this error is so egregious[16] that I am confounded at the universality with which it has been received. Mathematical axioms are *not* axioms of general truth. What is true of *relation*—of form and quantity—is often grossly false in regard to morals, for example. In this latter science it is very usually *un*true that the aggregated parts are equal to the whole. In chemistry also the axiom fails. In the consideration of motive it fails; for two motives, each of a given value, have not, necessarily, a value when united, equal to the sum of their values apart. There are numerous other mathematical truths which are only truths within the limits of *relation*. But the mathematician

---

15. *Il y a . . .:* You can count on the fact that all popular notions and accepted conventions are stupid, since they suit the majority.
16. egregious: (e gre´ jəs) *adj.*: Extraordinary.

argues, from his *finite truths,* through habit, as if they were of an absolutely general applicability—as the world indeed imagines them to be. Bryant, in his very learned *Mythology,* mentions an analogous source of error, when he says that 'although the Pagan fables are not believed, yet we forget ourselves continually, and make inferences from them as existing realities.' With the algebraists, however, who are Pagans themselves, the 'Pagan fables' *are* believed, and the inferences are made, not so much through lapse of memory, as through an unaccountable addling of the brains. In short, I never yet encountered the mere mathematician who could be trusted out of equal roots, or one who did not clandestinely hold it as a point of his faith that x^2+px was absolutely and unconditionally equal to q. Say to one of these gentlemen, by way of experiment, if you please, that you believe occasions may occur where x^2+px is *not* altogether equal to q, and, having made him understand what you mean, get out of his reach as speedily as convenient, for, beyond doubt, he will endeavor to knock you down.

"I mean to say," continued Dupin, while I merely laughed at his last observations, "that if the Minister had been no more than a mathematician, the Prefect would have been under no necessity of giving me this check. I knew him, however, as both mathematician and poet, and my measures were adapted to his capacity, with reference to the circumstances by which he was surrounded. I knew him as a courtier, too, and as a bold *intriguant.*[17] Such a man, I considered, could not fail to be aware of the ordinary policial modes of action. He could not have failed to anticipate—and events have proved that he did not fail to anticipate—the waylayings to which he was subjected. He must have foreseen, I reflected, the secret investigations of his premises. His frequent absences from home at night, which were hailed by the Prefect as certain aids to his success, I regarded only as *ruses,* to afford opportunity for thorough search to the police, and thus the sooner to impress them with the conviction to which G——, in fact, did finally arrive—the conviction that the letter was not upon the premises. I felt, also, that the whole train of thought, which I was at some pains in detailing to you just now, concerning the invariable principle of policial action in searches for articles concealed—I felt that this whole train of thought would necessarily pass through the mind of the Minister. It would imperatively lead him to despise all the ordinary *nooks* of concealment. *He* could not, I reflected, be so weak as not to see that the most intricate and remote recess of his hotel would be as open as his commonest closets to the eyes, to the probes, to the gimlets, and to the microscopes of the Prefect. I saw, in

17. *intriguant:* Schemer.

fine, that he would be driven, as a matter of course, to *simplicity*, if not deliberately induced to it as a matter of choice. You will remember, perhaps, how desperately the Prefect laughed when I suggested, upon our first interview, that it was just possible this mystery troubled him so much on account of its being so *very* self-evident."

"Yes," said I, "I remember his merriment well. I really thought he would have fallen into convulsions."

"The material world," continued Dupin, "abounds with very strict analogies to the immaterial; and thus some color of truth has been given to the rhetorical dogma, that metaphor, or simile, may be made to strengthen an argument, as well as to embellish a description. The principle of the *vis inertiæ*,[18] for example, seems to be identical in physics and metaphysics. It is not more true in the former, that a large body is with more difficulty set in motion than a smaller one, and that its subsequent *momentum* is commensurate with this difficulty, than it is, in the latter, that intellects of the vaster capacity, while more forcible, more constant, and more eventful in their movements than those of inferior grade, are yet the less readily moved, and more embarrassed and full of hesitation in the first few steps of their progress. Again: have you ever noticed which of the street signs, over the shop doors, are the most attractive of attention?"

"I have never given the matter a thought," I said.

"There is a game of puzzles," he resumed, "which is played upon a map. One party playing requires another to find a given word—the name of town, river, state or empire—any word, in short, upon the motley and perplexed surface of the chart. A novice in the game generally seeks to embarrass his opponents by giving them the most minutely lettered names; but the adept selects such words as stretch, in large characters, from one end of the chart to the other. These, like the over-largely lettered signs and placards of the street, escape observation by dint of being excessively obvious; and here the physical oversight is precisely analogous with the moral inapprehension by which the intellect suffers to pass unnoticed those considerations which are too obtrusively and too palpably self-evident. But this is a point, it appears, somewhat above or beneath the understanding of the Prefect. He never once thought it probable, or possible, that the Minister had deposited the letter immediately beneath the nose of the whole world, by way of best preventing any portion of that world from perceiving it.

"But the more I reflected upon the daring, dashing, and discriminating ingenuity of D——; upon the fact that the document

---

18. ***vis inertiae:*** Boredom.

must always have been *at hand,* if he intended to use it to good purpose; and upon the decisive evidence, obtained by the Prefect, that it was not hidden within the limits of that dignitary's ordinary search—the more satisfied I became that, to conceal this letter, the Minister had resorted to the comprehensive and sagacious expedient of not attempting to conceal it at all.

"Full of these ideas, I prepared myself with a pair of green spectacles, and called one fine morning, quite by accident, at the Ministerial hotel. I found D——at home, yawning, lounging, and dawdling, as usual, and pretending to be in the last extremity of *ennui.*[19] He is, perhaps, the most really energetic human being now alive—but that is only when nobody sees him.

"To be even with him, I complained of my weak eyes, and lamented the necessity of the spectacles, under cover of which I cautiously and thoroughly surveyed the apartment, while seemingly intent only upon the conversation of my host.

"I paid special attention to a large writing-table near which he sat, and upon which lay confusedly, some miscellaneous letters and other papers, with one or two musical instruments and a few books. Here, however, after a long and very deliberate scrutiny, I saw nothing to excite particular suspicion.

"At length my eyes, in going the circuit of the room, fell upon a trumpery filligree card-rack of paste-board, that hung dangling by a dirty blue ribbon, from a little brass knob just beneath the middle of the mantelpiece. In this rack, which had three or four compartments, were five or six visiting cards and a solitary letter. This last was much soiled and crumpled. It was torn nearly in two, across the middle—as if a design, in the first instance, to tear it entirely up as worthless, had been altered, or stayed, in the second. It had a large black seal, bearing the D—— cipher *very* conspicuously, and was addressed, in a diminutive female hand, to D——, the minister, himself. It was thrust carelessly, and even, as it seemed, contemptuously, into one of the upper divisions of the rack.

"No sooner had I glanced at this letter, than I concluded it to be that of which I was in search. To be sure, it was, to all appearance, radically different from the one of which the Prefect had read us so minute a description. Here the seal was large and black, with the D—— cipher; there it was small and red, with the ducal arms of the S—— family. Here, the address, to the Minister, was diminutive and feminine; there the superscription, to a certain royal personage, was markedly bold and decided; the size alone formed a point of correspondence. But, then, the *radicalness* of these differences, which was excessive; the dirt; the

---

19. *ennui:* (än´ wē) Weariness due to lack of interest.

soiled and torn condition of the paper, so inconsistent with the *true* methodical habits of D——, and so suggestive of a design to delude the beholder into an idea of the worthlessness of the document; these things, together with the hyperobtrusive situation of this document, full in the view of every visitor, and thus exactly in accordance with the conclusions to which I had previously arrived; these things, I say, were strongly corroborative of suspicion, in one who came with the intention to suspect.

"I protracted my visit as long as possible, and, while I maintained a most animated discussion with the Minister, on a topic which I knew well had never failed to interest and excite him, I kept my attention really riveted upon the letter. In this examination, I committed to memory its external appearance and arrangement in the rack; and also fell, at length, upon a discovery which set at rest whatever trivial doubt I might have entertained. In scrutinizing the edges of the paper, I observed them to be more *chafed*[20] than seemed necessary. They presented the *broken* appearance which is manifested when a stiff paper, having been once folded and pressed with a folder, is refolded in a reversed direction, in the same creases or edges which had formed the original fold. This discovery was sufficient. It was clear to me that the letter had been turned, as a glove, inside out, redirected, and resealed. I bade the Minister good morning, and took my departure at once, leaving a gold snuff-box upon the table.

"The next morning I called for the snuff-box, when we resumed, quite eagerly, the conversation of the preceding day. While thus engaged, however, a loud report, as if of a pistol, was heard immediately beneath the windows of the hotel, and was succeeded by a series of fearful screams, and the shoutings of a mob. D—— rushed to a casement, threw it open, and looked out. In the meantime, I stepped to the card-rack, took the letter, put it in my pocket, and replaced it by a *facsimile* (so far as regards externals,) which I had carefully prepared at my lodgings; imitating the D—— cipher, very readily, by means of a seal formed of bread.

"The disturbance in the street had been occasioned by the frantic behavior of a man with a musket. He had fired it among a crowd of women and children. It proved, however, to have been without ball, and the fellow was suffered to go his way as a lunatic or a drunkard. When he had gone, D—— came from the window, whither I had followed him immediately upon securing the object in view. Soon afterwards I bade him farewell. The pretended lunatic was a man in my own pay."

---

20. *chafed:* Worn away.

"But what purpose had you," I asked, "in replacing the letter by a *facsimile?* Would it not have been better, at the first visit, to have seized it openly, and departed?"

"D——," replied Dupin, "is a desperate man, and a man of nerve. His hotel, too, is not without attendants devoted to his interests. Had I made the wild attempt you suggest, I might never have left the Ministerial presence alive. The good people of Paris might have heard of me no more. But I had an object apart from these considerations. You know my political prepossessions. In this matter, I act as a partisan of the lady concerned. For eighteen months the Minister has had her in his power. She has now him in hers; since, being unaware that the letter is not in his possession, he will proceed with his exactions as if it was. Thus will he inevitably commit himself, at once, to his political destruction. His downfall, too, will not be more precipitate than awkward. It is all very well to talk about the *facilis descensus Averni,*[21] but in all kinds of climbing, as Catalani said of singing, it is far more easy to get up than to come down. In the present instance I have no sympathy—at least no pity—for him who descends. He is that *monstrum horrendum,* an unprincipled man of genius. I confess, however, that I should like very well to know the precise character of his thoughts, when, being defied by her whom the Prefect terms 'a certain personage,' he is reduced to opening the letter which I left for him in the card-rack."

"How? did you put anything particular in it?"

"Why—it did not seem altogether right to leave the interior blank—that would have been insulting. D——, at Vienna once, did me an evil turn, which I told him, quite good-humoredly, that I should remember. So, as I knew he would feel some curiosity in regard to the identity of the person who had outwitted him, I thought it a pity not to give him a clue. He is well acquainted with my MS., and I just copied into the middle of the blank sheet the words—

'—Un dessein si funeste,
S'il n'est digne d'Atrée, est digne de Thyeste.'[22]

They are to be found in Crébillon's *Atrèe.*"[23]

---

21. *facilis descensus Averni:* The easy descent to Hell.
22. *Un dessein si:* So deadly a scheme is worthy of Thyestes, if not of Atreus [that is, a good enough plan, but not a great one].
23. *Atree:* A play by a French writer (1674–1762).

*dgar Allan Poe

from Chapter of Suggestions

An excellent Magazine paper might be written upon the subject of the progressive steps by which any great work of art—especially of literary art—attained completion. How vast a dissimilarity always exists between the germ and the fruit—between the work and its original conception! Sometimes the original conception is abandoned, or left out of sight altogether. *Most* authors sit down to write with *no* fixed design, trusting to the inspiration of the moment; it is not, therefore, to be wondered at, that *most* books are valueless. Pen should never touch paper, until at least a well-digested *general* purpose be established. In fiction, the *dénouement*—in all other composition the intended *effect*, should be definitely considered and arranged, before writing the first word; and *no* word should be then written which does not tend, or form a part of a sentence which tends, to the development of the *dénouement*, or to the strengthening of the effect. Where *plot* forms a portion of the contemplated interest, too much preconsideration cannot be had. *Plot* is very imperfectly understood, and has never been rightly defined. Many persons regard it as mere complexity of incident. In its most rigorous acceptation, it is *that from which no component atom can be removed, and in which none of the component atoms can be displaced, without ruin to the whole*; and although a sufficiently good plot may be constructed, without attention to the whole rigor of this definition, still it is the definition which the true artist should always keep in view, and always endeavor to consummate in his works. Some authors appear, however, to be totally deficient in constructiveness, and thus, even with plentiful invention, fail signally in plot.

☑ Check Your Comprehension

1. Why do you think Poe refrains from stating the year of the "The Purloined Letter" or the names of Monsieur G——, Minister D——, the victim of the robbery, and the "other exalted personage"?

2. According to Dupin, why does D—— not hide the letter in a secret place?

3. How does Dupin manage to replace the letter with the facsimile?

4. Why does Dupin write a note inside the facsimile letter?

5. According to Poe in "Chapter of Suggestions," why are most books worthless?

◆ Critical Thinking

1. Is the "game of puzzles" in its use of a map a good analogy to D——'s hiding of the purloined letter? Why or why not? [Connect]

2. Which is more important in Dupin's finding of the letter, his methods of thinking or his powers of observation? Explain. **[Make a Judgment]**

3. Is it possible to understand the plot of "The Purloined Letter" and to follow the action without a knowledge of all of Dupin's quotations and examples from science, mathematics, and literature? Explain. **[Criticize]**

4. Why does Poe include all of Dupin's quotations and examples? **[Speculate]**

COMPARE LITERARY WORKS

5. Do you think Poe followed his own advice and writing standards as outlined in "Chapter of Suggestions," in his own work, "The Purloined Letter"? Why or why not? **[Connect]**

Edgar Allan Poe

Alone

From childhood's hour I have not been
As others were—I have not seen
As others saw—I could not bring
My passions from a common spring.
5   From the same source I have not taken
My sorrow; I could not awaken
My heart to joy at the same tone;
And all I loved, *I* loved alone.
Then—in my childhood—in the dawn
10   Of a most stormy life—was drawn
From every depth of good and ill
The mystery which binds me still:
From the torrent, or the fountain,
From the red cliff of the mountain,
15   From the sun that 'round me rolled
In its autumn tint of gold—
From the lightning in the sky
As it passed me flying by—
From the thunder and the storm,
20   And the cloud that took the form
(When the rest of Heaven was blue)
Of a demon in my view.

Edgar Allan Poe

Eldorado[1]

Gaily bedight,[2]
A gallant knight,
In sunshine and in shadow,
Had journeyed long,
5   Singing a song,
In search of Eldorado.

But he grew old—
This knight so bold—
And o'er his heart a shadow
10   Fell, as lie found
No spot of ground
That looked like Eldorado.

And, as his strength
Failed him at length
15   He met a pilgrim[3] shadow—
"Shadow," said he,
"Where can it be—
This land of Eldorado?"

"Over the Mountains
20   Of the Moon,
Down the Valley of the Shadow,
Ride, boldly ride,"
The shade[4] replied,—
"If you seek for Eldorado!"

---

1. **Eldorado** (el də rä´ dō): A legendary kingdom in South America, rich in gold and gems.
2. **bedight** (bi dīt´) _adj._: Adorned.
3. **pilgrim** _adj._: Wanderer.
4. **shade** _n._: Ghost.

To Helen

Helen, thy beauty, is to me
   Like those Nicean[1] barks[2] of yore,
That gently, o'er a perfumed sea,
   The weary, way-worn wanderer bore
5   To his own native shore.

On desperate seas long wont to roam,
   Thy hyacinth[3] hair, thy classic face,
Thy Naiad airs have brought me home
   To the glory that was Greece
10   And the grandeur that was Rome.

Lo! in yon brilliant window-niche
   How statue-like I see thee stand!
The agate lamp within thy hand,
Ah! Psyche, from the regions which
15   Are Holy Land!

---

1. **Nicean** (nī sē´ ən) *n.*: From the ancient city of Nicaea in Turkey.
2. **barks:** Sailing ships.
3. **hyacinth** (hī ə sinth´) *adj.*: Lustrous; yellow.

☑ Check Your Comprehension

1. In what ways has the speaker felt himself to be unlike the "others" in "Alone"?
2. What is the "mystery" of line 12 of "Alone"?
3. In "Eldorado" the knight is described as "gallant" and "bold." Considering his quest for Eldorado, how else could he be described?
4. What is the "Valley of the Shadow" that the shade directs the knight to at the end of the poem? Explain.
5. What is the effect of the "Nicean barks" on the wanderer of "To Helen"?

◆ Critical Thinking

INTERPRET

1. Does the speaker of "Alone" assume others will feel as he does about the "mystery"? Explain. **[Draw Conclusions]**
2. What are the different meanings of "shadow" in "Eldorado"? **[Connect]**
3. In "To Helen," why does Helen's beauty remind the speaker of "Nicean barks of yore"? **[Infer]**
4. Psyche, in mythology, is the human soul. Why does the speaker address Helen as "Psyche" at the end of the poem? **[Interpret]**

COMPARE LITERARY WORKS

5. Compare the speakers of "To Helen" and "Alone" with the knight of "Eldorado" in terms of their isolation. **[Compare and Contrast]**

$\mathcal{E}$dgar Allan Poe
$\mathcal{C}$omparing and $\mathcal{C}$onnecting the $\mathcal{A}$uthor's $\mathcal{W}$orks

◆ Literary Focus: Irony

There are two kinds of **irony** that can be found in Poe's works. The simpler kind is **verbal irony**, in which it is clear that a speaker or writer means the opposite of what he or she is saying. For example, in "The Purloined Letter," Dupin says to the Prefect that, compared to the Prefect, "No more sagacious agent could, I suppose, be desired, or even imagined." Dupin, of course, does not have a high regard for the Prefect's "sagacity." What makes the exchange humorous is that the pompous Prefect doesn't realize that Dupin is being ironic.

Another kind of irony is **situational irony**, in which the outcome of a situation is the opposite of what is expected.

1. What is ironic about the Prefect's efforts to find the purloined letter?
2. What is ironic about the lady's having the letter in her possession at the end of the story?
3. What is the irony at the end of "Eldorado"?

◆ Drawing Conclusions About Poe's Work

William Cullen Bryant, one of the most respected of American poets in his day, wrote the inscription for an 1875 monument to Poe in Baltimore. He described Poe as:

> Author of the Raven
> and other Poems,
> and of various works of Fiction
> Distinguished alike
> for originality in the conception,
> skill in word-painting,
> and power over the mind
> of the reader....

In the graphic organizer below, Poe may be viewed through the lens of an important poet and critic, William Cullen Bryant. Look at this organizer to see examples of how Poe's work exemplifies Bryant's words. Make your own graphic organizer, and then find more examples of how Poe's work reflects Bryant's inscription.

Bryant's Words	Poe's Work
originally in the conception	The quest for gold Turns into death at the end of a wasted life in "Eldorado."
skill in word-painting	"The glory that was Greece, /And the grandeur that was Rome" sums up the ancient world in two lines.
power over mind of the reader	The beginning of "Alone" is a memorable portrait of an unhappy, alienated person.

◆ Idea Bank

Writing

1. **Letter** Imagine that the speaker of "Alone" is a friend of yours. Would you understand his feelings? Would you have advice to give him? Write a letter to the speaker, expressing your feelings about his situation.
2. **Story Outline** Work with other students to develop the plot outline for an exciting short story. Follow Poe's suggestions in "Chapter of Suggestions" to start with the story's

denouement, or the "unknotting" after the climax.

3. **Parody** We think of Poe as a serious writer. Much of what he wrote, however, was intended to be humorous—hoaxes, comic sketches, and parodies of other writers. Write a parody of one of the Poe selections you have read. You could try to imitate his style of writing, or just create a light treatment of one of this themes.

Speaking and Listening

4. **Dramatization** Writers, movie directors, and composers have often based their works on Poe's creations. Working with other students, choose a poem or story of Poe's and prepare a dramatization of all or a portion of it. Write a script, round up sound effects and music, and decide on costumes and props and whether you need scenery or special lighting. Tape your performance or present it "live" to other students. **[Performing Arts Link]**

Researching and Representing

5. **Further Reading** Find a short story or novel that is an example of detective fiction. Write a report on the story or novel. Include a discussion of what it does or does not have in common with the detective-story elements Poe included in "The Purloined Letter."

6. **Classical and Gothic Architecture** In Poe's lifetime and later, two types of literature showed the influence of the Classical world (ancient Greece and Rome) and the Gothic era (the Middle Ages). There were also two popular styles of architecture: Classical, resembling the temples and other buildings of ancient Greece and Rome; and Gothic, based on the castles and cathedrals of the Middle Ages. Take photos of buildings in your community—or find pictures of American buildings—that show the two styles. Show the pictures to other students. Write a short essay explaining which style your prefer. **[Art Link]**

◆ Further Reading, Listening, and Viewing

- Suzanne LeVert and Vito Perrone: *Edgar Allan Poe: Library of Biography* (1992). Biography of the imaginative author and poet, focusing on his struggles to establish himself in the literary world

- Philip V. Stern (editor): *The Portable Edgar Allan Poe* (1976). Anthology presenting the many sides of Poe's works

- *The Poetry of Edgar Allan Poe* (2 cassettes), Vol. 2, (1996). Performed by David Warner and Christopher Cazenove. Poems exploring the love, anguish and despair of Poe's tragic life

- A&E Biography Video: *The Mystery of Edgar Allan Poe* (1994). Poe's complete story including dramatic readings of poems and expert commentary

- *Edgar Allan Poe: Terror of the Soul,* PBS American Masters series, 1995, 60 mins. A comprehensive film biography of Poe with dramatic recreations of important scenes from his life and work

On the Web:

http://www.phschool.com/atschool/literature
Go to the student edition of *The American Experience.* Proceed to Unit 3. Then, click Hot Links to find Web sites featuring Edgar Allan Poe

Walt Whitman In Depth

"I celebrate myself, and sing myself,
And what I assume you shall assume,
For every atom belonging to me as good belongs to you." —*Walt Whitman*

WALT WHITMAN'S poems not only look different from the poetry written before him—the content is different as well. Instead of traditional views of nature and morality, Whitman set out to write about everything in the world around him; he wanted to be the poet of American democracy. Before Whitman, poetry was a polite form of literature. It is not surprising that people felt either shocked or liberated by what he wrote.

Long Island Much of what Whitman knew about America came from a part of New York State known as Long Island. Native Americans called it "Paumanok," which meant "fish-shaped." Long Island was mostly rural, with farms, small villages, and isolated beaches. At its western end was the city of Brooklyn; which in Whitman's time became the fourth largest city in the United States. New York City, the largest, was a short ferry ride away.

Whitman was born in 1819 to a family that would include eight other children. His father was a farmer and carpenter who moved the family to Brooklyn in 1823, where he built houses as a contractor. Walt left school at the age of eleven to work as a printer's apprentice. When the family returned to rural Long Island in 1834, he stayed in Brooklyn.

Schools and Newspapers For several years Whitman worked as a teacher and as a printer and editor on newspapers in Long Island and New York City. He contributed articles, stories, and poems to several newspapers. In 1845, he met with Edgar Allan Poe, the editor of the *Broadway Journal*, who published an article he wrote.

By 1846, he was an editor of the *Brooklyn Daily Eagle*. He was a success until he got in trouble over the prohibition of slavery in the new United States territories. Whitman favored the prohibition; the owner of the *Eagle* was against it. After Whitman published an editorial stating his position, he was fired.

He was offered a job on a newspaper in New Orleans. Though he stayed only three months, the long trip to and from New Orleans was his main experience of the vast country he would speak for in his poems.

Leaves of Grass Except for editing the *Brooklyn Daily Freeman* in 1848–49, Whitman spent the next years working at odd jobs in carpentry and writing, living with his family, and working on his poems. In 1855 he paid to have one thousand copies of his poetry printed, doing some of the typesetting himself. In ninety-five pages, *Leaves of Grass* included twelve poems and a preface that stated his intention of writing a new kind of poetry for American readers.

A few of the reviews were positive— the writers recognized something fresh and exciting in the form and subject matter. The noted writer Ralph Waldo Emerson wrote, "I greet you at the beginning of a great career." Others, however, accused Whitman of writing something that was hardly poetry at all.

A year later, he published a second edition, adding several new poems; the book was three hundred forty-two pages long. It didn't sell. To support his family, Whitman became editor of the *Brooklyn Daily Times* from 1857–59. A new publishing company in Boston, Thayer and Eldridge, published a third edition of *Leaves of Grass* in 1861. As many as 5,000 copies may have been sold.

Civil War The main American crisis of Whitman's lifetime—over states' rights and slavery—broke out in 1861. Too old to enlist at forty-three, Whitman supported the Union effort in poems like "Beat! Beat! Drums!" He visited his brother George, slightly wounded at Fredericksburg, Virginia, and he stayed on in Washington. Over the next three years, he made hundreds of visits to hospitals, helping in the care of soldiers.

In 1865, he published his poems about the war, including tributes to Lincoln after his assassination. After his poems were published in England in 1868, the recognition he got in that country encouraged American magazines to treat his work more favorably.

Camden In 1873, Whitman suffered a stroke. He recovered sufficiently to travel to Camden, New Jersey, a city near Philadelphia. Whitman stayed in Camden, writing articles for New York newspapers, as well as writing new poems. He bought a small house, receiving important visitors there and traveling to receive awards. After a second stroke in 1888, he stayed at home, working on what became known as the "Deathbed Edition" of *Leaves of Grass*. He died in March, 1892. The recognition his work has received since his death fulfilled a prediction in the first edition of *Leaves of Grass*: "The proof of a poet is that his country absorbs him as affectionately as he has absorbed it."

◆ Whitman and the Newspaper World

Most of Walt Whitman's experience in the working world was as a newspaper

printer, reporter, and editor. Besides giving him practice in the craft of writing, his job exposed him to the stories of all the people he encountered in his trade.

The first American newspapers imitated English examples. England's first daily newspaper, in 1702, was the *Daily Courant*, and the first editorials were written in 1704 by Daniel Defoe, better known as the author of *Robinson Crusoe*. The first independent newspaper in America was the *New-England Courant*, published by Benjamin Franklin's brother James in 1721.

New kinds of printing and paper-making processes made larger editions at lower prices possible. By Whitman's time, most towns had at least one newspaper. In rapidly growing cities, different newspapers often supported different political parties or sides of issues like the prohibition of alcohol or the abolition of slavery. By 1851, when the *New York Times* began publication, the New York City papers sold 200,000 copies each day.

◆ Literary Works

Poetry Whitman collected all of his poems in *Leaves of Grass*. He prepared several editions from 1855 to 1891, usually adding new poems and rearranging and revising the old ones.

Song of Myself; There Was a Child Went Forth (1855)

Crossing Brooklyn Ferry; Song of the Open Road (1856)

Out of the Cradle Endlessly Rocking (1859)

I Hear America Singing (1860)

When Lilacs Last in The Dooryard Bloom'd (1865)

Prose

Democratic Vistas (1870)

Memoranda During the War (1876)

Specimen Days and Collect (1882)

T I M E L I N E

Whitman's Life	World Events
1819 Whitman is born in West Hills, Long Island, New York	**1812–15** War of 1812 between the United States and Britain
1823 Whitman family moves to Brooklyn	**1819–26** South American countries win independence from Spain
1825–30 Walt attends public school	**1820** Missouri Compromise
1831–36 Apprentice in print shops and on newspapers	**1822** Liberia, West Africa, becomes home for freed slaves
1836–41 Teaches school and works on newspapers on Long Island	**1827** Photography invented in France
1841–45 Works on newspapers in New York City	**1833** Slavery abolished in British Empire
1845–49 Edits newspapers in Brooklyn and New Orleans	**1838** Trail of Tears as Native Americans are moved west
1855 Publishes *Leaves of Grass*; father dies	**1842** Tennyson's *Morte d'Arthur* published
1856 Publishes second edition of *Leaves of Grass*	**1846–48** War between United States and Mexico
1860 Third edition published by Thayer and Eldridge	**1848** *Communist Manifesto* published; women's rights meeting held in Seneca Falls, N.Y.
1862–73 Works in Washington as government clerk; regularly visits hospitals during Civil War	**1849** Republican Party, opposed to slavery, is founded
1867 Fourth edition of *Leaves of Grass*	**1856** Darwin's *The Origin of Species* published
1868 *Poems of Walt Whitman* published in England	**1859** *Les Misérables* published
1873 Suffers stroke; mother dies; moves to Camden, New Jersey	**1865** Lincoln assassinated; Thirteenth Amendment ends slavery
1879–80 Trips to Colorado, Missouri, Canada	**1869** Suez Canal opens; transcontinental railroad completed in United States
1884 Buys house in Camden, New Jersey	**1876** Telephone invented; Queen Victoria becomes Empress of India
1888 Second stroke	**1877** Edison invents phonograph
1891 Prepares "Deathbed Edition" of *Leaves of Grass* and *Complete Prose Works*	**1883** Edison invents light bulb
1892 Whitman dies in Camden; is buried there	**1886** Statue of Liberty is dedicated; American Federation of Labor is founded

alt Whitman

As I Ebb'd with the Ocean of Life

1

As I ebb'd with the ocean of life,
As I wended the shores I know,
As I walk'd where the ripples continually wash you Paumanok[1]
Where they rustle up hoarse and sibilant,
5   Where the fierce old mother endlessly cries for her castaways,
I musing late in the autumn day, gazing off southward,
Held by this electric self out of the pride of which I utter
    poems,
Was seiz'd by the spirit that trails in the lines underfoot,
The rim, the sediment that stands for all the water and all
    the land of the globe.

10   Fascinated, my eyes reverting from the south, dropped, to
    follow those slender windrows[2],
Chaff, straw, splinters of wood, weeds, and the sea-gluten,
Scum, scales from shining rocks, leaves of salt-lettuce, left by
    the tide,
Miles walking, the sound of breaking waves the other side
    of me,
Paumanok there and then as I thought the old thought of
    likenesses,
15   These you presented to me you fish-shaped island,
As I wended the shores I know,
As I walk'd with that electric self seeking types.

2

As I wend to the shores I know not,
As I list to the dirge, the voices of men and women wreck'd,
20   As I inhale the impalpable breezes that set in upon me,
As the ocean so mysterious rolls toward me closer and closer,
I too but signify at the utmost a little wash'd-up drift,
A few sands and dead leaves to gather,
Gather, and merge myself as part of the sands and drift.

25   O baffled, balk'd, bent to the very earth,
Opppress'd with myself that I have dared to open my mouth,

---

1. Paumanok: Native American name for Long Island, New York.
2. windrows (wind′ rōz′) n.: Vegetation swept into a row by the wind or surge.

Aware now that amid all that blab whose echoes recoil upon
    me I have not once had the least idea who or what I am,
But that before all my arrogant poems the real Me stands yet
    untouch'd, untold, altogether unreach'd
Withdrawn far, mocking me with mock-congratulatory signs
    and bows,
30   With peals of distant ironical laughter at every word I have
    written,
Pointing in silence to these songs, and then to the sand
    beneath.

I perceive I have not really understood anything, not a
    single object, and that no man ever can,
Nature here in sight of the sea taking advantage of me to
    dart upon me and sting me,
Because I have dared to open my mouth to sing at all.

3

35   You oceans both, I close with you,
We murmur alike reproachfully rolling sands and drift,
    knowing not why,
These little shreds indeed standing for you and me and all.

You friable³ shore with trails of debris,
You fish-shaped island, I take what is underfoot,
40   What is yours is mine my father.

I too Paumanok,
I too have bubbled up, floated the measureless float, and
    been wash'd on your shores,
I too am but a trail of drift and debris,
I too leave little wrecks upon you, you fish-shaped island.

45   I throw myself upon your breast my father,
I cling to you so that you cannot unloose me,
I hold you so firm till you answer me something.

Kiss me my father,
Touch me with your lips as I touch those I love,
50   Breathe to me while I hold you close the secret of the
    murmuring I envy.

---

3. friable (fri ə bəl) : Crumbly; easily crushed.

4

Ebb, ocean of life, (the flow will return,)
Cease not your moaning you fierce old mother,
Endlessly cry for your castaways, but fear not, deny not me,
Rustle not up so hoarse and angry against my feet as I touch
    you or gather from you.

55   I mean tenderly by you and all,
I gather for myself and for this phantom looking down
    where we lead, and following me and mine.

Me and mine, loose windrows, little corpses,
Froth, snowy white, and bubbles,
(See, from my dead lips the ooze exuding at last,
60   See, the prismatic colors glistening and rolling,)
Tufts of straw, sands, fragments,
Buoy'd hither from many moods, one contradicting another,
From the storm, the long calm, the darkness, the swell,
Musing, pondering, a breath, a briny tear, a dab of liquid or
    soil,
65   Up just as much out of fathomless workings fermented and
    thrown,
A limp blossom or two, torn, just as much over waves floating,
    drifted at random,
Just as much for us that sobbing dirge of Nature,
Just as much whence we come that blare of the cloud-trumpets,
We, capricious, brought hither we know not whence, spread out
    before you,
70   You up there walking or sitting,
Whoever you are, we too lie in drifts at your feet.

Walt Whitman

Broadway

What hurrying human tides, or day or night!
What passions, winnings, losses, ardors, swim thy
    waters!
What whirls of evil, bliss and sorrow, stem thee!
What curious questioning glances—glints of love!
5   Leer, envy, scorn, contempt, hope, aspiration!
Thou portal—thou arena—thou of the myriad long-
    drawn lines and groups!
(Could but thy flagstones, curbs, façades, tell their
    inimitable tales,
Thy windows rich, and huge hotels—thy sidewalks
    wide;)
Thou of the endless sliding, mincing, shuffling feet!
10   Thou, like the parti-colored world itself—like infinite,
    teeming, mocking life!
Thou visor'd, vast, unspeakable show and lesson!

☑ Check Your Comprehension

1. In line 22 of "As I Ebb'd with the Ocean of Life," what does the speaker mean when he speaks of himself as "a little washed-up drift"?

2. What does the speaker address as his father in line 48? What does he see himself as in order to "cling" to the father?

3. Who is the "you" of the last lines of the poem?

4. In the first three lines of "Broadway," what is the street seen as?

◆ Critical Thinking

1. In lines 28–31 of "As I Ebb'd with the Ocean of Life," why does "the real Me" point to "these songs, and then to the sand beneath"? **[Drawing Conclusions]**

2. At the end of Part 3, what is the "secret of the murmuring I envy" that the speaker wants to learn from Paumanok? **[Speculate]**

3. Why is ebbing and flowing so important in the poem, as mentioned at the beginning of Parts 1 and 4? **[Assess]**

4. In "Broadway," why does Whitman include negative aspects of life—losses, evil, sorrow, envy, scorn, contempt, mocking—along with such positive aspects as winnings, bliss, love, hope, and aspiration? **[Infer]**

COMPARE LITERARY WORKS

5. Both "As I Ebb'd with the Ocean of Life" and "Broadway" include images of things that flow in water. What is different about the images in the two poems? **[Distinguish]**

Beat! Beat! Drums!

*This poem was written in response to the defeat of the
Union army by Confederate forces in the battle of Bull Run
in 1861. The Confederate victory shocked many people who
felt that the Union would easily win the war and made it
clear that a long and bloody struggle lay ahead.*

Beat! beat! drums!—blow! bugles! blow!
Through the windows—through doors—burst like a
    ruthless force,
Into the solemn church, and scatter the congregation,
Into the school where the scholar is studying;
5   Leave not the bridegroom quiet—no happiness must he
    have now with his bride,
Nor the peaceful farmer any peace, ploughing his field or
    gathering his grain,
So fierce you whirr and pound you drums—so shrill you
    bugles blow.

Beat! beat! drums!—blow! bugles! blow!
Over the traffic of cities—over the rumble of wheels in the
    streets;
10   Are beds prepared for sleepers at night in the houses? no
    sleepers must sleep in those beds,
No bargainers' bargains by day—no brokers or
    speculators —would they continue?
Would the talkers be talking? would the singer attempt to
    sing?
Would the lawyer rise in the court to state his case before
    the judge?
Then rattle quicker, heavier drums—you bugles wilder
    blow.

15   Beat! beat! drums!—blow! bugles! blow!
Make no parley—stop for no expostulation,
Mind not the timid—mind not the weeper or prayer,
Mind not the old man beseeching the young man,
Let not the child's voice be heard, nor the mother's
    entreaties,
20   Make even the trestles to shake the dead where they lie
    awaiting the hearses
So strong you thump O terrible drums—so loud you
    bugles blow.

alt Whitman

As Toilsome I Wander'd Virginia's Woods

As toilsome I wander'd Virginia's woods,
To the music of rustling leaves kicked by my feet,
   (for 'twas autumn,)
I marked at the foot of a tree the grave of a soldier;
Mortally wounded and buried on the retreat,
   (easily all could I understand,)
5   The halt of mid-day hour, when up! no time to
   lose—yet this sign left,
On a tablet scrawled and nailed on the tree by
   the grave,
Bold, cautious, true, and my loving comrade.
Long, long I muse, then on my way go wandering,
Many a changeful season to follow, and many a
   scene of life,
10   Yet at times through changeful season and scene,
   abrupt, alone, or in the crowded street,
Comes before me the unknown soldier's grave,
   comes the inscription rude in Virginia's woods,
Bold, cautious, true, and my loving comrade.

Death of President Lincoln

April 16, '65—I find in my notes of the time, this passage on the death of Abraham Lincoln: He leaves for America's history and biography, so far, not only its most dramatic reminiscence—he leaves, in my opinion, the greatest, best, most characteristic, artistic, moral personality. Not but that he had faults, and showed them in the Presidency; but honesty, goodness, shrewdness, conscience, and (a new virtue, unknown to other lands, and hardly yet really known here, but the foundation and tie of all, as the future will grandly develop,) UNIONISM, in its truest and amplest sense, formed the hard-pan of his character. These he seal'd with his life. The tragic splendor of his death, purging, illuminating all, throws round his form, his head, an aureole that will remain and will grow brighter through time, while history lives, and love of country lasts. By many has this Union been help'd; but if one name, one man, must be picked out, he, most of all, is the conservator of it, to the future. He was assassinated—but the Union is not assassinated—*ça ira!*[1] One falls, and another falls. The soldier drops, sinks like a wave—but the ranks of the ocean eternally press on. Death does its work, obliterates a hundred, a thousand—President, general, captain, private—but the Nation is immortal.

---

1. **Ça ira!** (sä ēr ä´): French for "that will continue."

☑ **Check Your Comprehension**

1. What does the speaker of "Beat! Beat! Drums!" want the drums and bugles to do?

2. After first seeing the grave in "As Toilsome I Wander'd Virginia's Woods," when does the speaker think of it again?

3. According to Whitman in "Death of President Lincoln," what was Lincoln's greatest accomplishment?

◆ **Critical Thinking**

1. Do you think the point of "Beat! Beat! Drums!" is pro-war or anti-war? Explain. **[Distinguish]**

2. In "As Toilsome I Wander'd Virginia's Woods," why does the "inscription rude" have such an impact on the speaker? **[Speculate]**

COMPARE/LITERARY WORKS

3. In "Beat! Beat! Drums!" and "As Toilsome I Wander'd Virginia's Woods," is war seen as a natural part of life? Explain your answer. **[Connect]**

Walt Whitman

Comparing and Connecting the Author's Works

◆ Literary Focus: Free Verse

Whitman's poems were considered revolutionary in his time because of both their content and their form. Readers who were accustomed to traditional verse were often shocked by his poetry. **Free verse**, without regular meter or line length, was developed by Whitman from the example of a few earlier writers' experiments and portions of the King James Version of the Bible.

The rhythms of free verse are closer to natural speech than the patterns of traditional verse. Free verse uses other devices to give it structure, such as repetition of words, phrases, and consonant and vowel sounds. For musical effect, Whitman often connects phrases in long, rolling sentences. He also arranges the accents of his lines in rhythmic patterns that are looser than traditional meters.

1. Read aloud several lines of one of Whitman's poems. Then read aloud a poem written in traditional verse from another unit of this book. Do you hear patterns in both? How are they different? Does one poem sound more natural than the other?

2. Do you prefer the free verse or the traditional verse? Explain.

◆ Drawing Conclusions About Whitman's Work

One early reader of the first edition of *Leaves of Grass* whose reactions were recorded was Abraham Lincoln. A colleague of Lincoln reported years later that Lincoln commended the new poet's verses, for their virility, freshness, unconventional sentiments, and unique forms of expression, and claimed that Whitman gave promise of a new school of poetry.

Draw a chart on your paper like the one below. Find two examples of unconventional sentiments and unique forms of expression. Write them in your chart.

Unconventional Sentiments	Unique Forms of Expression

◆ Idea Bank

Writing

1. **Remembrance** In "As Toilsome I Wander'd Virginia's Woods," the speaker remembers a grave he once saw. Think of something you once saw that had a strong impact on you. Write a short essay or a poem about your experience.

2. **Effects of War** Choose one of the scenes of daily life that are mentioned in "Beat! Beat! Drums!" Write a story or play about how the activities depicted are affected by the outbreak of war. The setting can be the Civil War or another war of your choosing, real or imaginary.

3. **Poem** Write a poem in a style similar to Whitman's. Try to include an example of what critics call his "catalogues," that is, repetitions of words or phrases. Test your writing by reading a draft aloud to see that your lines are rhythmical and natural.

Speaking and Listening

4. **Dramatic Reading** Working with other students, choose a poem of Whitman's and prepare a dramatic

reading of it. Assign lines and sections to individual readers or to more than one reader. Practice so that the lines are clear and rhythmical. Tape music to accompany your reading. Present it for other students. **[Performing Arts Link; Group Activity]**

Researching and Representing

5. **Comparison** Find a poem to compare with one of Whitman's. It can be either in a traditional verse form or in free verse, but it should be on a similar theme, for example, war, the ocean, a city. Compare the poem with Whitman's, pointing out similarities and differences. Give your opinion of which poem you prefer. Support your points with quotations from the poems.

6. **Art of the Times** While Whitman was writing the first edition of *Leaves of Grass*, the Hudson River School of painting became popular in the United States. Many of the early paintings were views of the Hudson River region of New York State, including the Catskill Mountains. Thomas Cole, Frederic Church, Asher Durand, and Albert Bierstadt exhibited landscape paintings that many Americans, including Whitman, saw. Find examples of their work in the library. Choose one that could serve to illustrate one of

Whitman's poems. Write a paragraph explaining your choice. **[Art Link]**

◆ Further Reading, Listening, and Viewing

• Audio — *To the Soul: Thomas Hampson sings the poetry of Walt Whitman*—audio CD, EMI Classics, 1997

• David Reynolds: *Walt Whitman's America: A Cultural Biography* (Knopf)

• *The Poetry Of Walt Whitman* (Dove Audio, 1997) Audiocassette

• *Orson Welles Reads Song Of Myself* (Audio Forum, 1984) Audiocassette

• *Walt Whitman* (South Carolina Educational Television Network, 1988) Video on Whitman's life and career

• *John Adams: The Wound Dresser* (audio CD, Elektra Nonesuch, 1989) Songs with orchestra based on work by Walt Whitman

• *Leaves Of Grass*, unabridged (13 audio-cassettes, Blackstone Audio Books, 1995) Read by Noah Waterman

On the Web:

http://www.phschool.com/atschool/literature
Go to the student edition of *The American Experience*. Proceed to Unit 3. Then, click Hot Links to find Web sites featuring Walt Whitman.

*M*ark Twain In Depth

"In our country we have three unspeakably precious things: freedom of speech, freedom of conscience, and the prudence never to produce either."

—*Mark Twain*

MARK TWAIN was an American original and a man of his time. The nineteenth century was a period of great change in the United States, and the themes Twain chose serve as a chronicle of a nation in transition. His topics included the American West, technological progress, and, most notably, the Mississippi river life of his youth. Twain was a creature of the new print media, and he would become its star— by far the most famous American author of his time. He was an incomparable humorist and a master of American regional dialects.

Childhood and Apprenticeship
Born Samuel Langhorne Clemens in 1835, Twain grew up in Hannibal, Missouri, along the banks of the Mississippi River. He started working in a print shop at age eleven, after his father's death. His early twenties were spent as a river boat pilot on the Mississippi.

When the Civil War stopped river traffic, Twain briefly joined a Confederate army unit before heading out west with his brother, Orion. Twain returned east to begin his writing career as a reporter for the Virginia City *Territorial Enterprise*, where he became known as a humorist. It was at this time that he assumed the pen name "Mark Twain." "Mark the twain" is a navigational warning used when measuring the depth of the river to ensure a boat's safe passage.

Early Literary Success
The short story, "The Notorious Jumping Frog of Calaveras County," published in newspapers nationwide in 1865, brought Mark Twain widespread attention. *Innocents Abroad* (1869–1870), a collection of satirical travel letters, enhanced the young author's reputation. With his marriage to heiress Olivia Hangdon and their move to Hartford, Connecticut, Twain, like some of his characters, was the very picture of American boom-time success.

Literary Greatness
In 1884 Twain published *The Adventures of Huckleberry Finn*, his best-known work. He drew on his memories of life on the Mississippi River in offering his account of a bustling, vital, yet often malevolent world. His vision is conveyed through the distinctive voice of the uneducated youth, Huckleberry Finn. In befriending the escaped slave Jim, Huck exhibits a healthy innocence that refuses to accept the social convention of racism. Ernest Hemingway wrote that *Huckleberry Finn* was the most influential book for modern American authors.

A Master of Satire
In 1889, Twain published *A Connecticut Yankee in King Arthur's Court*, a kind of "dream" travel novel. The place visited is no actual site on a map, but a mythical place in King Arthur's England in the sixth century. *Connecticut Yankee*, like many of Twain's works, affirms the American democratic spirit. Twain sought to criticize the traditions of chivalry and aristocratic privilege that underlay English and European society. He did not shirk from the chance for a scrape with adherents of Old World values. As with previous literary projects, Twain sought to gain great profits from this novel. *Connecticut Yankee* was finished on a tight deadline for issue at the peak of the Christmas season.

Last Years and Growing Pessimism

Twain's last years were unhappy ones. His wife and three of his four children died before him. From the time *Pudden'head Wilson* was published (1894), his writings assumed a more pessimistic world view. Twain began to argue that human motivation was fundamentally selfish and that all human conduct could be ascribed to this impulse. "A Fable" (1909) is an exception to this cynical view, exhibiting a playfulness rarely in evidence in Twain's later work.

More complicated than the good-natured humorist he was often taken for, Twain was a man of contradictions. He sought acceptance by the social elite even as he criticized it in his writings; he praised American progress while at the same time deploring the nation's policy of worldwide expansionism.

◆ The Author in the Newspaper Age

Mark Twain was a creation of the newspaper age, and a great American journalist who later became an even greater novelist. Newspapers assumed their modern character during Twain's lifetime. They became more popular in their appeal: Increasing numbers of newspapers that sold for one cent led to big increases in circulation during the 1830's and 1840's.

The Gold Rush fostered the spread of newspapers through the western territories of Colorado, Utah, Idaho, Oregon, Montana, and Wyoming. Nevada's first newspaper was started by the publisher of the paper where Twain worked as a reporter.

With the Industrial Revolution in the 1850's appeared giant printing presses able to print ten thousand complete newspapers in only an hour's time. By 1850, the United States had some 2,526 newspapers, among them the first week-lies to carry sketches made by "pictorial" reporters.

Twain's time in the West greatly influenced his writing style and his preference for plain speech. His talent for simplicity and humor and his gift with native speech patterns made him a natural for the growing newspaper industry. For every European writer like Charles Dickens or Matthew Arnold, who criticized the sensationalist and superficial aspects of the American newspapers, there were many others who defended them as the right medium for the expression of the American democratic spirit.

◆ Literary Works

Nonfiction Twain traveled widely and was a great observer of human nature. He turned his observations into witty letters home, which were published in newspapers and later in book form. His autobiography, published after his death, is full of his candid reflections on life.

The Innocents Abroad (1869)
Roughing It (1872)
Autobiography (1924)

The Fiction of His Peak Years

Considered Twain's most significant literary achievement, *The Adventures of Huckleberry Finn* demonstrated Twain's sensitivity to race and class issues, his gifts as an observer of human nature and societal convention, his knack for capturing the authentic patterns of regional speech, and his commitment to social justice.

The Adventures of Tom Sawyer (1876)
The Adventures of Huckleberry Finn (1885)
A Connecticut Yankee in King Arthur's Court (1889)
Pudd'nhead Wilson (1894)

TIMELINE

Twain's Life

1835 Born Samuel Langhorne Clemens in Florida, Missouri

1847 Father, John Clemens, dies; Clemens goes to work at a printing shop

1857 Pilots a steamboat on the Mississippi River until the start of the Civil War in 1861

1862 Works as a reporter for the Virginia City *Territorial Enterprise*

1863 Adopts pen name "Mark Twain"

1865 "The Notorious Jumping Frog of Calaveras County" is published in newspapers nationwide

1869–70 *Innocents Abroad* earns Twain wide renown

1870–71 Marries Olivia Langdon and establishes home at Nook Farm, a suburb of Hartford, Conn.

1874 "A True Story, Repeated Word for Word as I Heard It," one of Twain's most powerful anti-slavery writings, is published

1876 *The Adventures of Tom Sawyer* published

1881 *The Prince and the Pauper* published

1884 Adventures of Huckleberry Finn published in England; published in the U.S. in 1885

1885 *Huckleberry Finn* banned by the Concord, Mass., Free Public Library

1889 *A Connecticut Yankee in King Arthur's Court* is published

1894 *Pudd'nhead Wilson* is published

1894 Failed business investments leave Twain bankrupt

1895 Embarks on five-year worldwide lecture tour

1910 Dies of heart disease; buried with rest of family in Elmira, NY

World Events

1832 Andrew Jackson is reelected U.S. President

1848 California's Gold Rush begins

1852 Harriet Beecher Stowe's *Uncle Tom's Cabin* is published

1855 Walt Whitman's first edition of *Leaves of Grass* is published

1861 Harriet Jacob's Incidents in the *Life of a Slave Girl* is published

1863 President Lincoln delivers Gettysburg Address

1867–68 Charles Dickens lectures in America

1871 P.T. Barnum opens his "Greatest Show on Earth" in New York City

1880 Thomas Edison constructs an electricity-generating station in New York City

1881 Russia's Tsar Alexander II is assassinated

1882 Matthew Arnold publishes "A Word About America," criticizing Twain

1883 The Indonesian volcano Krakatoa explodes with one of the most catastrophic eruptions ever witnessed

1891 Death of Walt Whitman

1898 The U.S. defeats Spain in Cuba to win the Spanish-American war

1900 Hurricane causes 6,000 deaths in Galveston, Texas

1901 McKinley assassinated; Theodore Roosevelt becomes President

1903 Henry Ford founds Ford Motor Company

1904 Death of England's Queen Victoria

from Perplexing Lessons

As a boy, Mark Twain dreamed of becoming a steamboat pilot on the Mississippi River. By chance, Twain meets Mr. Bixby, a famous pilot on the Mississippi and convinces Bixby to teach him to navigate the river. The following events occur.

AT the end of what seemed a tedious while, I had managed to pack my head full of islands, towns, bars, "points," and bends; and a curiously inanimate mass of lumber it was, too. However, inasmuch as I could shut my eyes and reel off a good long string of these names, without leaving out more than ten miles of river in every fifty, I began to feel that I could take a boat down to New Orleans if I could make her skip those little gaps. But of course my complacency could hardly get start enough to lift my nose a trifle into the air, before Mr. Bixby would think of something to fetch it down again. One day he turned on me suddenly with this settler:

"What is the shape of Walnut Bend?"

He might as well have asked me my grandmother's opinion of protoplasm. I reflected respectfully, and then said I didn't know it had any particular shape. My gun-powdery chief went off with a bang, of course, and then went on loading and firing until he was out of adjectives.

I had learned long ago that he only carried just so many rounds of ammunition, and was sure to subside into a very placable and even remorseful old smoothbore as soon as they were all gone. That word "old" is merely affectionate; he was not more than thirty-four. I waited. By and by he said:

"My boy, you've got to know the *shape* of the river perfectly. It is all there is left to steer by on a very dark night. Everything else is blotted out and gone. But mind you, it hasn't the same shape in the night that it has in the daytime."

"How on earth am I ever going to learn it, then?"

"How do you follow a hall at home in the dark? Because you know the shape of it. You can't see it."

"Do you mean to say that I've got to know all the million trifling variations of shape in the banks of this interminable river as well as I know the shape of the front hall at home?"

"On my honor, you've got to know them *better* than any man ever did know the shapes of the halls in his own house."

"I wish I was dead!"

"Now I don't want to discourage you, but—"

"Well, pile it on me; I might as well have it now as another time."

"You see, this has got to be learned; there isn't any getting around it. A clear starlight night throws such heavy shadows that, if you didn't know the shape of a shore perfectly, you would claw away from every bunch of timber, because you would take the black shadow of it for a solid cape; and you see you would be getting scared to death every fifteen minutes by the watch. You would be fifty yards from shore all the time when you ought to be within fifty feet of it. You can't see a snag in one of those shadows, but you know exactly where it is, and the shape of the river tells you when you are coming to it. Then there's your pitch-dark night; the river is a very different shape on a pitch-dark night from what it is on a star-light night. All shores seem to be straight lines, then, and mighty dim ones, too; and you'd *run* them for straight lines, only you know better. You boldly drive your boat right into what seems to be a solid, straight wall (you knowing very well that in reality there is a curve there), and that wall falls back and makes way for you. Then there's your gray mist. You take a night when there's one of these grisly, drizzly, gray mists, and then there isn't *any* par- ticular shape to a shore. A gray mist would tangle the head of the oldest man that ever lived. Well, then, different kinds of *moonlight* change the shape of the river in different ways. You see—"

"Oh, don't say any more, please! Have I got to learn the shape of the river according to all these five hundred thousand differ- ent ways? If I tried to carry all that cargo in my head it would make me stoop-shouldered."

"*No!* you only learn *the* shape of the river; and you learn it with such absolute certainty that you can always steer by the shape that's *in your head*, go and never mind the one that's before your eyes."

"Very well, I'll try it . . . "

I went to work now to learn the shape of the river; and of all the eluding and ungraspable objects that ever I tried to get mind or hands on, that was the chief. I would fasten my eyes upon a sharp, wooded point, that projected far into the river some miles ahead of me, and go to laboriously photographing its shape upon my brain; and just as I was beginning to succeed to my satisfaction, we would draw up toward it and the exasperating thing would begin to melt away and fold back into the bank! If there had been a conspicuous dead tree standing upon the very point of the cape, I would find that tree inconspicuously merged into the general forest, and occupying the middle of a straight shore, when I got abreast of it! No prominent hill would stick to its shape long enough for me to make up my mind what its form really was, but it was as dissolving and changeful as if it had been a mountain of butter in the hottest corner of the tropics. Nothing ever had the same shape when I was coming down-stream that it had borne when I went up. I mentioned these little difficulties to Mr. Bixby. He said:

"That's the very main virtue of the thing. If the shapes didn't change every three seconds they wouldn't be of any use. Take this place where we are now, for instance. As long as that hill over yonder is only one hill, I can boom right along the way I'm going; but the moment it splits at the top and forms a V, I know I've got to scratch to starboard in a hurry, or I'll bang this boat's brains out against a rock; and then the moment one of the prongs of the V swings behind the other, I've got to waltz to larboard[1] again, or I'll have a misunderstanding with a snag that would snatch the keelson out of this steamboat as neatly as if it were a sliver in your hand. If that hill didn't change its shape on bad nights there would be an awful steamboat graveyard around here inside of a year."

It was plain that I had got to learn the shape of the river in all the different ways that could be thought of—upside down wrong end first, inside out, fore-and-aft, and "thort-ships "—and then know what to do on gray nights when it hadn't any shape at all.

During the afternoon watch the next day, Mr. Bixby asked me if I knew how to run the next few miles. I said:

"Go inside the first snag above the point, outside the next one, start out from the lower end of Higgins's woodyard, make a square crossing, and—"

"That's all right. I'll be back before you close up on the next point."

But he wasn't. He was still below when I rounded it and entered upon a piece of the river which I had some misgivings about. I did not know that he was hiding behind a chimney to see how I would perform. I went gaily along, getting prouder and prouder, for he had never left the boat in my sole charge such a length of time before. I even got to "setting" her and letting the wheel go entirely, while I vaingloriously turned my back and inspected the stem marks and hummed a tune, a sort of easy indifference which I had prodigiously admired in Bixby and other great pilots. Once I inspected rather long, and when I faced to the front again my heart flew into my mouth so suddenly that if I hadn't clapped my teeth together I should have lost it. One of those frightful bluff reefs was stretching its deadly length right across our bows! My head was gone in a moment; I did not know which end I stood on; I gasped and could not get my breath; I spun the wheel down with such rapidity that it

---

1. **larboard** (lär´ bərd) *n.*: Left-hand side of a boat when it faces forward; port.

wove itself together like a spider's web; the boat answered and turned square away from the reef, but the reef followed her! I fled, but still it followed, still it kept—right across my bows! I never looked to see where I was going, I only fled. The awful crash was imminent. Why didn't that villain come? If I committed the crime of ringing a bell I might get thrown overboard. But better that than kill tile boat. So in blind desperation, I started such a rattling "shivaree"[2] down below as never had astounded an engineer in this world before, I fancy. Amidst the frenzy of the bells the engines began to back and fill in a curious way, and my reason forsook its throne—we were about to crash into the woods on the other side of the river. Just then Mr. Bixby stepped calmly into view on the hurricane-deck. My soul went out to him in gratitude. My distress vanished; I would have felt safe on the brink of Niagara with Mr. Bixby on the hurricane-deck. He blandly and sweetly took his toothpick out of his mouth between his fingers, as if it were a cigar—we were just in the act of climbing an overhanging big tree, and the passengers were scudding astern like rats—and lifted up these commands to me ever so gently:

"Stop the starboard! Stop the larboard! Set her back on both!"

The boat hesitated, halted, pressed her nose among the boughs a critical instant, then reluctantly began to back away.

"Stop the larboard! Come ahead on it! Stop the starboard! Come ahead on it! Point her for the bar!"

I sailed away as serenely as a summer's morning. Mr. Bixby came in and said, with mock simplicity:

"When you have a hail, my boy, you ought to tap the big bell three times before you land, so that the engineers can get ready."

I blushed under the sarcasm, and said I hadn't had any hail.

"Ah! Then it was for wood, I suppose. The officer of the watch will tell you when he wants to wood up."

I went on consuming, and said I wasn't after wood.

"Indeed? Why, what could you want over here in the bend, then? Did you ever know of a boat following a bend up-stream at this stage of the river?"

"No. sir—and *I* wasn't trying to follow it. I was getting away from a bluff reef."[3]

"No, it wasn't a bluff reef; there isn't one within three miles of where you were."

"But I saw it. It was as bluff as that one yonder."

"Just about. Run over it!"

"Do you give it as an order?"

---

2. **shivaree** (shiv´ ə re) *n.*: Noisy demonstration.
3. **reef** (rēf) *n.*: Ridge of rock or sand near the surface of the water.

"Yes. Run over it!"

"If I don't, I wish I may die."

"All right; I am taking the responsibility."

I was just as anxious to kill the boat, now, as I had been to save it before. I impressed my orders upon my memory, to be used at the inquest, and made a straight break for the reef. As it disappeared under our bows I held my breath; but we slid over it like oil.

"Now, don't you see the difference? It wasn't anything but a *wind* reef. The wind does that."

"So I see. But it is exactly like a bluff reef. How am I ever going to tell them apart?"

"I can't tell you. It is an instinct. By and by you will just naturally *know* one from the other, but you never will be able to explain why or how you know them apart."

It turned out to be true. The face of the water, in time, became a wonderful book—a book that was a dead language to the uneducated passenger, but which told its mind to me without reserve, delivering its most cherished secrets as clearly as if it uttered them with a voice. And it was not a book to be read once and thrown aside, for it had a new story to tell every day. Throughout the long twelve hundred miles there was never a page that was void of interest, never one that you could leave unread without loss, never one that you would want to skip, thinking you could find higher enjoyment in some other thing. There never was so wonderful a book written by man; never one whose interest was so absorbing, so unflagging, so sparkingly renewed with every reperusal. The passenger who could not read it was charmed with a peculiar sort of faint dimple on its surface (on the rare occasions when he did not overlook it altogether); but to the pilot that was an *italicized* passage; indeed, it was more than that, it was a legend of the largest capitals, with a string of shouting exclamation-points at the end of it, for it meant that a wreck or a rock was buried there that could tear the life out of the strongest vessel that ever floated. It is the faintest and simplest expression the water ever makes, and the most hideous to a pilot's eye. In truth, the passenger who could not read this book saw nothing but all manner of pretty pictures in it, painted by the sun and shaded by the clouds, whereas to the trained eye these were not pictures at all, but the grimmest and most dead-earnest of reading-matter.

Now when I had mastered the language of this water, and had come to know every trifling feature that bordered the great river as familiarly as I knew the letters of the alphabet, I had made a valuable acquisition. But I had lost something, too. I had lost something which could never be restored to me while I lived. All the grace, the beauty, the poetry, had gone out of the majestic river! I still kept in mind a certain wonderful sunset which I witnessed when steamboating was new to me. A broad expanse of the river was turned to blood; in the middle distance the red hue brightened into gold, through which a solitary log came floating, black and conspicuous; in one place a long, slanting mark lay sparkling upon the water; in another the surface was broken by boiling, tumbling rings, that were as many-tinted as an opal; where the ruddy flush was faintest, was a smooth spot that was covered with graceful circles and radiating lines, ever so delicately traced; the shore on our left was densely wooded, and the somber shadow that fell from this forest was broken in one place by a long, ruffled trail that shone like silver; and high above the forest wall a clean-stemmed dead tree waved a single leafy bough that glowed like a flame in the unobstructed splendor that was flowing from the sun. There were graceful curves, reflected images, woody heights, soft distances; and over the whole scene, far and near, the dissolving lights drifted steadily, enriching it every passing moment with new marvels of coloring.

I stood like one bewitched. I drank it in, in a speechless rapture. The world was new to me, and I had never seen anything like this at home. But as I have said, a day came when I began to cease from noting the glories and the charms which the moon and the sun and the twilight wrought upon the river's face; another day came when I ceased altogether to note them.

☑ Check Your Comprehension

1. What kinds of things must the narrator learn to become a licensed steamboat pilot?

2. Specify the kinds of "ammunition" the "gun-powdery chief," Mr. Bixby, "loads" and "fires."

3. What does Mr. Bixby mean when he tells the narrator, "you've got to know the shape of the river?"

4. As he tells the narrator how to read the riverbank, what does Mr. Bixby say a pilot should do when a hill "splits at the top and forms a V?"

5. What mistake does the narrator make that puts his steamboat in jeopardy?

◆ Critical Thinking

INTERPRET

1. What does Twain mean when he writes of the Mississippi river that, "The face of the water, in time, became a wonderful book—a book that was a dead language to the uneducated passenger, but which told its mind to me without reserve ..." **[Interpret]**

2. Can you think of some part of your everyday life that you read like a book, in the way that Mark Twain reads the Mississippi river like a book? Describe this in a journal entry. **[Apply]**

3. When Twain makes a distinction between the "uneducated passenger" and the person with a "trained eye," what expertise does he grant this "trained eye?" **[Analyze]**

4. Write a detailed account of something for which you have a "trained eye." **[Extend]**

5. What change takes place in the way Twain reads the Mississippi? **[Interpret]**

Mark Twain

An Encounter with an Interviewer

The nervous, dapper, "peart"[1] young man took the chair I offered him, and said he was connected with the *Daily Thunderstorm*, and added: "Hoping it's no harm, I've come to interview you."

"Come to what?"

"*Interview* you."

"Ah! I see. Yes—yes. Um! Yes—yes."

I was not feeling bright that morning. Indeed, my powers seemed a bit under a cloud. However, I went to the bookcase, and when I had been looking six or seven minutes I found I was obliged to refer to the young man. I said:

"How do you spell it?"

"Spell what?"

"Interview."

"Oh, my goodness! what do you want to spell it for?"

"I don't want to spell it; I want to see what it means."

"Well, this is astonishing, I must say. *I* can tell you what it means, if you—if you—"

"Oh, all right! That will answer, and much obliged to you, too."

"In, *in*, ter, *ter*, inter—"

"Then you spell it with an *I*?"

"Why, certainly!"

"Oh, that is what took me so long."

"Why, my *dear* sir, what did *you* propose to spell it with?"

"Well, I—I—hardly know. I had the Unabridged, and I was ciphering around in the back end, hoping I might tree her among the pictures. But it's a very old edition."

"Why, my friend, they wouldn't have a *picture* of it in even the latest—My dear sir, I beg your pardon, I mean no harm in the world, but you do not look as—as—intelligent as I had expected you would. No harm—I mean no harm at all."

"Oh, don't mention it! It has often been said, and by people who would not flatter and who could have no inducement to flatter, that I am quite remarkable in that way. Yes—yes; they always speak of it with rapture."

"I can easily imagine it. But about this interview. You know it is the custom, now, to interview any man who has become notorious."

---

1. **peart** (pyərt) *adj.*: Lively; chipper; variation of pert.

"Indeed, I had not heard of it before. It must be very interesting. What do you do it with?

"Ah, well—well—well—this is disheartening. It *ought* to be done with a club in some cases; but customarily it consists in the interviewer asking questions and the interviewed answering them. It is all the rage now. Will you let me ask you certain questions calculated to bring out the salient points of your public and private history?"

"Oh, with pleasure—with pleasure. I have a very bad memory, but I hope you will not mind that. That is to say, it is an irregular memory—singularly irregular. Sometimes it goes in a gallop, and then again it will be as much as a fortnight passing a given point. This is a great grief to me."

"Oh, it is no matter, so you will try to do the best you can."

"I will. I will put my whole mind on it."

"Thanks. Are you ready to begin?"

"Ready."

Q. How old are you?

A. Nineteen, in June.

Q. Indeed. I would have taken you to be thiry-five or six. Where were you born?

A. In Missouri.

Q. When did you begin to write?

A. In 1836.

Q. Why, how could that be, if you are only nineteen now?

A. I don't know. It does seem curious, somehow.

Q. It does, indeed. Whom do you consider the most remarkable man you ever met?

A. Aaron Burr.[2]

Q. But you never could have met Aaron Burr, if you are only nineteen years—

A. Now, if you know more about me than I do, what do you ask me for?

Q. Well, it was only a suggestion; nothing more. How did you happen to meet Burr?

A. Well, I happened to be at his funeral one day, and he asked me to make less noise, and—

Q. But, good heavens! if you were at his funeral, he must have been dead, and if he was dead how could he care whether you made a noise or not?

A. I don't know. He was always a particular kind of a man that way.

Q. Still, I don't understand it at all. You say he spoke to you,

---

2. Aaron Burr: Political leader who tied with Thomas Jefferson for the presidency in the election of 1800. He lost in a congressional vote but became vice-president (1756–1836).

and that he was dead?

A. I didn't say he was dead.

Q. But wasn't he dead?

A. Well, some said he was, some said he wasn't.

Q. What did you think?

A. Oh, it was none of my business! It wasn't any of my funeral.

Q. Did you— However, we can never get this matter straight. Let me ask about something else. What was the date of your birth?

A. Monday, October 31, 1693.

Q. What! Impossible! That would make you a hundred and eighty years old. How do you account for that?

A. I don't account for it at all.

Q. But you said at first you were only nineteen, and now you make yourself out to be one hundred and eighty. It is an awful discrepancy.

A. Why, have you noticed that? (Shaking hands.) Many a time it has seemed to me like a discrepancy, but somehow I couldn't make up my mind. How quick you notice a thing!

Q. Thank you for the compliment, as far as it goes. Had you, or have you, any brothers or sisters?

A. Eh! I—I—I—think so—yes—but I don't remember.

Q. Well, that is the most extraordinary statement I ever heard!

A. Why, what makes you think that?

Q. How could I think otherwise? Why, look here! Who is this a picture of on the wall? Isn't that a brother of yours?

A. Oh, yes, yes, yes! Now you remind me of it; that *was* a brother of mine. That's William—*Bill* we called him. Poor old Bill!

Q. Why? Is he dead, then?

A. Ah! Well, I suppose so. We never could tell. There was a great mystery about it.

Q. That is sad, very sad. He disappeared, then?

A. Well, yes, in a sort of general way. We buried him.

Q. *Buried* him! *Buried* him, without knowing whether he was dead or not?

A. Oh, no! Not that. He was dead enough.

Q. Well, I confess that I can't understand this. If you buried him, and you knew he was dead—

A. No! no! We only thought he was.

Q. Oh, I see! He came to life again?

A. I bet he didn't.

Q. Well, I never heard anything like this. *Somebody* was dead. *Somebody* was buried. Now, where was the mystery?

A. Ah! that's just it! That's it exactly. You see, we were twins—defunct and I—and we got mixed in the bathtub when we were only two weeks old, and one of us was drowned. But we didn't know which. Some think it was Bill. Some think It was me.

Q. Well, that *is* remarkable. What do *you* think?

A. Goodness knows! I would give whole worlds to know. This solemn, this awful mystery has cast a gloom over my whole life. But I will tell you a secret now, which I never have revealed to any creature before. One of us had a peculiar mark—a large mole on the back of his left hand; that was *me. That child was the one that was drowned!*

Q. Very well, then, I don't see that there is any mystery about it, after all.

A. You don't? Well, *I* do. Anyway, I don't see how they could ever have been such a blundering lot as to go and bury the wrong child, But, 'sh!—don't mention it where the family can hear of it. Heaven knows they have heartbreaking troubles enough without adding this.

Q. Well, I believe I have got material enough for the present, and I am very much obliged to you for the pains you have taken. But I was a good deal interested in that account of Aaron Burr's funeral. Would you mind telling me what particular circumstance it was that made you think Burr was such a remarkable man?

A. Oh! it was a mere trifle! Not one man in fifty would have noticed it at all. When the sermon was over, and the procession all ready to start for the cemetery, and the body all arranged nice in the hearse, he said he wanted to take a last look at the scenery, and so he *got up and rode with the driver.*

Then the young man reverently withdrew. He was very pleasant company, and I was sorry to see him go.

1875

$\mathcal{M}$ark Twain

A General Reply

When I was sixteen or seventeen years old, a splendid idea burst upon me—a bran-new one, which had never occurred to anybody before: I would write some "pieces" and take them down to the editor of the "Republican," and ask him to give me his plain, unvarnished opinion of their value! Now, as old and threadbare as the idea was, it was fresh and beautiful to me, and it went flaming and crashing through my system like the genuine lightning and thunder of originality. I wrote the pieces. I wrote them with that placid confidence and that happy facility which only want of practice and absence of literary experience can give. There was not one sentence in them that cost half an hour's weighing and shaping and trimming and fixing. Indeed, it is possible that there was no one sentence whose mere wording cost even one-sixth of that time. If I remember rightly, there was not one single erasure or interlineation in all that chaste manu-script. (I have since lost that large belief in my powers, and like-wise that marvellous perfection of execution.) I started down to the "Republican" office with my pocket full of manuscripts, my brain full of dreams, and a grand future opening out before me. I knew perfectly well that the editor would be ravished with my pieces. But presently—

However, the particulars are of no consequence. I was only about to say that a shadowy sort of doubt just then intruded upon my exaltation. Another came, and another. Pretty soon a whole procession of them. And at last, when I stood before the "Republican" office and looked up at its tall, unsympathetic front, it seemed hardly *me* that could have "chinned" its towers ten minutes before, and was now so shrunk up and pitiful that if I dared to step on the gratings I should probably go through.

At about that crisis the editor, the very man I had come to consult, came down stairs, and halted a moment to pull at his wristbands and settle his coat to its place, and he happened to notice that I was eyeing him wistfully. He asked me what I wanted, I answered, "NOTHING!" with a boy's own meekness and shame; and, dropping my eyes, crept humbly round till I was fairly in the alley, and then drew a big grateful breath of relief, and picked up my heels and ran!

I was satisfied. I wanted no more. It was my first attempt to get a "plain unvarnished opinion" out of a literary man concern-ing my compositions, and it has lasted me until now. And in these latter days, whenever I receive a bundle of MS. through the mail, with request that I will pass judgment upon its merits, I feel like saying to the author, "If you had only taken your piece to some grim and stately newspaper office, where you did not know anybody, you would not have so fine an opinion of your production as it is easy to see you have now."

Every man who becomes editor of a newspaper or magazine straightway begins to receive MSS.[1] from literary aspirants, together with requests that he will deliver judgment upon the same. And after complying in eight or ten instances, he finally takes refuge in a general sermon upon the subject, which he inserts in his publication, and always afterward refers such correspondents to that sermon for answer. I have at last reached this station in my literary career. I now cease to reply privately to my applicants for advice, and proceed to construct my public sermon.

As all letters of the sort I am speaking of contain the very same matter, differently worded, I offer as a fair average specimen the last one I have received:

Oct 3.

MARK TWAIN, Esq,

DEAR SIR: I am a youth, just out of school and ready to start in life. I have looked around, but don't see anything that suits exactly. Is a literary life easy and profitable, or is it the hard times it is generally put up for? It *must* be easier than a good many if not most of the occupations, and I feel drawn to launch out on it, make or break, sink or swim, survive or perish. Now, what are the conditions of success in literature? You need not be afraid to paint the thing just as it is. I can't do any worse than fail. Everything else offers the same. When I thought of the law—yes, and five or six other professions—I found the same thing was the case every time, viz: *all full — overrun—every profession so crammed that success is rendered impossible—too many hands and not enough work.* But I must try *something*, and so I turn at last to literature. Something tells me that that is the true bent of my genius, if I have any. I enclose some of my pieces. Will you read them over and give me your candid, unbiased opinion of them? And now I hate to trouble you, but you have been a young man yourself, and what I want is for you to get me a news-paper job of writing to do. You know many newspaper people, and I am entirely unknown. And will you make the best terms you can for me? though I do not expect what might be called high

---

1. **MSS:** Abbreviation for manuscripts.

wages at first, of course. Will you candidly say what such articles as these I enclose are worth? I have plenty of them. If you should sell these and let me know, I can send you more, as good and may be better than these. An early reply, etc.

Yours truly, etc.

I will answer you in good faith. Whether my remarks shall have great value or not, or my suggestions be worth following, are problems which I take great pleasure in leaving entirely to you for solution. To begin: There are several questions in your letter which only a man's life experience can eventually answer for him—not another man's words. I will simply skip those.

I. Literature, like the ministry, medicine, the law, and all *other* occupations, is cramped and hindered for want of men to do the work, not want of work to do. When people tell you the reverse, they speak that which is not true. If you desire to test this, you need only hunt up a first-class editor, reporter, business manager, foreman of a shop, mechanic, or artist in any branch of industry, and t*ry to hire him.* You will find that he is already hired. He is sober, industrious, capable, and reliable, and is always in demand. He cannot get a day's holiday except by courtesy of his employer, or his city, or the great general public. But if you need idlers, shirkers, half-instructed, unambitious, and comfort-seeking editors, reporters, lawyers, doctors, and mechanics, apply anywhere. There are millions of them to be had at the dropping of a handkerchief.

2. No; I must not and will not venture any opinion whatever as to the literary merit of your productions. The public is the only critic whose judgment is worth anything at all. Do not take my poor word for this, but reflect a moment and take your own. For instance, if Sylvanus Cobb or T.S. Arthur had submitted their maiden MSS. to you, you would have said, with tears in your eyes, "Now please don't write any more!" But you see yourself how popular they are. And if it had been left to you, you would have said the "Marble Faun" was tiresome, and that even "Paradise Lost" lacked cheerfulness; but you know they sell. Many wiser and better men than you pooh-poohed Shakespeare, even as late as two centuries ago; but still that old party has outlived those people. No, I will not sit in judgment upon your literature. If I honestly and conscientiously praised it, I might thus help to inflict a lingering and pitiless bore upon the public; if I honestly and conscientiously condemned it, I might thus rob the world of all undeveloped and unsuspected Dickens or Shakespeare.

3. 1 shrink from hunting up literary labor for you to do and

receive pay for. Whenever your literary productions have proved for themselves that they have a real value, you will never have to go around hunting for remunerative literary work to do. You will require more hands than you have now, and more brains than you probably ever will have, to do even half the work that will be offered you. Now, in order to arrive at the proof of value hereinbefore spoken of, one needs only to adopt a very simple and certainly very sure process; and that is, to *write without pay until somebody offers pay.* If nobody offers pay within three years, the candidate may look upon this circumstance with the most implicit confidence as the sign that sawing wood is what he was intended for. If he has any wisdom at all, then, he will retire with dignity and assume his heaven-appointed vocation.

In the above remarks I have only offered a course of action which Mr. Dickens and most other successful literary men had to follow; but it is a course which will find no sympathy with my client, perhaps. The young literary aspirant is a very, very curious creature. He knows that if he wished to become a tinner, the master smith would require him to prove the possession of a good character, and would require him to promise to stay in the shop three years—possibly four—and would make him sweep out and bring water and build fires all the first year, and let him learn to black stoves in the intervals; and for these good honest services would pay him two suits of cheap clothes and his board; and next year he would begin to receive instructions in the trade, and a dollar a week would be added to his emoluments; and two dollars would be added the third year, and three the fourth; and then, if he had become a first-rate tinner he would get about fifteen or twenty, or may be thirty dollars a week, with never a possibility of getting seventy-five while he lived. If he wanted to become a mechanic of any other kind, he would have to undergo this same tedious, ill-paid apprenticeship. If he wanted to become a lawyer or a doctor, he would have fifty times worse; for he would get nothing at all during his long apprenticeship, and in addition would have to pay a large sum for tuition, and have the privilege of boarding and clothing himself. The literary aspirant knows all this, and yet he has the hardihood to present himself for reception into the literary guild and ask to share its high honors and emoluments, without a single twelve-month's apprenticeship to show in excuse for his presumption! I He would smile pleasantly if he were asked to make even so simple a thing as a ten-cent tin dipper without previous instruction in the art; but, all green and ignorant, wordy, pompously-assertive, ungrammatical, and with a vague, distorted knowledge of men and the world acquired in a back country village, he will serenely take up so dangerous a weapon as a pen, and attack the most formidable subject that finance, commerce, war, or politics can furnish him withal. It would be laughable if it were not so sad and so pitiable. The poor fellow would not intrude upon the tin shop without an apprenticeship, but is willing to seize and wield with unpracticed hand an instrument which is able to overthrow dynasties, change religions, and decree the weal or woe of nations.

If my correspondent will write free of charge for the newspaper of his neighborhood it will be one of the strangest things that ever happened if he does not get all the employment he can attend to on those terms. And as soon as ever his writings are worth money, plenty of people will hasten to offer it.

And by way of serious and well-meant encouragement, I wish to urge upon him once more the truth that acceptable writers for the press are so scarce that book and periodical publishers are seeking them constantly, and with a vigilance that never grows heedless for a moment.

November 1870

☑ Check Your Comprehension

1. According to the interviewer, what purpose do interviews have?
2. Where did the interviewed man meet Aaron Burr?
3. Which twin brother drowned in the bathtub?
4. For what situation has Twain constructed his general reply?
5. For what reasons has the young man who writes Twain chosen a career in literature?
6. For Twain, who is the only critic that matters?
7. What does Twain recommend the literary aspirant do to get employment?

◆ Critical Thinking

INTERPRET
1. (a) How does the narrator of "An Encounter with an Interviewer" regard the interview process? (b) Does he succeed in showing you by the way he behaves towards the interviewer? [Evaluate]
2. Is the interviewer fooled by the narrator's behavior? How do you know? [Interpret]
3. Why did the interviewer finally leave? [Infer]
4. (a) After reading these two pieces, what conclusions might you draw about Twain's attitude about the practice and profession of writing? (b) What particular points about writing are made in each essay? [Infer]

COMPARE LITERARY WORKS
5. (a) Compare the different attitudes of the interviewed man in "Encounter with an Interviewer" and the writer replying to literary aspirants in "A General Reply." (b) Compare the attitudes of the young men encountered by Twain in each story.

M ark Twain

The Boss

from A Connecticut Yankee in King Arthur's Court

A Yankee, a factory worker in nineteenth century Connecticut, is knocked unconscious. He awakes in sixth century England in King Arthur's Court where he is taken prisoner. By using his knowledge of science and history to predict a solar eclipse and to dynamite a tower, the Yankee convinces the court that he has greater powers than Merlin, the court magician. The following excerpt occurs after the Yankee is released from prison.

To be vested with enormous authority is a fine thing; but to have the onlooking world consent to it is a finer. The tower episode solidified my power, and made it impregnable. If any were perchance disposed to be jealous and critical before that, they experienced a change of heart, now. There was not any one in the kingdom who would have considered it good judgment to meddle with my matters.

I was fast getting adjusted to my situation and circumstances. For a time, I used to wake up, mornings, and smile at my "dream," and listen for the Colt's factory whistle; but that sort of thing played itself out, gradually, and at last I was fully able to realize that I was actually living in the sixth century, and in Arthur's court, not a lunatic asylum. After that, I was just as much at home in that century as I could have been in any other; and as for preference, I wouldn't have traded it for the twentieth. Look at the opportunities here for a man of knowledge, brains, pluck, and enterprise to sail in and grow up with the country. The grandest field that ever was; and all my own; not a competitor; not a man who wasn't a baby to me in acquirements and capacities; whereas, what would I amount to in the twentieth century? I should be foreman of a factory, that is about all; and could drag a seine down-street any day and catch a hundred better men than myself.

What a jump I had made! I couldn't keep from thinking about it, and contemplating it, just as one does who has struck oil. There was nothing back of me that could approach it...I had done my entire public a kindness in sparing the sun, and was popular by reason of it.

I was no shadow of a king; I was the substance; the king himself was the shadow. My power was colossal; and it was not a mere name, as such things have generally been, it was the genuine article. I stood here, at the very spring and source of the second great period of the world's history; and could see the trickling stream of that history gather and deepen and broaden, and roll its mighty tides down the far centuries; and I could note the upspringing of adventurers like myself in the shelter of its long array of thrones: De Montforts, Gavestons, Mortimers, Villierses; the war-making, campaign-directing wantons of France, and Charles the Second's scepter-wielding drabs; but nowhere in the procession was my full-sized fellow visible. I was a Unique; and glad to know that that fact could not be dislodged or challenged for thirteen centuries and a half, for sure.

Yes, in power I was equal to the king. At the same time there was another power that was a trifle stronger than both of us put together. That was the Church. I do not wish to disguise that fact. I couldn't, if I wanted to. But never mind about that, now; it will show up, in its proper place, later on. It didn't cause me any trouble in the beginning—at least any of consequence.

Well, it was a curious country, and full of interest. And the people! They were the quaintest and simplest and trustingest race; why, they were nothing but rabbits. It was pitiful for a person born in a wholesome free atmosphere to listen to their humble and hearty outpourings of loyalty toward their king and Church and nobility; as if they had any more occasion to love and honor king and Church and noble than a slave has to love and honor the lash, or a dog has to love and honor the stranger that kicks him! Why, dear me, *any* kind of royalty, howsoever modified, *any* kind of aristocracy, howsoever pruned, is rightly an insult; but if you are born and brought up under that sort of arrangement you probably never find it out for yourself, and don't, believe it when somebody else tells you. It is enough to make a body ashamed of his race to think of the sort of froth that has always occupied its thrones without shadow of right or reason, and the seventh-rate people that have always figured as its aristocracies—a company of monarchs and nobles who, as a rule, would have achieved only poverty and obscurity if left, like their betters, to their own exertions.

The most of King Arthur's British nation were slaves, pure and simple, and bore that name, and wore the iron collar on their necks; and the rest were slaves in fact, but without the name; they imagined themselves men and freemen, and called themselves so. The truth was, the nation as a body was in the world for one object, and one only: to grovel before king and Church and noble; to slave for them, sweat blood for them, starve that they might be fed, work that they might play, drink misery to the dregs that they might be happy, go naked that they might wear silks and jewels, pay taxes that they might be spared from paying them, be familiar all their lives with the degrading language and postures of adulation that they might walk in pride and think themselves the gods of this world. And for all this, the thanks they got were cuffs and contempt; and so poor-spirited were they that they took even this sort of attention as an honor.

Inherited ideas are a curious thing, and interesting to observe and examine. I had mine, the king and his people had theirs. In both cases they flowed in ruts worn deep by time and habit, and the man who should have proposed to divert them by reason and argument would have had a long contract on his hands. For instance, those people had inherited the idea that all men without title and a long pedigree, whether they had great natural gifts and acquirements or hadn't, were creatures of no more consideration than so many animals, bugs, insects; whereas I had inherited the idea that human daws who can consent to masquerade in the peacock shams of inherited dignities and unearned titles, are of no good but to be laughed at. The way I was looked upon was odd, but it was natural. You know how the keeper and the public regard the elephant in the menagerie: well, that is the idea. They are full of admiration of his vast bulk and his prodigious strength; they speak with pride of the fact that he can do a hundred marvels which are far and away beyond their own powers; and they speak with the same pride of the fact that in his wrath he is able to drive a thousand men before him. But does that make him one of *them*? No; the raggedest tramp in the pit would smile at the idea. He couldn't comprehend it; couldn't take it in; couldn't in any remote way conceive of it. Well, to the king, the nobles, and all the nation, down to the very slaves and tramps, I was just that kind of an elephant, and nothing more. I was admired, also feared; but it was as an animal is admired and feared. The animal is not reverenced, neither was I; I was not even respected. I had no pedigree, no inherited title; so in the king's and nobles' eyes I was mere dirt; the people regarded me with wonder and awe, but there was no reverence mixed with it; through the force of inherited ideas they were not able to conceive of anything being entitled to that except pedigree or lordship . . .

Even down to my birth-century that a poison was still in the blood of Christendom, and the best of English commoners was still content to see his inferiors impudently continuing to hold a number of positions, such as lordships and the throne, to which the grotesque laws of his country did not allow him to aspire; in fact, he was not merely contented with this strange condition of things, he was even able to persuade himself that he was proud of it. It seems to show that there isn't anything you can't stand, if you are only born and bred to it. Of course that taint, that reverence for rank and title, had been in our American blood, too—I know that; but when I left America it had disappeared—at least to all intents and purposes. The remnant of it was restricted to the dudes and dudesses. When a disease has worked its way down to that level, it may fairly be said to be out of the system.

But to return to my anomalous position in King Arthur's kingdom. Here I was, a giant among pygmies, a man among children, a master intelligence among intellectual moles; by all rational measurement the one and only actually great man in that whole British world; and yet there and then, just as in the remote England of my birth-time, the sheep-witted earl who could claim long descent from a king. . . was a better man than I was. Such a personage was fawned upon in Arthur's realm and reverently looked up to by everybody, even though his dispositions were as mean as his intelligence. . . . There were times when *he* could sit down in the king's presence, but I couldn't. I could have got a title easily enough, and that would have raised me a large step in everybody's eyes; even in the king's, the giver of it. But I didn't ask for it; and I declined it when it was offered. I couldn't have enjoyed such a thing with my notions; and it wouldn't have been fair, anyway, because as far back as I could go, our tribe had always been short of the bar sinister. I couldn't have felt really and satisfactorily fine and proud and set-up over any title except one that should come from the nation itself, the only legitimate source; and such an one I hoped to win; and in the course of years of honest and honorable endeavor, I did win it and did wear it with a high and clean pride. This title fell casually from the lips of a blacksmith, one day, in a village, was caught up as a happy thought and tossed from mouth to mouth with a laugh and an affirmative vote; in ten days it had swept the kingdom, and was become as familiar as the king's name. I was never known by any other designation afterward, whether in the nation's talk or in grave debate upon matters of state at the council-board of the sovereign. This title, translated into modern speech, would be THE BOSS. Elected by the nation. That suited me. And it was a pretty high title. There were very few THE's, and I was one of them. If you spoke of the duke, or the earl, or the bishop, how could anybody tell which one you meant? But if you spoke of The King or The Queen or The Boss, it was different.

Well, I liked the king, and *as* king I respected him—respected the office; at least respected it as much as I was capable of respecting any unearned supremacy; but as *men* I looked down upon him and his nobles—privately. And he and they liked me, and respected my office; but as an animal, without birth or sham title, they looked down upon me—and were not particularly private about it, either. I didn't charge for my opinion about them, and they didn't charge for their opinion about me: the account was square, the books balanced, everybody was satisfied.

Mark Twain

The Yankees Fight With the Knights

from A Connecticut Yankee in King Arthur's Court

Up to the day set, there was no talk in all Britain of anything but this combat. All other topics sank into insignificance and passed out of men's thoughts and interest. It was not because a tournament was a great matter; it was not because Sir Sagramor had found the Holy Grail, for he had not, but had failed; it was not because the second (official) personage in the kingdom was one of the duelists; no, all these features were commonplace. Yet there was abundant reason for the extraordinary interest which this coming fight was creating. It was born of the fact that all the nation knew that this was not to be a duel between mere men, so to speak, but a duel between two mighty magicians; a duel not of muscle but of mind, not of human skill but of superhuman art and craft; a final struggle for supremacy between the two master enchanters of the age. It was realized that the most prodigious achievements of the most renowned knights could not be worthy of comparison with a spectacle like this; they could be but child's play, contrasted with this mysterious and awful battle of the gods. Yes, all the world knew it was going to be in reality a duel between Merlin and me, a measuring of his magic powers against mine. It was known that Merlin had been busy whole days and nights together, imbuing Sir Sagramor's arms and armor with supernal powers of offense and defense, and that he had procured for him from the spirits of the air a fleecy veil which would render the wearer invisible to his antagonist while still visible to other men. Against Sir Sagramor, so weaponed and protected, a thousand knights could accomplish nothing; against him no known enchantments could prevail. These facts were sure; regarding them there was no doubt, no reason for doubt. There was but one question: might there be still other enchantments, *unknown* to Merlin, which could render Sir Sagramor's veil transparent to me, and make his enchanted mail vulnerable to my weapons? This was the one thing to be decided in the lists. Until then the world must remain in suspense.

So the world thought there was a vast matter at stake here, and the world was right, but it was not the one they had in their minds. No, a far vaster one was upon the cast of this die: *the* life *of knight-errantry*[1]. I was a champion, it was true, but not the champion of the frivolous black arts, I was the champion of hard unsentimental common sense and reason. I was entering the lists to either destroy knight-errantry or be its victim.

Vast as the show-grounds were, there were no vacant spaces in them outside of the lists, at ten o'clock on the morning of the 16th. The mammoth grand-stand was clothed in flags, streamers, and rich tapestries, and packed with several acres of small-fry tributary kings, their suites, and the British aristocracy; with our own royal gang in the chief place, and each and every individual a flashing prism of gaudy silks and velvets —well, I never saw anything to begin with it but a fight between an Upper Mississippi sunset and the aurora borealis. The huge camp of beflagged and gay-colored tents at one end of the lists, with a stiff-standing sentinel at everydoor and a shining shield hanging by him for challenge, was another fine sight. You see, every knight was there who had any ambition or any caste feeling; for my feeling toward their order was not much of a secret, and so here was their chance. If I won my fight with Sir Sagramor, others would have the right to call me out as long as I might be willing to respond.

Down at our end there were but two tents; one for me, and another for my servants. At the appointed hour the king made a sign, and the heralds, in their tabards,[2] appeared and made proclamation, naming the combatants and stating the cause of quarrel. There was a pause, then a ringing bugle-blast, which was the signal for us to come forth. All the multitude caught their breath, and an eager curiosity flashed into every face.

Out from his tent rode great Sir Sagramor, an imposing tower of iron, stately and rigid, his huge spear standing upright in its socket and grasped in his strong hand, his grand horse's face and breast cased in steel, his body clothed in rich trappings that almost dragged the ground—oh, a most noble picture. A great shout went up, of welcome and admiration.

And then out I came. But I didn't get any shout. There was a wondering and eloquent silence for a moment, then a great wave of laughter began to sweep along that human sea, but a warning bugle-blast cut its career short. I was in the simplest and comfortablest of gymnast costumes—flesh-colored tights from neck to heel, with blue silk puffings about my loins, and bareheaded.

1. **knight-errantry** (nīt er' ən trē) *n.*: Actions of a medieval knight wandering in search of adventure.
2. **tabard** (tab' ərd) *n.*: A heavy, emblazoned cloak, worn by a knight over armor.

My horse was not above medium size, but he was alert, slender-limbed, muscled with watch-springs, and just a grey-hound to go. He was a beauty, glossy as silk, and naked as he was when he was born except for bridle and ranger-saddle.

The iron tower and the gorgeous bed-quilt came cumbrously but gracefully pirouetting down the lists, and we tripped lightly up to meet them. We halted; the tower saluted, I responded; then we wheeled and rode side by side to the grand-stand and faced our king and queen, to whom we made obeisance. The queen exclaimed:

"Alack, Sir Boss, wilt fight naked[3] and without lance or sword or—"

But the king checked her and made her understand, with a polite phrase or two, that this was none of her business. The bugles rang again; and we separated and rode to the ends of the lists, and took position. Now old Merlin stepped into view and cast a dainty web of gossamer threads over Sir Sagramor which turned him into Hamlet's ghost; the king made a sign, the bugles blew, Sir Sagramor laid his great lance in rest, and the next moment here he came thundering down the course with his veil flying out behind, and I went whistling through the air like an arrow to meet him—cocking my ear the while, as if noting the invisible knight's position and progress by hearing, not sight. A chorus of encouraging shouts burst out for him, and one brave voice flung out a heartening word for me—said:

"Go it, slim Jim!"

It was an even bet that Clarence had procured that favor for me—and furnished the language, too. When that formidable lance-point was within a yard and a half of my breast I twitched my horse aside without an effort, and the big knight swept by, scoring a blank. I got plenty of applause that time. We turned, braced up, and down we came again. Another blank for the knight, a roar of applause for me. This same thing was repeated once more; and it fetched such a whirlwind of applause that Sir Sagramor lost his temper, and at once changed his tactics and set himself the task of chasing me down. Why, he hadn't any show in the world at that; it was a game of tag, with all the advantage on my side; I whirled out of his path with ease when-ever I chose, and once I slapped him on the back as I went to the rear. Finally I took the chase into my own hands; and after that, turn, or twist, or do what he would, he was never able to

---

3. **naked** *adj.*: Clothed, but without armor.

get behind me again; he found himself always in front at the end of his manoeuver. So he gave up that business and retired to his end of the lists. His temper was clear gone now, and he forgot himself and flung an insult at me which disposed of mine. I slipped my lasso from the horn of my saddle, and grasped the coil in my right hand. This time you should have seen him come!—it was a business trip, sure; by his gait there was blood in his eye. I was sitting my horse at ease, and swinging the great loop of my lasso in wide circles about my head; the moment he was under way, I started for him; when the space between us had narrowed to forty feet, I sent the snaky spirals of the rope a-cleaving through the air, then darted aside and faced about and brought my trained animal to a halt with all his feet braced under him for a surge. The next moment the rope sprang taut and yanked Sir Sagramor out of the saddle! Great Scott, but there was a sensation!

Unquestionably, the popular thing in this world is novelty. These people had never seen anything of that cowboy business before, and it carried them clear off their feet with delight. From all around and everywhere, the shout went up:

"Encore! encore!"

I wondered where they got the word, but there was no time to cipher on philological matters, because the whole knight-errantry hive was just humming now, and my prospect for trade couldn't have been better. The moment my lasso was released and Sir Sagramor had been assisted to his tent, I hauled in the slack, took my station and began to swing my loop around my head again. I was sure to have use for it as soon as they could elect a successor for Sir Sagramor, and that couldn't take long where there were so many hungry candidates. Indeed, they elected one straight off—Sir Hervis de Revel.

Bzz! Here he came, like a house afire; I dodged: he passed like a flash, with my horse-hair coils settling around his neck; a second or so later, *fst!* his saddle was empty.

I got another encore; and another, and another, and still another. When I had snaked five men out, things began to look serious to the ironclads, and they stopped and consulted together. As a result, they decided that it was time to waive etiquette and send their greatest and best against me. To the astonishment of that little world, I lassoed Sir Lamorak de Galis, and after him Sir Galahad. So you see there was simply nothing to be done now, but play their right bower—bring out the superbest of the superb, the mightiest of the mighty, the great Sir Launcelot himself!

A proud moment for me? I should think so. Yonder was Arthur, King of Britain; yonder was Guinever; yes, and whole tribes of little provincial kings and kinglets; and in the tented camp yonder, renowned knights from many lands; and likewise the selectest body known to chivalry, the Knights of the Table Round, the most illustrious in Christendom; and biggest fact of all, the very sun of their shining system was yonder couching his lance, the focal point of forty thousand adoring eyes; and all by myself, here was I laying for him. Across my mind flitted the dear image of a certain girl of West Hartford, and I wished she could see me now. In that moment, down came the Invincible, with the rush of a whirlwind—the courtly world rose to its feet and bent forward—the fateful coils went circling through the air, and before you could wink I was towing Sir Launcelot across the field on his back, and kissing my hand to the storm of waving kerchiefs and the thunder-crash of applause that greeted me!

Said I to myself, as I coiled my lariat and hung it on my saddle-horn, and sat there drunk with glory, "The victory is perfect—no other will venture against me—knight-errantry is dead." Now imagine my astonishment—and everybody else's, too—to hear the peculiar bugle-call which announces that another competitor is about to enter the lists! There was a mystery here; I couldn't account for this thing. Next, I noticed Merlin gliding away from me; and then I noticed that my lasso was gone! The old sleight-of-hand expert had stolen it, sure, and slipped it under his robe.

The bugle blew again. I looked, and down came Sagramor riding again, with his dust brushed off and his veil nicely rearranged. I trotted up to meet him, and pretended to find him by the sound of his horse's hoofs. He said:

"Thou'rt quick of ear, but it will not save thee from this!" and he touched the hilt of his great sword. "An ye are not able to see it, because of the influence of the veil, know that it is no cumbrous lance, but a sword—and I ween ye will not be able to avoid it."

His visor was up; there was death in his smile. I should never be able to dodge his sword, that was plain. Somebody was going to die this time. If he got the drop on me, I could name the corpse. We rode forward together, and saluted the royalties. This time the king was disturbed. He said:

"Where is thy strange weapon?"

"It is stolen, sire."

"Hast another at hand?"

"No, sire, I brought only the one."

Then Merlin mixed in:

"He brought but the one because there was but the one to bring. There exists none other but that one. It belongeth to the king of the Demons of the Sea. This man is a pretender, and ignorant; else he had known that that weapon can be used in but eight bouts only, and then it vanisheth away to its home under the sea."

"Then is he weaponless," said the king. "Sir Sagramor, ye will grant him leave to borrow."

"And I will lend!" said Sir Launcelot, limping up. " He is as brave a knight of his hands as any that be on live, and he shall have mine."

He put his hand on his sword to draw it, but Sir Sagramor said:

"Stay, it may not be. He shall fight with his own weapons; it was his privilege to choose them and bring them. If he has erred, on his head be it."

"Knight!" said the king. "Thou'rt overwrought with passion; it disorders thy mind. Wouldst kill a naked man?"

"An he do it, he shall answer it to me," said Sir Launcelot.

"I will answer it to any he that desireth!" retorted Sir Sagramor hotly.

Merlin broke in, rubbing his hands and smiling his low-downest smile of malicious gratification:

"'Tis well said, right well said! And 'tis enough of parleying, let my lord the king deliver the battle signal."

The king had to yield. The bugle made proclamation, and we turned apart and rode to our stations. There we stood, a hundred yards apart, facing each other, rigid and motionless, like horsed statues. And so we remained, in a soundless hush, as much as a full minute, everybody gazing, nobody stirring. It seemed as if the king could not take heart to give the signal. But at last he lifted his hand, the clear note of a bugle followed, Sir Sagramor's long blade described a flashing curve in the air, and it was superb to see him come. I sat still. On he came. I did not move. People got so excited that they shouted to me:

"Fly, fly! Save thyself! This is murther!

I never budged so much as an inch till that thundering apparition had got within fifteen paces of me; then I snatched a dragoon revolver out of my holster, there was a flash and a roar, and the revolver was back in the holster before anybody could tell what had happened.

Here was a riderless horse plunging by, and yonder lay Sir Sagramor, stone dead.

The people that ran to him were stricken dumb to find that the life was actually gone out of the man and no reason for it visible, no hurt upon his body, nothing like a wound. There was a hole through the breast of his chain-mail, but they attached no importance to a little thing like that; and as a bullet-wound there produces but little blood, none came in sight because of the clothing and swaddlings under the armor. The body was dragged over to let the king and the swells look down upon it. They were stupefied with astonishment naturally. I was requested to come and explain the miracle. But I remained in my tracks, like a statue, and said:

"If it is a command, I will come, but my lord the king knows that I am where the laws of combat require me to remain while any desire to come against me."

I waited. Nobody challenged . . .

The day was mine. Knight-errantry was a doomed institution. The march of civilization was begun. How did I feel? Ah, you never could imagine it.

And Brer Merlin? His stock was flat again. Somehow, every time the magic of fol-de-rol[4] tried conclusions with the magic of science, the magic of fol-de-rol got left.

---

4. **fol-de-rol** (fäl' də räl') *n*.: Showy but worthless objects; mere nonsense.

☑ Check Your Comprehension

1. What does the Yankee think "pitiful" about the people's attitude to king, Church, and noble?
2. What does the Yankee say would happen to aristocrats "if left to their own exertions?"
3. Who gives the Yankee the name "The Boss?"
4. What power does the "fleecy veil" give to Sir Sagamor?
5. How does the crowd react to the Yankee's first appearance in the jousting arena?
6. What modern "inventions" does the Yankee use to defeat the other knights?

◆ Critical Thinking

INTERPRET

1. About midway through the chapter headed "The Boss," the narrator says that, "Inherited ideas are a curious thing, and interesting to observe and examine." Analyze one inherited idea in King Arthur's England that the narrator discusses. **[Analyze]**

2. What does the narrator mean when he says that the king and the people regard him as an "elephant in the menagerie?" **[Interpret]**
3. Write a description of someone who has been your boss. Compare this person to the narrator. **[Apply]**
4. Near the beginning of the battle scene selection, the Yankee speaks of the need to discover "other enchantments, unknown to Merlin," if he is to defeat Sir Sagramor. Would you classify what he comes up with as "enchantments?" Explain your answer. **[Analyze]**
5. What does the Yankee mean when, in the last paragraph of the battle scene, he says "the march of civilization was begun?" **[Interpret]**
6. Research the story of the quest for the Holy Grail in an encyclopedia (the Holy Grail is mentioned at the beginning of the battle scene selection). Then research a modern expedition into outer space. Contrast these two quests in an essay. **[Extend; Science Link]**

Mark Twain
Comparing and Connecting the Author's Works

◆ Literary Focus: Humor and Criticism

A comic writer like Mark Twain combines the techniques of a vaudevillian performer with the serious intent of a novelist. He is like a juggler: He keeps all the particulars of his developing narrative up in the air until the right moment when, with one rip-roaring detail, he brings the scene to a delightful climax. We feel this when, just before the Yankee's duel with Sir Sagramor, the dismayed queen exclaims, "Alack, Sir Boss, wilt fight naked," because the Yankee has chosen not to use a sword; or when, just afterwards, a single English voice cries out, in support of him, "Go it, slim Jim." It is Twain's comic purpose to hold no subject so sacred as to be safe from his satire. He draws on all his skill for exaggeration in making the Knights of the Round Table seem vain and selfish as they succumb pitifully to the Yankee's makeshift lasso. And yet his laugh-filled narrative also has a serious underside: Twain wants to reexamine the values of the heroic past and to compare them with modern American democratic values.

Main Features of Twain's Humor Writing

• Creates brilliantly exaggerated descriptions of characters and scenes

• Adapts a comic performer's sense of timing to the technique of narrative

• Makes his first-person narrator a colorful personality whose thoughts evoke laughter

1. Write down the parts of Twain's descriptions in the selection, "The Yankee's Fight with the Knights," that you think are funny. Then describe a crowd scene (downtown during mid-day traffic, a stadium, a school lunchroom, or an auditorium, adopting Twain's techniques of exaggeration to create a comic effect.

2. Write a dialogue between the Yankee and an Englishman/woman of King Arthur's time who addresses him as "The Boss." Have them discuss the issue of equality in Arthurian society. Try to incorporate some of Twain's humorous effects, such as his exaggerated descriptions and the Yankee's excitable tone.

◆ Drawing Conclusions About Twain's Work

The name Mark Twain *differs because it is more like a brand in a commercial world of celebrity, advertisement, and packaged products.* Mark Twain *was an enterprise that included popular travel writing, coast-to-coast lecturing, door-to-door subscription sales of his books, a publishing house, and speculations in various inventions. The name was a trademark, secured by constant public witticisms and cartoons, and stabilized by a fixed and well-known eccentric appearance.*

—*Philip Fisher*

The above passage makes clear that Twain was a famous man and that he tried hard to be one. All the selections deal with the fame. Draw a diagram to compare uses of this theme of fame.

Ways in which fame is discussed in selections	Twain's ideas on fame as suggested by details

◆ Idea Bank

Writing

1. **Message to the Author** Write a note to Twain in the form of an e-mail message. Give him your thoughts on the narrator of *A Connecticut Yankee in King Arthur's Court.* Specify what you like and don't like about this character.

2. **Interview** Interview someone whose life you view as noteworthy—a classmate, a teacher, a relative, a family friend, etc. Prepare a list of questions. Organize what you learn into a written profile of the person.

3. **Compare and Contrast** Write an essay analyzing the thoughts and experiences of the young Twain as recounted in *Life on the Mississippi.* Compare and contrast the narrator's state of mind at the beginning of the selection and at the end.

Speaking and Listening

4. **Enacting the Interview** With a partner, read "Encounter with an Interviewer." Each of you should read one character's part. Stress the differences in their word choices, tone, and personality.

5. **Debate** Twain writes of Sir Drinadan, in *A Connecticut Yankee in King Arthur's Court,* that "he liked to have a fresh market for his jokes, the most of them having reached that stage of wear where the teller has to do the laughing himself while the other person looks sick." With this comment in mind, debate the lasting appeal of Twain's humor. One side should argue that Twain's humor doesn't appeal to readers today; the other should argue that it retains its appeal.

Research and Representing

6. **Compare and Contrast** No two creative artists could be more different than Twain and the Impressionist painter Vincent van Gogh (1853–1890). Yet, both men have written powerful descriptions of Nature. Twain described the Mississippi river world, while van Gogh described the rural landscapes of France. Find a copy of van Gogh's letters to his brother, Theo, and compare and contrast his descriptions of Nature with those by Twain.

◆ Further Reading, Listening, and Viewing

- Shelley Fisher Fishkin: *Was Huck Black?: Mark Twain and African American Voices.* (1993) A groundbreaking study that looks at the African-American sources for the speech patterns of Huck Finn

- Justin Kaplan: *Mr. Clemens and Mark Twain.* (1966) An important biography by a leading Twain scholar

- J. R. LeMaster and James D. Wilson, eds. *The Mark Twain Encyclopedia* (1993)

- J. Steinbrink. *Getting to be Mark Twain* (1991)

- Mark Twain. *The Connecticut Yankee in King Arthur's Court.* Norton Critical Edition. Allison R. Ensor, ed. (1982) With illustrations from the original edition by Dan Beard

- *Mark Twain Tonight!* (1967) Film directed by Peter Bogart

On the Web:

http://www.phschool.com/atschool/literature
Go to the student edition of *The American Experience.* Proceed to Unit 4. Then, click Hot links to find Web sites featuring Mark Twain.

Willa Cather In Depth

WILLA CATHER is one of the most distinguished American novelists of the early twentieth century. She is particularly associated with her beautiful, sweeping descriptions of frontier America, especially the prairie of the Midwest where she grew up. Although Cather's early writing was greatly influenced by Henry James, critics assert that she was fiercely original in her sensitive depiction of her characters, especially those figures she drew from the immigrant families she knew as a child. Critics praise her seemingly effortless ability to weave a good story.

A Life-Altering Decision Willa Cather was born on December 7, 1873, in what is now known as Gore, Virginia. There she enjoyed exploring the farm and the beauties of nature with her siblings. When she was nine years old, Cather's idyllic existence came to an abrupt halt when her parents decided to move to Red Cloud, Nebraska.

Cather was shocked by the contrast of the flat starkness of the Nebraska plains with the lush greenery of the Blue Ridge Mountains. She wrote that she had "come to the end of everything—it [the prairie] was a kind of erasure of personality. . . . I thought I would go under." However, Cather began to see the beauty in the prairie—a land "buried in wheat and corn"—and used it as a setting for many of her stories. The immigrant settlers from Scandinavia, Germany, France, and Eastern Europe provided inipration for her characters.

Literary Debut Cather started a course of science study at the University of Nebraska in Lincoln. Fate stepped in in the guise of a professor who submitted an essay of hers to the local newspaper. So impressed was the editor that Cather was hired as a drama critic. Cather gave up her goal of medicine to pursue a literary career. From her often opinionated and disparaging style of writing, Cather earned a reputation for being bright, brash, and unconventional.

In 1896, Cather was offered a job as editor of a magazine in Pittsburgh. She moved back east, where she was to live for the rest of her life. She worked at this magazine and later for *The Daily Leader* as editor and reviewer. She gave up editing to teach high-school English and Latin, and devote more time to her writing. It was during her teaching stint that her first books, *April Twilights* (1903), a book of poetry, and *The Troll Garden* (1905), a collection of stories, appeared.

Magazine Life In 1906, impressed by the Cather's stories and poems, S. S. McClure invited Cather to come to New York to join the staff of *McClure's Magazine*. Within a year, Cather was promoted to managing editor. Working for the magazine enabled Cather to meet many of its famous literary contributors. One of these, Sarah Orne Jewett, told her that she must have her "own quiet center of life" in order to write, and that "a true artist draws on what he knows

Willa Cather

from My Ántonia

I

I FIRST heard of Ántonia[1] on what seemed to be an interminable journey across the great midland plain of North America. I was ten years old then; I had lost both my father and mother within a year, and my Virginia relatives were sending me out to my grandparents, who lived in Nebraska. I travelled in the care of a mountain boy, Jake Marpole, one of the 'hands' on my father's old farm under the Blue Ridge, who was now going West to work for my grandfather. Jake's experience of the world was not much wider than mine. He had never been in a railway train until the morning when we set out together to try our fortunes in a new world.

We went all the way in day-coaches, becoming more sticky and grimy with each stage of the journey. Jake bought everything the newsboys offered him: candy, oranges, brass collar buttons, a watch-charm, and for me a 'Life of Jesse James,' which I remember as one of the most satisfactory books I have ever read. Beyond Chicago we were under the protection of a friendly passenger conductor, who knew all about the country to which we were going and gave us a great deal of advice in exchange for our confidence. He seemed to us an experienced and worldly man who had been almost everywhere; in his conversation he threw out lightly the names of distant states and cities. He wore the rings and pins and badges of different fraternal orders to which he belonged. Even his cuff-buttons were engraved with hieroglyphics, and he was more inscribed than an Egyptian obelisk.

Once when he sat down to chat, he told us that in the immigrant car ahead there was a family from 'across the water' whose destination was the same as ours.

'They can't any of them speak English, except one little girl, and all she can say is "We go Black Hawk, Nebraska." She's not much older than you, twelve or thirteen, maybe, and she's as bright as a new dollar.

'Don't you want to go ahead and see her, Jimmy? She's got the pretty brown eyes, too!'

This last remark made me bashful, and I shook my head and

---

1. Ántonia: In the novel, Ántonia is an immigrant girl from Bohemia (a region of Czech Republic) who arrives in Nebraska on the same train as Jim.

settled down to 'Jesse James.' Jake nodded at me approvingly.

I do not remember crossing the Missouri River, or anything about the long day's journey through Nebraska. Probably by that time I had crossed so many rivers that I was dull to them. The only thing very noticeable about Nebraska was that it was still, all day long, Nebraska.

I had been sleeping, curled up in a red plush seat, for a long while when we reached Black Hawk. Jake roused me and took me by the hand. We stumbled down from the train to a wooden siding, where men were running about with lanterns. I couldn't see any town, or even distant lights; we were surrounded by utter darkness. The engine was panting heavily after its long run. In the red glow from the fire-box, a group of people stood huddled together on the platform, encumbered by bundles and boxes. I knew this must be the immigrant family the conductor had told us about. The woman wore a fringed shawl tied over her head, and she carried a little tin trunk in her arms, hugging it as if it were a baby. There was an old man, tall and stooped. Two half-grown boys and a girl stood holding oilcloth bundles, and a little girl clung to her mother's skirts. Presently a man with a lantern approached them and began to talk, shouting and exclaiming. I pricked up my ears, for it was positively the first time I had ever heard a foreign tongue.

Another lantern came along. A bantering voice called out: 'Hello, are you Mr. Burden's folks? If you are, it's me you're looking for. I'm Otto Fuchs. I'm Mr. Burden's hired man, and I'm to drive you out. Hello, Jimmy, ain't you scared to come so far west?'

I looked up with interest at the new face in the lantern-light. He might have stepped out of the pages of 'Jesse James.' He wore a sombrero hat, with a wide leather band and a bright buckle, and the ends of his moustache were twisted up stiffly, like little horns. He looked lively and ferocious, I thought, and as if he had a history. A long scar ran across one cheek and drew the corner of his mouth up in a sinister curl. The top of his left ear was gone, and his skin was brown as an Indian's. Surely this was the face of a desperado. As he walked about the platform in his high-heeled boots, looking for our trunks, I saw that he was a rather slight man, quick and wiry, and light on his feet. He told us we had a long night drive ahead of us, and had better be on the hike. He led us to a hitching-bar where two farm-wagons were tied, and I saw the foreign family crowding into one of them. The other was for us. Jake got on the front seat with Otto Fuchs, and I rode on the straw in the bottom of the wagon-box, covered up with a buffalo hide. The immigrants rumbled off into the empty darkness, and we followed them.

I tried to go to sleep, but the jolting made me bite my tongue, and I soon began to ache all over. When the straw settled down, I had a hard bed. Cautiously I slipped from under the buffalo hide, got up on my knees and peered over the side of the wagon. There seemed to be nothing to see; no fences, no creeks or trees, no hills or fields. If there was a road, I could not make it out in the faint starlight. There was nothing but land: not a country at all, but the material out of which countries are made. No, there was nothing but land—slightly undulating, I knew, because often our wheels ground against the brake as we went down into a hollow and lurched up again on the other side. I had the feeling that the world was left behind, that we had got over the edge of it, and were outside man's jurisdiction. I had never before looked up at the sky when there was not a familiar mountain ridge against it. But this was the complete dome of heaven, all there was of it. I did not believe that my dead father and mother were watching me from up there; they would still be looking for me at the sheep-fold down by the creek, or along the white road that led to the mountain pastures. I had left even their spirits behind me. The wagon jolted on, carrying me I knew not whither. I don't think I was homesick. If we never arrived anywhere, it did not matter. Between that earth and that sky I felt erased, blotted out. I did not say my prayers that night: here, I felt, what would be would be.

II

I do not remember our arrival at my grandfather's farm sometime before daybreak, after a drive of nearly twenty miles with heavy work-horses. When I awoke, it was afternoon. I was lying in a little room, scarcely larger than the bed that held me, and the window-shade at my head was flapping softly in a warm wind. A tall woman, with wrinkled brown skin and black hair, stood looking down at me; I knew that she must be my grandmother. She had been crying, I could see, but when I opened my eyes she smiled, peered at me anxiously, and sat down on the foot of my bed.

'Had a good sleep, Jimmy?' she asked briskly. Then in a very different tone she said, as if to herself, 'My, how you do look like your father!' I remembered that my father had been her little boy; she must often have come to wake him like this when he overslept. 'Here are your clean clothes,' she went on, stroking my coverlid with her brown hand as she talked. 'But first you come down to the kitchen with me, and have a nice warm bath behind the stove. Bring your things; there's nobody about.'

'Down to the kitchen' struck me as curious; it was always 'out in the kitchen' at home. I picked up my shoes and stockings and followed her through the living-room and down a flight of stairs into a basement. This basement was divided into a dining-room at the right of the stairs and a kitchen at the left. Both rooms were plastered and whitewashed—the plaster laid directly upon the earth walls, as it used to be in dugouts. The floor was of hard cement. Up under the wooden ceiling there were little half-windows with white curtains, and pots of geraniums and wandering Jew in the deep sills. As I entered the kitchen, I sniffed a pleasant smell of gingerbread baking. The stove was very large, with bright nickel trimmings, and behind it there was a long wooden bench against the wall, and a tin washtub, into which grandmother poured hot and cold water. When she brought the soap and towels, I told her that I was used to taking my bath without help.

'Can you do your ears, Jimmy? Are you sure? Well, now, I call you a right smart little boy.'

It was pleasant there in the kitchen. The sun shone into my bath-water through the west half-window, and a big Maltese cat came up and rubbed himself against the tub, watching me curiously. While I scrubbed, my grandmother busied herself in the dining-room until I called anxiously, 'Grandmother, I'm afraid the cakes are burning!' Then she came laughing, waving her apron before her as if she were shooing chickens.

She was a spare, tall woman, a little stooped, and she was apt to carry her head thrust forward in an attitude of attention, as if she were looking at something, or listening to something, far away. As I grew older, I came to believe that it was only because she was so often thinking of things that were far away. She was quick-footed and energetic in all her movements. Her voice was high and rather shrill, and she often spoke with an anxious inflection, for she was exceedingly desirous that everything should go with due order and decorum. Her laugh, too, was high, and perhaps a little strident, but there was a lively intelligence in it. She was then fifty-five years old, a strong woman, of unusual endurance.

After I was dressed, I explored the long cellar next the kitchen. It was dug out under the wing of the house, was plastered and cemented, with a stairway and an outside door by which the men came and went. Under one of the windows there was a place for them to wash when they came in from work.

While my grandmother was busy about supper, I settled

myself on the wooden bench behind the stove and got acquainted with the cat—he caught not only rats and mice, but gophers,
I was told. The patch of yellow sunlight on the floor travelled
back toward the stairway, and grandmother and I talked about
my journey, and about the arrival of the new Bohemian family;
she said they were to be our nearest neighbours. We did not talk
about the farm in Virginia, which had been her home for so
many years. But after the men came in from the fields, and we
were all seated at the supper table, then she asked Jake about
the old place and about our friends and neighbours there.

My grandfather said little. When he first came in he kissed
me and spoke kindly to me, but he was not demonstrative. I felt
at once his deliberateness and personal dignity, and was a little
in awe of him. The thing one immediately noticed about him was
his beautiful, crinkly, snow-white beard. I once heard a mission-
ary say it was like the beard of an Arabian sheik. His bald crown
only made it more impressive.

Grandfather's eyes were not at all like those of an old man;
they were bright blue, and had a fresh, frosty sparkle. His teeth
were white and regular—so sound that he had never been to a
dentist in his life. He had a delicate skin, easily roughened by
sun and wind. When he was a young man his hair and beard
were red; his eyebrows were still coppery.

As we sat at the table, Otto Fuchs and I kept stealing covert
glances at each other. Grandmother had told me while she was
getting supper that he was an Austrian who came to this country a young boy and had led an adventurous life in the Far West
among mining-camps and cow outfits. His iron constitution was
somewhat broken by mountain pneumonia, and he had drifted
back to live in a milder country for a while. He had relatives in
Bismarck, a German settlement to the north of us, but for a year
now he had been working for grandfather.

The minute supper was over, Otto took me into the kitchen to
whisper to me about a pony down in the barn that had been
bought for me at a sale; he had been riding him to find out
whether he had any bad tricks, but he was a 'perfect gentleman,'
and his name was Dude. Fuchs told me everything I wanted to
know: how he had lost his ear in a Wyoming blizzard when he
was a stage-driver, and how to throw a lasso. He promised to
rope a steer for me before sundown next day. He got out his
'chaps' and silver spurs to show them to Jake and me, and his
best cowboy boots, with tops stitched in bold design—roses, and
true-lover's knots, and undraped female figures. These, he
solemnly explained, were angels.

Before we went to bed, Jake and Otto were called up to the living-room for prayers. Grandfather put on silver-rimmed spectacles and read several Psalms. His voice was so sympathetic and he read so interestingly that I wished he had chosen one of my favourite chapters in the Book of Kings. I was awed by his intonation of the word 'Selah.' 'He shall choose our inheritance for us, the excellency of Jacob whom He loved. Selah.' I had no idea what the word meant; perhaps he had not. But, as he uttered it, it became oracular, the most sacred of words.

Early the next morning I ran out-of-doors to look about me. I had been told that ours was the only wooden house west of Black Hawk—until you came to the Norwegian settlement, where there were several. Our neighbours lived in sod houses and dugouts—comfortable, but not very roomy. Our white frame house, with a storey and half-storey above the basement, stood at the east end of what I might call the farmyard, with the windmill close by the kitchen door. From the windmill the ground sloped westward, down to the barns and granaries and pig-yards. This slope was trampled hard and bare, and washed out in winding gullies by the rain. Beyond the corncribs, at the bottom of the shallow draw, was a muddy little pond, with rusty willow bushes growing about it. The road from the post-office came directly by our door, crossed the farmyard, and curved round this little pond, beyond which it began to climb the gentle swell of unbroken prairie to the west. There, along the western sky-line it skirted a great cornfield, much larger than any field I had ever seen. This cornfield, and the sorghum patch behind the barn, were the only broken land in sight. Everywhere, as far as the eye could reach, there was nothing but rough, shaggy, red grass, most of it as tall as I.

North of the house, inside the ploughed fire-breaks, grew a thick-set strip of box-elder trees, low and bushy, their leaves already turning yellow. This hedge was nearly a quarter of a mile long, but I had to look very hard to see it at all. The little trees were insignificant against the grass. It seemed as if the grass were about to run over them, and over the plum-patch behind the sod chicken-house.

As I looked about me I felt that the grass was the country, as the water is the sea. The red of the grass made all the great prairie the colour of wine-stains, or of certain seaweeds when they are first washed up. And there was so much motion in it; the whole country seemed, somehow, to be running.

I had almost forgotten that I had a grandmother, when she came out, her sunbonnet on her head, a grain-sack in her hand,

and asked me if I did not want to go to the garden with her to dig potatoes for dinner.

The garden, curiously enough, was a quarter of a mile from the house, and the way to it led up a shallow draw past the cattle corral. Grandmother called my attention to a stout hickory cane, tipped with copper, which hung by a leather thong from her belt. This, she said, was her rattlesnake cane. I must never go to the garden without a heavy stick or a corn-knife; she had killed a good many rattlers on her way back and forth. A little girl who lived on the Black Hawk road was bitten on the ankle and had been sick all summer.

I can remember exactly how the country looked to me as I walked beside my grandmother along the faint wagon-tracks on that early September morning. Perhaps the glide of long railway travel was still with me, for more than anything else I felt motion in the landscape; in the fresh, easy-blowing morning wind, and in the earth itself, as if the shaggy grass were a sort of loose hide, and underneath it herds of wild buffalo were galloping, galloping . . .

Alone, I should never have found the garden—except, perhaps, for the big yellow pumpkins that lay about unprotected by their withering vines—and I felt very little interest in it when I got there. I wanted to walk straight on through the red grass and over the edge of the world, which could not be very far away. The light air about me told me that the world ended here: only the ground and sun and sky were left, and if one went a little farther there would be only sun and sky, and one would float off into them, like the tawny hawks which sailed over our heads making slow shadows on the grass. While grandmother took the pitchfork we found standing in one of the rows and dug potatoes, while I picked them up out of the soft brown earth and put them into the bag, I kept looking up at the hawks that were doing what I might so easily do.

When grandmother was ready to go, I said I would like to stay up there in the garden awhile.

She peered down at me from under her sunbonnet. 'Aren't you afraid of snakes?'

'A little,' I admitted, 'but I'd like to stay, anyhow.'

'Well, if you see one, don't have any thing to do with him. The big yellow and brown ones won't hurt you; they're bull-snakes and help to keep the gophers down. Don't be scared if you see anything look out of that hole in the bank over there. That's a badger hole. He's about as big as a big 'possum, and his face is striped, black and white. He takes a chicken once in a while, but

I won't let the men harm him. In a new country a body feels friendly to the animals. I like to have him come out and watch me when I'm at work.'

Grandmother swung the bag of potatoes over her shoulder and went down the path, leaning forward a little. The road followed the windings of the draw; when she came to the first bend, she waved at me and disappeared. I was left alone with this new feeling of lightness and content.

I sat down in the middle of the garden, where snakes could scarcely approach unseen, and leaned my back against a warm yellow pumpkin. There were some ground-cherry bushes growing along the furrows, full of fruit. I turned back the papery triangular sheaths that protected the berries and ate a few. All about me giant grasshoppers, twice as big as any I had ever seen, were doing acrobatic feats among the dried vines. The gophers scurried up and down the ploughed ground. There in the sheltered draw-bottom the wind did not blow very hard, but I could hear it singing its humming tune up on the level, and I could see the tall grasses wave. The earth was warm under me, and warm as I crumbled it through my fingers. Queer little red bugs came out and moved in slow squadrons around me. Their backs were polished vermilion, with black spots. I kept as still as I could. Nothing happened. I did not expect anything to happen. I was something that lay under the sun and felt it, like the pumpkins, and I did not want to be anything more. I was entirely happy. Perhaps we feel like that when we die and become a part of something entire, whether it is sun and air, or goodness and knowledge. At any rate, that is happiness; to be dissolved into something complete and great. When it comes to one, it comes as naturally as sleep.

Willa Cather

Prairie Spring

Evening and the flat land,
Rich and sombre and always silent;
The miles of fresh-plowed soil,
Heavy and black, full of strength and harshness;
5   The growing wheat, the growing weeds,
The toiling horses, the tired men;
The long empty roads,
Sullen fires of sunset, fading,
The eternal, unresponsive sky.
10   Against all this, Youth,
Flaming like the wild roses,
Singing like the larks over the plowed fields,
Flashing like a star out of the twilight;
Youth with its insupportable sweetness,
15   Its fierce necessity,
Its sharp desire,
Singing and singing,
Out of the lips of silence,
Out of the earthy dusk.

☑ Check Your Comprehension

1. How does Jim feel when the friendly conductor tells him about Ántonia, the daughter of the immigrant family in the next car?
2. (a)What can Jim tell about Nebraska from looking out the window of the train? (b) What can he see from looking over the side of the wagon?
3. How does Cather let the reader know what kind of person Jim's grandmother is?
4. What does Otto Fuchs do to make Jim feel at home?
5. (a) In "Prairie Spring," what adjectives does Cather use to describe the land? (b) What words does the poet use to describe the qualities of youth?

◆ Critical Thinking

INTERPRET

1. (a) In *My Ántonia*, why does Jim feel "erased, blotted out" when he rides in the wagon to his new home? (b) List three phrases Jim uses to tell how he feels about his new home. **[Interpret; Support]**
2. Why does Jim say, when he gets to the garden, "I wanted to walk straight on through the red grass and over the edge of the world, which could not be very far away." **[Interpret]**
3. By the end of the story Jim says he was "entirely happy." How do you account for his change of mood? **[Draw Conclusions]**

EVALUATE

4. (a) In "Prairie Spring," to what does Cather compare and/or contrast the prairie? (b) Why do you think she makes this comparison? **[Compare; Contrast; Infer]**

COMPARE LITERARY WORKS

5. Look at the paragraph from *My Ántonia* just before Jim goes to the garden, and look at lines 10–14 from "Prairie Spring." What comparisons does Cather make in these passages? **[Analyze; Connect]**

Willa Cather

The Sentimentality of William Tavener

It takes a strong woman to make any sort of success of living in the West, and Hester undoubtedly was that. When people spoke of William Tavener as the most prosperous farmer in McPherson County, they usually added that his wife was a "good manager." She was an executive woman, quick of tongue and something of an imperatrix. The only reason her husband did not consult her about his business was that she did not wait to be consulted.

It would have been quite impossible for one man, within the limited sphere of human action, to follow all Hester's advice, but in the end William usually acted upon some of her suggestions. When she incessantly denounced the "shiftlessness" of letting a new threshing machine stand unprotected in the open, he eventually built a shed for it. When she sniffed contemptuously at his notion of fencing a hog corral with sod walls, he made a spiritless beginning on the structure—merely to "show his temper," as she put it—but in the end he went off quietly to town and bought enough barbed wire to complete the fence. When the first heavy rains came on, and the pigs rooted down the sod wall and made little paths all over it to facilitate their ascent, he heard his wife relate with relish the story of the little pig that built a mud house, to the minister at the dinner table, and William's gravity never relaxed for an instant. Silence, indeed, was William's refuge and his strength.

William set his boys a wholesome example to respect their mother. People who knew him very well suspected that he even admired her. He was a hard man towards his neighbors, and even towards his sons: grasping, determined and ambitious.

There was an occasional blue day about the house when William went over the store bills, but he never objected to items relating to his wife's gowns or bonnets. So it came about that many of the foolish, unnecessary little things that Hester bought for boys, she had charged to her personal account.

One spring night Hester sat in a rocking chair by the sitting room window, darning socks. She rocked violently and sent her long needle vigorously back and forth over her gourd, and it took only a very casual glance to see that she was wrought up over something. William sat on the other side of the table reading his farm paper. If he had noticed his wife's agitation, his calm, clean-shaven face betrayed no sign of concern. He must have noticed the sarcastic turn of her remarks at the supper table, and he must have noticed the moody silence of the older boys as they ate. When supper was but half over little Billy, the youngest, had suddenly pushed back his plate and slipped away from the table, manfully trying to swallow a sob. But William Tavener never heeded ominous forecasts in the domestic horizon, and he never looked for a storm until it broke.

After supper the boys had gone to the pond under the willows in the big cattle corral, to get rid of the dust of plowing. Hester could hear an occasional splash and a laugh ringing clear through the stillness of the night, as she sat by the open window. She sat silent for almost an hour reviewing in her mind many plans of attack. But she was too vigorous a woman to be much of a strategist, and she usually came to her point with directness. At last she cut her thread and suddenly put her darning down, saying emphatically:

"William, I don't think it would hurt you to let the boys go to that circus in town tomorrow."

William continued to read his farm paper, but it was not Hester's custom to wait for an answer. She usually divined his arguments and assailed them one by one before he uttered them.

"You've been short of hands all summer, and you've worked the boys hard, and a man ought use his own flesh and blood as well as he does his hired hands. We're plenty able to afford it, and it's little enough our boys ever spend. I don't see how you can expect 'em to be steady and hard workin', unless you encourage 'em a little. I never could see much harm in circuses, and our boys have never been to one. The animals are real instructive, an' our boys don't get to see much out here on the prairie. It was different where we were raised, but the boys have got no advantages here, an' if you don't take care, they'll grow up to be greenhorns."

Hester paused a moment, and William folded up his paper, but vouchsafed no remark. His sisters in Virginia had often said that only a quiet man like William could ever have lived with Hester Perkins. Secretly, William was rather proud of his wife's "gift of speech," and of the fact that she could talk in prayer meeting as fluently as a man. He confined his own efforts in that line to a brief prayer at Covenant meetings.

Hester shook out another sock and went on.

"Nobody was ever hurt by goin' to a circus. Why, law me! I remember I went to one myself once, when I was little. I had most forgot about it. It was over at Pewtown, an' I remember how I had set my heart on going. I don't think I'd ever forgiven my father if he hadn't taken me, though that red clay road was in a frightful way after the rain. I mind they had an elephant and six poll parrots, an' a Rocky Mountain Lion, an' a cage of monkeys, an' two camels. My! but they were a sight to me then!"

Hester dropped the black sock and shook her head and smiled at the recollection. She was not expecting anything from William yet, and she was fairly startled when he said gravely, in much the same tone in which he announced the hymns in prayer meeting:

"No, there was only one camel. The other was a dromedary."

She peered around the lamp and looked at him keenly.

"Why, William, how come you to know?"

William folded his paper and answered with some hesitation, "I was there, too."

Hester's interest flashed up. "Well, I never, William! To think of my finding it out after all these years! Why, you couldn't have been much bigger'n our Billy then. It seems queer I never saw you when you was little, to remember about you. But then you Back Creek folks never have anything to do with us Gap people. But how come you to go? Your father was stricter with you than you are with your boys."

"I reckon I shouldn't 'a gone," he said slowly, "but boys will do foolish things. I had done a good deal of fox hunting the winter before, and father let me keep the bounty money. I hired Tom Smith's Tap to weed the corn for me, an' I slipped off unbeknownst to father an' went to the show."

Hester spoke up warmly: "Nonsense, William! It didn't do you no harm, I guess. You was always worked hard enough. It must have been a big sight for a little fellow. That clown must have just tickled you to death."

William crossed his knees and leaned back in his chair.

"I reckon I could tell all that fool's jokes now. Sometimes I can't help thinkin' about 'em in meetin' when the sermon's long. I mind I had on a pair of new boots that hurt me like the mischief but I forgot all about 'em when that fellow rode the donkey. I recall I had to take them boots off as soon as I got out of sight o' town, and walked home in the mud barefoot."

"O poor little fellow!" Hester ejaculated, drawing her chair nearer and leaning her elbows on the table. "What cruel shoes they did use to make for children. I remember I went up to Back Creek to see the circus wagons go by. They came down from Romney, you know. The circus men stopped at the creek to water the animals, an' the elephant got stubborn an' broke a big limb off the yellow willow tree that grew there by the toll house porch, an' the Scribners were 'fraid as death he'd pull the house down. But this much I saw him do; he waded in the creek an' filled his trunk with water and squirted it in at the window and nearly ruined Ellen Scribner's pink lawn dress that she had just ironed an' laid out on the bed ready to wear to the circus."

"I reckon that must have been a trial to Ellen," chuckled William, "for she was mighty prim in them days."

Hester drew her chair still nearer William's. Since the children had begun growing up, her conversation with her husband had been almost wholly confined to questions of economy and expense. Their relationship had become purely a business one, like that between landlord and tenant. In her desire to indulge her boys she had unconsciously assumed a defensive and almost hostile attitude towards her husband. No debtor ever haggled with his usurer more doggedly than did Hester with her husband in behalf of her sons. The strategic contest had gone on so long that it had almost crowded out the memory of a closer relationship. This exchange of confidences tonight, when common recollections took them unawares and opened their hearts, had all the miracle of romance. They talked on and on; of old neighbors, of old familiar faces in the valley where they had grown up, of long forgotten incidents of their youth—weddings, picnics, sleighing parties and baptizings. For years they had talked of nothing else but butter and eggs and the prices of things, and now they had as much to say to each other as people who meet after a long separation.

When the clock struck ten, William rose and went over to his walnut secretary and unlocked it. From his red leather wallet he took out a ten dollar bill and laid it on the table beside Hester.

"Tell the boys not to stay late, an' not to drive the horses hard," he said quietly, and went off to bed.

Hester blew out the lamp and sat still in the dark a long time. She left the bill lying on the table where William had placed it. She had a painful sense of having missed something, or lost something; she felt that somehow the years had cheated her.

The little locust trees that grew by the fence were white with blossoms. Their heavy odor floated in to her on the night wind and recalled a night long ago, when the first whippoorwill of the Spring was heard, and the rough, buxom girls of Hawkins Gap had held her laughing and struggling under the locust trees. Two of those same girls had been her bridesmaids. Hester had been a very happy bride. She rose and went softly into the room where William lay. He was sleeping heavily, but occasionally moved his hand before his face to ward off the flies. Hester went into the parlor and took the piece of mosquito net from the basket of wax apples and pears that her sister had made before she died. One of the boys had brought it all the way from Virginia, packed in a tin pall, since Hester would not risk shipping so precious an ornament by freight. She went back to the bedroom and spread the net over William's head. Then she sat down by the bed and listened to his deep, regular breathing until she heard the boys returning. She went out to meet them and warn them not to waken their father.

"I'll be up early to get your breakfast, boys. Your father says you can go to the show." As she handed the money to the eldest, she felt a sudden throb of allegiance to her husband and said sharply, "And you be careful of that, an' don't waste it. Your father works hard for his money."

The boys looked at each other in astonishment and felt that they had lost a powerful ally.

☑ Check Your Comprehension

1. What request does Hester make of her husband? Why does she think he would disapprove?

2. What are some of the arguments Hester uses to support her case?

3. How does Cather describe Hester and William's current relationship?

4. What happens when Hester and William start to talk about the circus they had both gone to when they were young?

◆ Critical Thinking

INTERPRET

1. What is the significance of Hester's putting the mosquito net over William's head as he sleeps? **[Interpret]**

2. Why does Cather say that the boys "felt that they had lost a powerful ally"? **[Infer]**

3. What does the title of this story mean? How is William Tavener sentimental? **[Interpret]**

EVALUATE

4. Why does William give Hester the money for the boys to go to the circus at the end of his conversation with her? **[Analyze Cause and Effect; Infer]**

5. Why does Cather say, "[Hester] had a painful sense of having missed something, or lost something; she felt that somehow the years had cheated her"? **[Draw Conclusions]**

APPLY

6. Do you think things will be different between Hester and William from now on? Why or why not? **[Speculate]**

Willa Cather

Comparing and Connecting the Author's Works

◆ Literary Focus: Lyric Description

Description is the portrayal in words of something that can be perceived by the five senses. Authors use descriptions well when they create a picture in the minds of the readers. Authors use vivid verbs and adjectives, as well as concrete, specific nouns to describe details. Note how the nouns and verbs underlined in this passage from *My Ántonia* enable you to hear, see, and even feel what the author is describing: "The engine was <u>panting</u> heavily after its long run. In the red <u>glow</u> from the tire-box, a group of people stood <u>huddled</u> together on the platform, <u>encumbered</u> by <u>bundles</u> and boxes."

1. (a) Find and write down five vivid verbs and/or adjectives from "Prairie Spring." (b) What noun-adjective combinations help to create an exact picture in your mind?

◆ Drawing Conclusions About Cather's Work

Willa Cather wrote the following about her idea of what art should be:

Art is not thought or emotion, but expression, expression, always expression. To keep an idea living, intact, tinged with all its original feeling, its original mood, preserving in it all the ecstasy which attended its birth, to keep it so all the way from the brain to the hand and transfer it on paper a living thing with color, odor, sound, life all in it, that is what art means, that is the greatest of all the gifts of the gods."

The following diagram shows how Cather in "Prairie Spring" was able to "transfer" something "with color, odor, sound" to the reader. Each circle represents one of the five senses. Words that

suggest one of the senses are put into the appropriate box. Note that some words fit in more than one box.

Create a similar diagram focusing on the last paragraph of the selection from *My Ántonia*. Write a short paragraph detailing how Cather lived up to her own definition of what art is.

◆ Idea Bank

Writing

1. **Letter** What would it be like to move to a strange new place as Jim did in *My Ántonia*? Imagine a place very different from where you now live. Think of as much detail as you can to describe the place, particularly words that suggest the five senses. Then write a letter to a friend back home describing your new home and your feelings about it.

2. **Compare and Contrast** Write a short essay in which you discuss the similarities and differences in the characters of Hester and William Tavener. Before you begin, make a

Venn diagram to organize your thoughts. The similarities should go in the space where the circles overlap; William's differences should go in one circle and Hester's in the other. The Venn diagram below shows you how to begin.

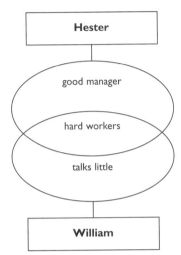

Hester

good manager

hard workers

talks little

William

3. **Poem** Write a poem about a place in nature that you have visited. Use words that appeal to the five senses and imagery, such as similes, personification, and metaphors.

Speaking and Listening

4. **Dramatization** With a partner, recreate the scene between Hester and William Tavener. Before you begin, discuss the following questions: What does each character think about the other one? What does the scene show about their life together? Practice your parts and then present the scene to the class. (Parts need not be memorized.)

5. **Listening to a Symphony** Antonin Dvořák, a composer from former Czechoslovakia where Ántonia and her family came from, visited the United States in 1892. He was so fascinated by this country that he com-

posed a symphony about it that he called *From the New World* (Symphony No. 9). With a group of students, listen to at least one movement of the symphony. Discuss how the music seems to describe parts of our country with which you are familiar. Compare the effect Dvořák produces in music with the effect Cather produces in her writing. **[Music Link]**

Researching and Representing

6. **Writing a Report** In small groups, research one of the following topics: (1) European immigration to the United States in the nineteenth century, (2) American authors of the late nineteenth/early twentieth centuries, or (3) an important American author, artist, or composer of this period. Decide what you want to cover in your report and divide the material so everyone does some of the work. When you have finished, present your report to the class. **[Group Activity]**

◆ Further Reading, Listening, and Viewing

- Bernice Slote and Lucia Woods: *Willa Cather: A Pictorial Memoir* (1973). Very readable, brief biography with wonderful pictures and quotations

- Marion Marsh Brown and Ruth Crone: *Willa Cather: The Woman and Her Works* (1970). An engaging, short biography

- *My Ántonia.* Videotape produced by Paramount Home Video, Hollywood, California, 1994. Starring Jason Robards and Eve Marie Saint. 92 mins.

On the Web:

http://www.phschool.com/atschool/literature
Go to the student edition of *The American Experience.* Click on Unit 4. Then click Hot Links to find Web sites featuring Willa Cather.

Robert Frost In Depth

"He has bequeathed his nation a body of imperishable verse from which Americans will forever gain joy and understanding."
— **President John F. Kennedy, on the occasion of Frost's death**

ROBERT **F**ROST was one of the most popular and beloved poets of the United States. Although he and his work are strongly identified with New England, Frost was born in 1874 in San Francisco. He and his younger sister spent their early childhood on the West Coast. Then in 1885, Frost's father died from tuberculosis. He had requested to be buried back in New England—which he considered home—and the family moved to Lawrence, Massachusetts.

Early New England Years Frost attended Lawrence High School, where he was an excellent student. Upon graduation in 1892, Frost and Elinor White were co-valedictorians. That fall, Frost entered Dartmouth College, but soon quit to become a teacher. Within two years, he published his first poem, "My Butterfly," and married his former classmate Elinor White. His wife encouraged him to continue writing poetry. Frost decided to return to college, but once again he did not stay long enough to earn a degree.

A Time of Changes Frost experienced devastating loss in 1900. His mother and his first son, Elliott, both died that year. After the death of his son, Frost and his family moved to a farm near Derry, New Hampshire. Frost dreamed of being able to support his family by writing poetry, but book and magazine publishers often rejected his poems. In 1912, after more than ten years on the farm, Frost decided to move to England. He hoped that in England his work would achieve greater attention.

During his three-year stay overseas, Frost published two books of poetry, *A Boy's Will* (1913) and *North of Boston* (1914). Edward Thomas reviewed the latter collection, which includes "The Death of the Hired Man," as "one of the most revolutionary books of modern times." Frost also befriended other writers in England, including the influential poet Ezra Pound. Before long, however, the rumblings of World War I brought Frost and his family back to the United States.

Acclaim and Sadness Upon returning home, Frost found that he was on the road to fame. Instead of pursuing a career as a full-time poet, however, he decided to begin teaching again. Frost and his family once again settled on a New Hampshire farm, and in 1917 he became a professor of English at Amherst College in Massachusetts. He would teach on and off at the college for the next twenty years.

In 1924, Frost was awarded the prestigious Pulitzer Prize for Poetry for his collection of poems entitled *New Hampshire*. Frost turned fifty that year, and it has been said that at this time he first began to think of himself as "a creature of literature." He continued to publish several more poetry collections and won two more Pulitzer Prizes for his work. Unfortunately, his great professional success was overshadowed by the death of his wife, Elinor, in 1938. Shortly thereafter, Frost resigned from his teaching position at Amherst and retreated to a new home in Vermont.

His Later Years In the years after his wife's death, Frost wrote a great number of poems. Both critics and the public enjoyed these depictions of New England scenes and characters. Although many commented on the simple and straightforward style of his work, Frost's best poems contain hidden meanings and serious messages beneath their simple exteriors. Just prior to his seventieth birthday, in 1943, Frost won a fourth Pulitzer Prize for his poetry collection, *A Witness Tree*. Then, in 1949, his *Complete Poems* was published. The elderly Frost was now one of the best-known living poets, and his face and name were as recognizable as were his most popular poems.

He continued to receive many public awards and honors and, in 1961, John F. Kennedy selected Frost to recite a poem as part of his presidential inauguration. Two years later, in 1963, both men—two icons of twentieth-century America—would be dead. On January 29, 1963, ten months before Kennedy's assassination, Frost died in his beloved New England. Across the country, many people gathered to listen to radio and television reports of the poet's death. Many felt as if they had lost an old friend.

◆ Career Influences

Frost began writing at a time when many other poets, including T. S. Eliot (1888–1965) and Ezra Pound (1885–1972), were pursuing radical new directions in their work. Although Frost was certainly well aware of the literary changes gaining attention during his lifetime, his work was more greatly influenced by earlier poets. Fellow New Englanders Emily Dickinson (1830–1886) and Ralph Waldo Emerson (1803–1882)

were his favorites. Many of Frost's poems also include reflections of his own life experiences and of his love and respect for his natural surroundings.

◆ Literary Works

Many of Frost's poems are beloved and have been widely anthologized and studied. Two of his best-known works are "Birches" (1915), about trees bent to the ground by ice storms, and "Stopping by Woods on a Snowy Evening" (1923), in which the narrator stops his horse to reflect upon the beauty around him.

In Frost's famous poem "The Road Not Taken" (1915), the narrator is undecided about which route to take when he comes to a fork in the road. He chooses to take the one that is less traveled. Long walks that Frost had taken with a friend through the English countryside inspired this poem.

Two of the poet's darker works include "The Fear" (1913) and "Home Burial" (1914). In "The Fear," a man and woman are frightened by something they perceive in the dark. "Home Burial" presents the death of a child and how it affects a husband and wife. Such works remind us of the sadness and loneliness Frost must have suffered by outliving many of his own family members.

Frost published his first two collections while living in England.
A Boy's Will (1913)
North of Boston (1914)

Frost won a Pulitzer Prize for each of these four collections:
New Hampshire (1924)
Collected Poems (1931)
A Further Range (1937)
A Witness Tree (1943)

This was Frost's last book:
Complete Poems (1949)

TIMELINE

Frost's Life		World Events	
1874	Robert Lee Frost born March 26, San Francisco	1876	Alexander Graham Bell invents the telephone
1885	Frost's father dies; the family moves to New England	1880	Birth of Helen Keller
1892	Graduates high school as co-valedictorian with Elinor White	1890	Emily Dickinson's poems published, four years after her death
1893	Publishes first poem, "My Butterfly"	1895	Poet William Butler Yeats becomes a leader of the Irish Renaissance
1894–99	Attends Harvard	1900	Death of Queen Victoria, British ruler since 1837
1900	Death of Frost's mother and first son; family moves to a New Hampshire farm	1912	Sinking of the *Titanic*
1912	Moves to England	1913	Premiere of composer Igor Stravinsky's *Rite of Spring*
1913	Publishes first book of poems	1914–18	World War I
1914	The Frosts return to New England	1918	More than 20 million die in global influenza epidemic
1917	Becomes Professor of English at Amherst College, Massachusetts	1920	Amendment gives U.S. women voting rights
1924	Wins the Pulitzer Prize for *New Hampshire*	1922	Poet T. S. Eliot publishes *The Waste Land;* discovery of King Tut's tomb in Egypt
1931	Second Pulitzer Prize for *Collected Poems*	1925	U.S. poet Ezra Pound publishes sections of his Cantos
1937	Third Pulitzer Prize for *A Further Range*	1929	Stock market crash
1938	Death of wife, Elinor; Frost resigns from Amherst College	1939	Demonstration of television at the New York World's Fair
1939	Moves to a farm in Vermont	1941	The U.S. enters World War II
1943	Fourth Pulitzer Prize for *A Witness Tree*	1948	T. S. Eliot wins the Nobel Prize for Literature
1949	Publication of *Complete Poems*	1950–53	The Korean War
1954	Frost celebrates his eightieth birthday	1961	Russian cosmonaut Yuri Gagarin is the first person in space
1961	Recites at John F. Kennedy's presidential inauguration	1963	Assassination of President John F. Kennedy, November 22
1963	Frost dies January 29, Boston		

Robert Frost

The Death of the Hired Man

Mary sat musing on the lamp-flame at the table,
Waiting for Warren. When she heard his step,
She ran on tiptoe down the darkened passage
To meet him in the doorway with the news

5   And put him on his guard. "Silas is back."
She pushed him outward with her through the door
And shut it after her. "Be kind," she said.
She took the market things from Warren's arms
And set them on the porch, then drew him down

10   To sit beside her on the wooden steps.

"When was I ever anything but kind to him?
But I'll not have the fellow back," he said.
"I told him so last haying, didn't I?
If he left then, I said, that ended it.

15   What good is he? Who else will harbor him
At his age for the little he can do?
What help he is there's no depending on.
Off he goes always when I need him most.
He thinks he ought to earn a little pay,

20   Enough at least to buy tobacco with,
So he won't have to beg and be beholden.
'All right,' I say, 'I can't afford to pay
Any fixed wages, though I wish I could.'
'Someone else can.' 'Then someone else will have to.'

25   I shouldn't mind his bettering himself
If that was what it was. You can be certain,
When he begins like that, there's someone at him
Trying to coax him off with pocket money—
In haying time, when any help is scarce.

30   In winter he comes back to us. I'm done."

"Sh! not so loud: he'll hear you," Mary said.

"I want him to: he'll have to soon or late."

"He's worn out. He's asleep beside the stove.
When I came up from Rowe's I found him here,
35   Huddled against the barn door fast asleep,
A miserable sight, and frightening, too—
You needn't smile—I didn't recognize him—
I wasn't looking for him—and he's changed.
Wait till you see."

               "Where did you say he'd been?"

40   "He didn't say. I dragged him to the house,
And gave him tea and tried to make him smoke.
I tried to make him talk about his travels.
Nothing would do: he just kept nodding off."
"What did he say? Did he say anything?"

"But little."

45   "Anything? Mary, confess
He said he'd come to ditch the meadow for me."

"Warren!"

         "But did he? I just want to know."
"Of course he did. What would you have him say?
Surely you wouldn't grudge the poor old man
50   Some humble way to save his self-respect.
He added, if you really care to know,
He meant to clear the upper pasture, too.
That sounds like something you have heard before?
Warren, I wish you could have heard the way
55   He jumbled everything. I stopped to look
Two or three times—he made me feel so queer—
To see if he was talking in his sleep.
He ran on Harold Wilson—you remember—
The boy you had in haying four years since.
60   He's finished school, and teaching in his college.
Silas declares you'll have to get him back.
He says they two will make a team for work:
Between them they will lay this farm as smooth!
The way he mixed that in with other things.
65   He thinks young Wilson a likely lad, though daft
On education—you know how they fought
All through July under the blazing sun,
Silas up on the cat to build the load,
Harold along beside to pitch it on."

70   "Yes, I took care to keep well out of earshot."

      "Well, those days trouble Silas like a dream.
      You wouldn't think they would. How some things linger!
      Harold's young college-boy's assurance piqued him.
      After so many years he still keeps finding
75   Good arguments he sees he might have used.
      I sympathize. I know just how it feels
      To think of the right thing to say too late.
      Harold's associated in his mind with Latin.
      He asked me what I thought of Harold's saying
80   He studied Latin, like the violin,
      Because he liked it—that an argument!
      He said he couldn't make the boy believe
      He could find water with a hazel prong—
      Which showed how much good school had ever done him.
85   He wanted to go over that. But most of all
      He thinks if he could have another chance
      To teach him how to build a load of hay—"

      "I know, that's Silas' one accomplishment.
      He bundles every forkful in its place,
90   And tags and numbers it for future reference,
      So he can find and easily dislodge it
      In the unloading. Silas does that well.
      He takes it out in bunches like big birds' nests.
      You never see him standing on the hay
95   He's trying to lift, straining to lift himself."

      "He thinks if he could teach him that, he'd be
      Some good perhaps to someone in the world.
      He hates to see a boy the fool of books.
      Poor Silas, so concerned for other folk,
100   And nothing to look backward to with pride,
      And nothing to look forward to with hope,
      So now and never any different."

      Part of a moon was failing down the west,
      Dragging the whole sky with it to the hills.
105   Its light poured softly in her lap. She saw it
      And spread her apron to it. She put out her hand
      Among the harplike morning-glory strings,
      Taut with the dew from garden bed to eaves,
      As if she played unheard some tenderness
110   That wrought on him beside her in the night.
      "Warren," she said, "he has come home to die:
      You needn't be afraid he'll leave you this time."

"Home," he mocked gently.

                              "Yes, what else but home?
It all depends on what you mean by home.
115   Of course he's nothing to us, any more
Than was the hound that came a stranger to us
Out of the woods, worn out upon the trail."

"Home is the place where, when you have to go there,
They have to take you in."

                              "I should have called it
120   Something you somehow haven't to deserve."

Warren leaned out and took a step or two,
Picked up a little stick, and brought it back
And broke it in his hand and tossed it by.
"Silas has better claim on us you think
125   Than on his brother? Thirteen little miles
As the road winds would bring him to his door.
Silas has walked that far no doubt today.
Why doesn't he go there? His brother's rich,
A somebody—director in the bank."

"He never told us that."

130   "We know it, though."

"I think his brother ought to help, of course.
I'll see to that if there is need. He ought of right
To take him in, and might be willing to—
He may be better than appearances.
135   But have some pity on Silas. Do you think
If he had any pride in claiming kin
Or anything he looked for from his brother,
He'd keep so still about him all this time?"

"I wonder what's between them."

                              "I can tell you.
140   Silas is what he is—we wouldn't mind him—
But just the kind that kinsfolk can't abide.
He never did a thing so very bad.
He don't know why he isn't quite as good
As anybody. Worthless though he is,
145   He won't be made ashamed to please his brother."

"I can't think Si ever hurt anyone."

"No, but he hurt my heart the way he lay
And rolled his old head on that sharp-edged chair-back.
He wouldn't let me put him on the lounge.

150 　You must go in and see what you can do.
　　 I made the bed up for him there tonight.
　　 You'll be surprised at him—how much he's broken.
　　 His working days are done; I'm sure of it."

　　 "I'd not be in a hurry to say that."

155 　"I haven't been. Go, look, see for yourself.
　　 But, Warren, please remember how it is:
　　 He's come to help you ditch the meadow.
　　 He has a plan. You mustn't laugh at him.
　　 He may not speak of it, and then he may.
160 　I'll sit and see if that small sailing cloud
　　 Will hit or miss the moon."
　　　　　　　　　　　　 It hit the moon.
　　 Then there were three there, making a dim row,
　　 The moon, the little silver cloud, and she.

　　 Warren returned—too soon, it seemed to her—
165 　Slipped to her side, caught up her hand and waited.
　　 "Warren?" she questioned.

　　　　　　　　　　 "Dead," was all he answered.

Robert Frost

The Sound of Trees

I wonder about the trees.
Why do we wish to bear
Forever the noise of these
More than another noise

5   So close to our dwelling place?
We suffer them by the day
Till we lose all measure of pace,
And fixity in our joys,
And acquire a listening air.

10   They are that that talks of going
But never gets away;
And that talks no less for knowing,
As it grows wiser and older,
That now it means to stay.

15   My feet tug at the floor
And my head sways to my shoulder
Sometimes when I watch trees sway,
From the window or the door.
I shall set forth for somewhere,

20   I shall make the reckless choice
Some day when they are in voice
And tossing so as to scare
The white clouds over them on.
I shall have less to say,

25   But I shall be gone.

A Brook in the City

The farmhouse lingers, though averse to square
With the new city street it has to wear
A number in. But what about the brook
That held the house as in an elbow crook?
5   I ask as one who knew the brook, its strength
And impulse, having dipped a finger length
And made it leap my knuckle, having tossed
A flower to try its currents where they crossed.
The meadow grass could be cemented down
10   From growing under pavements of a town;
The apple trees be sent to hearthstone flame.
Is water wood to serve a brook the same?
How else dispose of an immortal force
No longer needed? Staunch[1] it at its source
15   With cinder loads dumped down? The brook was thrown
Deep in a sewer dungeon under stone
In fetid darkness still to live and run—
And all for nothing it had ever done,
Except forget to go in fear perhaps.
20   No one would know except for ancient maps
That such a brook ran water. But I wonder
If from its being kept forever under,
The thoughts may not have risen that so keep
This new-built city from both work and sleep.

---

1. Staunch (stanch) *v.*: Restrain the flow of.

Robert Frost
Nothing Gold Can Stay

Nature's first green is gold,
Her hardest hue to hold.
Her early leaf's a flower;
But only so an hour.
5   Then leaf subsides to leaf.
So Eden sank to grief,
So dawn goes down to day.
Nothing gold can stay.

☑ **Check Your Comprehension**

1. Why is Warren annoyed with Silas in "The Death of the Hired Man"?
2. In the same poem, why does Mary think Silas has returned?
3. In "The Sound of Trees," what sometimes happens to the narrator when he watches the trees?
4. (a) Why is the brook "no longer needed" in the poem "A Brook in the City"? (b) How does the narrator know about the brook?
5. In "Nothing Gold Can Stay," name at least two examples that echo the brief stay of a tree's early gold growth?

◆ **Critical Thinking**

1. How does Frost use the setting of "The Death of the Hired Man" to create a somber mood? **[Evaluate]**
2. In the same poem, why do you think Silas does not go to stay with his brother? **[Infer]**
3. (a) In "The Sound of Trees," what do you think the narrator means when he says "I shall set forth for somewhere"? (b) What clues help support your conclusion? **[Interpret; Draw Conclusions]**

COMPARE LITERARY WORKS

4. What do the poems "Nothing Gold Can Stay" and "A Brook in the City" have in common? **[Connect]**

The Tuft of Flowers

I went to turn the grass once after one
Who mowed it in the dew before the sun.

The dew was gone that made his blade so keen
Before I came to view the leveled scene.

5   I looked for him behind an isle of trees;
I listened for his whetstone on the breeze.

But he had gone his way, the grass all mown,
And I must be, as he had been—alone,

"As all must be," I said within my heart,
10   "Whether they work together or apart."

But as I said it, swift there passed me by
On noiseless wing a bewildered butterfly,

Seeking with memories grown dim o'er night
Some resting flower of yesterday's delight.

15   And once I marked his flight go round and round,
As where some flower lay withering on the ground.

And then he flew as far as eye could see,
And then on tremulous wing came back to me.

I thought of questions that have no reply,
20   And would have turned to toss the grass to dry;

But he turned first, and led my eye to look
At a tall tuft of flowers beside a brook,

A leaping tongue of bloom the scythe had spared
Beside a reedy brook the scythe had bared.

25   The mower in the dew had loved them thus,
By leaving them to flourish, not for us,

Nor yet to draw one thought of ours to him,
But from sheer morning gladness at the brim.

The butterfly and I had lit upon,
30   Nevertheless, a message from the dawn,

That made me hear the wakening birds around,
And hear his long scythe whispering to the ground,

And feel a spirit kindred to my own;
So that henceforth I worked no more alone;

35   But glad with him, I worked as with his aid,
And weary, sought at noon with him the shade;

And dreaming, as it were, held brotherly speech
With one whose thought I had not hoped to reach.

"Men work together," I told him from the heart,
40   "Whether they work together or apart."

Robert Frost

Take Something Like a Star

O Star (the fairest one in sight),
We grant your loftiness the right
To some obscurity of cloud—
It will not do to say of night,
5   Since dark is what brings out your light.
Some mystery becomes the proud.
But to be wholly taciturn[1]
In your reserve is not allowed.
Say something to us we can learn
10   By heart and when alone repeat.
Say something! And it says, "I burn."
But say with what degree of heat.
Talk Fahrenheit, talk Centigrade.
Use language we can comprehend.
15   Tell us what elements you blend.
It gives us strangely little aid,
But does tell something in the end.
And steadfast as Keats' Eremite,[2]
Not even stooping from its sphere,
20   It asks a little of us here.
It asks of us a certain height,
So when at times the mob is swayed
To carry praise or blame too far,
We may take something like a star
25   To stay our minds on and be staid.[3]

---

1. **taciturn** (tas´i tərn´) *adj.*: Saying little; uncommunicative.

2. **Eremite:** A reference to a work by the British poet John Keats (1795–1821). The sonnet begins "Bright star, would I were steadfast as thou art!"

3. **staid:** Of quiet and steady character; sedate.

On "Choose Something Like a Star"[1]

I AM NOT partial with my poems, any more than a mother with her children. But your choice, "Choose Something Like a Star," is one I like to say.

I seem to fancy it as rather Horatian[2] in its ending. Then I like the two ways of spelling 'staid'; that's playing the words. And I like to mingle science and spirit here—as I do so deliberately in my new book.

But there are things beyond all this which I care more about, and hope we all do.

Poet's Choice, 1962

---

1. Frost changed the title of this poem from "Choose Something Like a Star" to "Take Something Like a Star" after it was first published in 1943.
2. Horatian: This refers to the work of the ancient Roman lyric poet Horace (65–8 B.C.). Horace used everyday language and occasional slang in his verse.

Robert Frost

Fragmentary Blue

Why make so much of fragmentary blue
In here and there a bird, or butterfly,
Or flower, or wearing-stone, or open eye,
When heaven presents in sheets the solid hue?

5   Since earth is earth, perhaps, not heaven (as yet)—
Though some savants[1] make earth include the sky;
And blue so far above us comes so high,
It only gives our wish for blue a whet.[2]

---

1. **savants** (sa vänts´): Learned persons.
2. **whet:** Small quantity of something that stimulates one's appetite.

Misgiving

All crying, "We will go with you, O Wind!"
The foliage follow him, leaf and stem;
But a sleep oppresses them as they go,
And they end by bidding him stay with them.

5 Since ever they flung abroad in spring
The leaves had promised themselves this flight,
Who now would fain seek sheltering wall,
Or thicket, or hollow place for the night.

And now they answer his summoning blast
10 With an ever vaguer and vaguer stir,
Or at utmost a little reluctant whirl
That drops them no further than where they were.

I only hope that when I am free,
As they are free, to go in quest
15 Of the knowledge beyond the bounds of life
It may not seem better to me to rest.

*R*obert Frost
For Once, Then, Something

Others taunt me with having knelt at well-curbs
Always wrong to the light, so never seeing
Deeper down in the well than where the water
Gives me back in a shining surface picture
5   Me myself in the summer heaven, godlike,
Looking out of a wreath of fern and cloud puffs.
Once, when trying with chin against a well-curb,
I discerned, as I thought, beyond the picture,
Through the picture, a something white, uncertain,
10   Something more of the depths—and then I lost it.
Water came to rebuke¹ the too clear water.
One drop fell from a fern, and lo, a ripple
Shook whatever it was lay there at bottom,
Blurred it, blotted it out. What was that whiteness?
15   Truth? A pebble of quartz? For once, then, something.

---

1. **rebuke:** Express disapproval for a fault.

☑ Check Your Comprehension

1. In "The Tuft of Flowers," how does the narrator change from the beginning to the end of the poem?
2. When does the narrator recommend that we "Take something like a star," in the poem of that title?
3. (a) List some blue objects that Frost names in the poem "Fragmentary Blue"? (b) Why are they examples of "fragmentary" blue?
4. In "Misgiving," what happens to the leaves when they follow the wind as promised?
5. (a) What activity does "For Once, Then, Something" describe? (b) To what does the poem's title refer?

◆ Critical Thinking

1. (a) List five words in the first half of "The Tuft of Flowers" that convey loneliness and something finished? (b) List five words in the second half that convey togetherness and a beginning? **[Analyze]**
2. In "On 'Choose Something Like a Star,'" what do you think Frost means by "things beyond all this which I care more about"? **[Infer]**

COMPARE LITERARY WORKS

3. Read the last stanza of "Misgiving." What quests are also present in "Take Something Like a Star," "Fragmentary Blue," and "For Once, Then, Something"? **[Connect]**

Richard Poirier

from *Paris Review* Interview

FROST. I never write except with a writing board. I've never had a table in my life. And I use all sorts of things. Write on the sole of my shoe.

POIRIER. Why have you never liked a desk? Is it because you've moved around so much and lived in so many places?

FROST. Even when I was younger I never had a desk. I've never had a writing room.

POIRIER. When you were in England from 1912 to 1915, did you ever think you might possibly stay there?

FROST. No. No, I went over there to be poor for a while, nothing else. I didn't think of printing a book over there. I'd never offered a book to anyone here. I was thirty-eight years old, wasn't I? Something like that. And I thought the way to a book was the magazines. I hadn't too much luck with them, and nobody ever noticed me except to send me a check now and then. So I didn't think I was ready for a book. But I had written three books when I went over.

POIRIER. Did you feel when you left London to go live on a farm in Gloucestershire that you were making a choice against the kind of literary society you'd found in the city?

FROST. No, my choices had been not connected with my going to England even. My choice was almost unconscious in those days. I didn't know whether I had any position in the world at all, and I wasn't choosing positions. You see, my instinct was not to belong to any gang. . . .

POIRIER. [Karl Shapiro][1] was saying that most modern poetry is obscure and overdifficult, that this is particularly true of Pound and Eliot, but that it isn't true of you.

FROST. Well, I don't want to be difficult. I like to fool—oh, you know, you like to be mischievous. But not in that dull way

---

1. **Karl Shapiro:** Shapiro (b. 1913) is an American poet and critic. He is known for praising accessible poetry rather than the work of modernists, such as Pound and Eliot.

of just being dogged and doggedly obscure.

POIRIER. The difficulty of your poetry is perhaps
in your emphasis on variety in tones of voice. You once said
that consciously or unconsciously it was tones of voice that
you counted on to double the meaning of every one of your
statements.

FROST. Yes, you could do that. Could unsay everything I
said, nearly. Talking contraries—it's in one of the poems.
Talk by contraries with people you're very close to. They know
what you're talking about. This whole thing of suggestiveness
and *double entendre* and hinting—comes down to the word
"hinting." With people you can trust you can talk in hints and
suggestiveness. Families break up when people take hints you
don't intend and miss hints you do intend. You can watch that
going on, as a psychologist. I don't know. No, don't . . . no don't
you . . . don't think of me . . . See, I haven't led a literary life.
These fellows, they *really* work away with their prose trying to
describe themselves and understand themselves, and so on. I
don't do that. I don't want to know too much about myself. It
interests me to know that Shapiro thinks I'm not difficult. That's
all right. I never wrote a review in my life, never wrote articles.
I'm constantly refusing to write articles. These fellows are all literary men. I don't have hours; I don't work at it, you know. I'm
not a farmer, that's no pose of mine. But I have farmed some,
and I putter around. And I walk and I live with other people.
Like to talk a lot. But I haven't had a very literary life, and I'm
never very much with the gang. . . .

POIRIER. Making couplets "offhand" is something like writing on schedule, isn't it? I know a young poet who claims he can
write every morning from six to nine, presumably before class.

FROST. Well, there's more than one way to skin a cat. I don't
know what that would be like, myself. When I get going on
something, I don't want to just—you know . . . Very first one I
wrote I was walking home from school and I began to make it—a
March day—and I was making it all afternoon and making it so
I was late at my grandmother's for dinner. I finished it, but it

burned right up, just burned right up, you know. And what started that? What burned it? So many talk, I wonder how falsely, about what it costs them, what agony it is to write. I've often been quoted: "No tears in the writer, no tears in the reader. No surprise for the writer, no surprise for the reader." But another distinction I made is: however sad, no grievance, grief without grievance. How could I, how could anyone have a good time with what cost me too much agony, how could they? What do I want to communicate but what a *hell* of a good time I had writing it?

The Paris Review, Summer–Fall 1960

☑ **Check Your Comprehension**

1. (a) For what reason does Frost say he moved to England? (b) What do you think he means by his explanation?
2. What does Poirier believe is perhaps the one difficulty of Frost's poetry?
3. Based on this interview, write a two-to-three sentence description that gives your impression of Frost.

◆ **Critical Thinking**

1. Frost mentions that at age thirty-eight he had not yet published a book of poems. Why do you think publishing might be important to a writer? **[Draw Conclusions]**
2. This interview was conducted in 1960 when Frost was eighty-six years old. How might an interview with Frost as a young man have been different? What other questions might Poirier have asked? **[Infer]**
3. In this interview, Frost says "I haven't had a very literary life." (a) What do you think the poet means? (b) Do you think this is true? Support your opinions. **[Interpret]**

Robert Frost
Comparing and Connecting the Author's Works

◆ Literary Focus: Narration

Narration is writing that tells a story. It is a form of discourse and may be true or fictional. Narration can be used in plays, poems, novels, short stories, and biographies. Robert Frost's poem "The Tuft of Flowers" is an example of a narrative poem because it tells a story. Not all poems are narrative however. Some may simply describe a scene, an image, or even just a feeling.

The person telling the story in a narrative work is called the **narrator**. The narrator may be a main character in the story, a supporting character, or a speaker who stands outside the action, uninvolved in the events. A narrator may speak in the first person (using "I" and "me"), as in the poem "The Sound of Trees," or in the third person (using "he," "she," "it," and "they"), as in "The Death of the Hired Man."

Main Features of a Narration

- Tells a story.
- May be used in plays, poems, novels, short stories, and biographies.
- Includes a narrator, who tells the story.
- The narrator may speak in either the first or third person.

1. Read the first five lines of "The Sound of Trees" and "Nothing Gold Can Stay" aloud. How do the forms of narration create a different voice in each poem? How do these voices make you feel?
2. Carefully reread the poem "Misgiving." What change occurs in narration between the third and fourth stanzas? How does this change affect the feeling of the poem?

◆ Drawing Conclusions About Frost's Work

You have read about Frost's personal experiences in both the biography on pages 140–141 and in the interview on pages 157–159. One way to gain a deeper understanding of his writing is to connect Frost's personal statements and the events in his life to individual poems.

In the interview excerpt, Frost says "I don't want to be difficult." The comment emphasizes that he viewed his poems as being more straightforward and simpler to understand than the works of many of his contemporaries. In talking about his fellow poets, Frost also once said "I'm waiting for them to say something I can get hold of." In another comment specifically directed at his poem "Take Something Like a Star," Frost suggested that the "Star" might represent a great poet.

The following chart shows how specific lines from that poem can be read as supporting Frost's stance. Create a similar chart in which you compare information from Frost's biography and/or interview with "The Sound of Trees," "Nothing Gold Can Stay," or lines 103–120 of "The Death of the Hired Man."

Examples from the Poem	Details from Frost's Comments
"O Star..."	"Star" may represent a great poet, such as Keats (see Line 18) or Horace (see "On 'Choose Something...'")
"Use language we can understand."	"I don't want to be difficult."
"Say something to us we can learn / By heart and when alone repeat."	"I'm waiting for them to say something I can get hold of."

◆ Idea Bank

Writing

1. **Compare and Contrast** Write a paragraph that compares and contrasts two of Frost's poems. Before you begin writing, create a chart like the following one to help you organize your findings.

For Once, Then ...	Nothing Gold ...
Narrative	Not narrative
First person	Third person
Unrhymed	Rhymed
Fictional	Factual

2. **Poem** The setting of New England is a significant aspect of many of Frost's poems. Write a short poem that describes a setting with which you are familiar—your neighborhood or town, a favorite place, or nearby city.

3. **Autobiographical Essay** Frost experienced many sad events in his life. After the death of his wife, his friend Kathleen Morrison was a great support to him. Frost said "She found me . . . hopeless, sick, run down. She . . . cared for me like a child." Write a brief essay about how a special friend, neighbor, or family member has helped you in some way.

Speaking and Listening

4. **Group Activity** Conduct a staged reading of "The Death of the Hired Man." Speaking parts should include Mary, Warren, and a narrator. Use a few props to help create a mood for the reading. **[Performing Arts Link]**

5. **Oral Introductions** When poets read their work in public, they often introduce each poem with an explanation or story. Choose one Frost poem to read aloud. Plan some remarks about Frost or the poem itself to share with a group of students who may not be familiar with the poet or his work.

Researching and Representing

6. **Group Activity** Create a classroom art exhibit. Conduct research to find additional poems by Frost that include vivid visual images or descriptions of nature. Display a selection of these poems on a wall or bulletin board, accompanied by pictures from magazines, original drawings and paintings; or display photographs you have taken. **[Art Link]**

◆ Further Reading, Listening, and Viewing

- Jay Parini: *Robert Frost: A Life* (1999). Combines commentary on the poetry and good anecdotes about Frost

- Joseph Brodsky: *Homage to Robert Frost* (1996). Collection of essays by three Nobel laureates—Joseph Brodsky, Seamus Heaney, and Derek Walcott.

- *Robert Frost* (South Carolina Educational Television Network, 1988). Videocassette, 60 minutes; *Voices and Visions*, Vol. 5. Life and career related through photographs, readings and comments

- *The Poetry of Robert Frost* (Dove Audio, 1996). Audiocassette, 60 minutes

- *Robert Frost Reads His Poetry* (Caedmon, 1992). Two audiocassettes, 100 minutes

On the Web:

http://www.phschool.com/atschool/literature
Go to the student edition of *The American Experience*. Proceed to Unit 5. Then, click Hot Links to find Web sites featuring Robert Frost.

$\mathcal{L}$angston Hughes In Depth

> "Ironically, we may fail to recognize the sheer boldness of his innovation, in large part because . . . it has been adopted, accepted, and naturalized by his literary successors."
>
> —*Henry Louis Gates, Jr.*

LANGSTON HUGHES although born in Joplin, Missouri, on February 1, 1902, called many places home. While growing up, he lived, alternately with his parents and with his grandmother, in Ohio, Illinois, Kansas, and even Mexico. As a young man, he traveled to Africa and France and began a career as a versatile and prolific writer. His work included poetry, novels, plays, essays, journalism, and two autobiographies. Hughes settled at last in New York City, there to become one of the major figures of the Harlem Renaissance.

Student Years At his graduation from elementary school in Lincoln, Illinois, in 1915, the young Hughes recited his first poem. He wrote his first short story during high school in Cleveland, Ohio. Hughes's early work drew the attention of W.E.B. Du Bois, an influential writer and teacher. The African American literary magazine *The Crisis,* edited by Du Bois, became one of the first to publish Hughes's poetry.

In 1921, Hughes moved to New York City and started college. He attended Columbia University, which is located near Harlem, a predominantly African American neighborhood in upper Manhattan. After one year, however, Hughes dropped out of Columbia and began to travel again. He pursued a series of odd jobs—including working on merchant ships that journeyed to Europe and Africa—that left him time to write.

Early Success When still in his early twenties, Hughes began to win accolades

for his poetry. At this time he also became acquainted with members of the Harlem Renaissance movement—a flowering of the arts partially fueled by the great number of African Americans who moved north in the early twentieth century. By 1926, when Hughes published his first book of poems, *The Weary Blues,* he had joined these talented ranks.

Shortly thereafter, however, Hughes was on the move again. He had earned a scholarship to Lincoln University in Pennsylvania. While enrolled at Lincoln, Hughes toured the southern U.S. with fellow African American writer Zora Neale Hurston. Their goal was to collect traditional African American folktales, a genre that would influence the later works of both writers. In 1929, Hughes received his B.A. degree.

Maturity During the 1930's, Hughes continued to write and travel. He collaborated with Hurston on the play *Mule Bone,* an African American folk comedy. In addition, Hughes published a novel, a short story collection, two books of verse, and three more plays. He visited Haiti and Russia and went to Spain as a correspondent covering the Spanish Civil War. Hughes also began to speak out publicly against poverty and discrimination.

This pattern of creative diversity would continue for the rest of Hughes's life. When he wasn't writing fiction, or traveling, or teaching, he pursued new challenges. In the 1940's, he published *The Big Sea,* an autobiography that recounts his experiences up to age twenty-eight, and he wrote the lyrics for *Street Scene,* a new opera by the prestigious German-born playwright and composer Kurt Weill (1900–1950). With Arna Bontemps, he also edited *The Poetry of the Negro, 1746–1949.* In the 1950's, Hughes translated *Gypsy Ballads,* a work by the revered Spanish poet and playwright Federico Garcia Lorca. Other literary endeavors of this period include books for children and a second volume of autobiography.

His Final Years By the end of the 1950's, Hughes—nicknamed Harlem's "Poet Laureate"—had long been an internationally renowned writer. Despite occasional financial difficulties, he purchased a home in Harlem that became an oasis for other creative artists. In 1960, Hughes was awarded the Springarn Medal from the National Association for the Advancement of Colored People (NAACP). In 1961, he was elected to the National Institute of Arts and Letters, and in 1963, he received an honorary doctorate from Howard University.

Hughes continued to write until he died on May 22, 1967, in his beloved New York City. At his memorial service, friends read from his poems, and jazz musicians performed a blues song. Hughes's final collection of poems, *The Panther and the Lash,* was published posthumously.

◆ The Harlem Renaissance

During the 1920's and 1930's, Harlem was the U.S. capital of African American culture. It was home to myriad theaters, clubs, newspapers, and magazines owned and managed by African Americans. Among the talents of the movement were Jean Toomer, author of *Cane* (1923); Claude McKay, who became the first African American best-selling author with his novel *Home to Harlem* (1928); poet Countee Cullen; Zora Neal Hurston, author of the 1937 classic *Their Eyes Were Watching God;* James Weldon Johnson, who helped found the NAACP; Arna Bontemps, librarian and historian of African American culture; and novelist and short story writer Nella Larsen. Although the movement dwindled after the Great Depression, its achievements continue to influence writers and artists today.

◆ Literary Works

Greatest Books Hughes's works are known for both their colloquial language and their basic theme of freedom. Much of his writing also reflects the rhythm and mood of jazz, the blues, and be-bop—musical forms that had been part of the popular Harlem nightlife.

Hughes's most acclaimed works include the following:
The Weary Blues (1926), poems
The Big Sea (1940), autobiography
Montage of a Dream Deferred (1951), poems

Other Publications These additional works are only a sampling of Hughes's enormous creative output.
Not Without Laughter (1930), Hughes's first novel
The Dream Keeper (1932), poems
The Ways of White Folks (1934), short stories
Troubled Island (1936), play
Shakespeare in Harlem (1942), poems
I Wonder as I Wander (1956), autobiography
Tambourines to Glory (1958)
Something in Common and Other Stories (1963)
The Prodigal Son (1965), play

T I M E L I N E

Hughes's Life	World Events
1902 Langston Hughes born February 1 in Joplin, Missouri	**1901** Booker T. Washington's autobiography, *Up from Slavery*, published
1921 Moves to New York City; enters Columbia University, but drops out	**1910** Founding of the NAACP
	1914–18 World War I
1926 *The Weary Blues* published; wins scholarship to Lincoln University	**1914–19** The Great Migration: 500,000 African Americans move north
1929 Receives B.A. from Lincoln University	**1920** Paul Robeson opens in Eugene O'Neill's play *The Emperor Jones*
1930 *Not Without Laughter* published; the play *Mule Bone* opens	**1922** *Book of Negro Poetry* published, edited by James Weldon Johnson
1934 Hughes's father dies	**1927** Duke Ellington and his orchestra open at the Cotton Club in Harlem
1935 Success of his Broadway play *Mulatto*	
1937 Hired as correspondent to cover Spanish Civil War; his mother dies	**1929** Stock market crashes
1938 Founds the Harlem Suitcase Theater	**1939** African American singer Marian Anderson performs at the Lincoln Memorial
1940 *The Big Sea* published	
1942 Moves to Harlem; founds Skyloft Players	**1940** Richard Wright's *Native Son* published
1943 Begins writing column for *Chicago Defender*	**1941** U.S. enters World War II
	1947 Jackie Robinson becomes first African American major-league baseball player
1947 Teaches writing at Atlanta University	
1948 Writes lyrics for Kurt Weill's *Street Scene*	**1948** President Truman ends segregation of U.S. armed forces
1956 *I Wonder as I Wander* published	**1950–53** 250,000 gather to hear Martin Luther King, Jr., in Washington, D.C.
1960 Receives the Springarn Medal from the NAACP	
1961 Elected to the National Institute of Arts and Letters	**1964** Civil Rights Act passed
	1968 Assassination of Martin Luther King, Jr.
1967 Dies in New York City	

Langston Hughes

Pictures to the Wall

Shall I tell you of my old, old dreams
Lost at the earth's strange turnings,
Some in the sea when the waves foamed high,
Some in a garret candle's burnings?

5 Shall I tell you of bitter, forgotten dreams—
You who are still so young, so young?
You with your wide brown singing eyes
And laughter at the tip of your tongue.

Shall I tell you of weary, weary, dreams,—
10 You who have lost no dreams at all,
Or shall I keep quiet and let turn
My ugly pictures to the wall?

*L*angston Hughes

Miss Blues'es Child

If the blues would let me,
Lord knows I would smile.
If the blues would let me,
I would smile, smile, smile.
5   Instead of that I'm cryin'—
I must be Miss Blues'es child.

You were my moon up in the sky,
At night my wishing star.
I love you, oh, I love you so—
10   But you have gone so far!

Now my days are lonely,
And night-time drives me wild.
In my heart I'm crying,
I'm just Miss Blues'es child!

Give Us Our Peace

Give us a peace equal to the war
Or else our souls will be unsatisfied,
And we will wonder what we have fought for
And why the many died.

5   Give us a peace accepting every challenge—
The challenge of the poor, the black, of all denied,
The challenge of the vast colonial world
That long has had so little justice by its side.

Give us a peace that dares us to be wise.
10   Give us a peace that dares us to be strong.
Give us a peace that dares us still uphold
Throughout the peace our battle against wrong.

Give us a peace that is not cheaply used.
A peace that is no clever scheme,
15   A people's peace which men can enthuse,
A peace that brings reality to our dream.

Give us a peace that will produce great schools—
As the war produced great armament,
A peace that will wipe out our slums—
20   As war wiped out our foes on evil bent.

Give us a peace that will enlist
A mighty army serving human kind,
Not just an army geared to kill,
But trained to help the living mind,

25   An army trained to shape our common good
And bring about a world of brotherhood.

Langston Hughes

Luck

Sometimes a crumb falls
From the tables of joy,
Sometimes a bone
Is flung.

5   To some people
Love is given,
To others
Only heaven.

☑ Check Your Comprehension

1. (a) What adjectives does the narrator use to describe his dreams in "Pictures to the Wall"? (b) How does he describe the person to whom he speaks?
2. In "Miss Blues'es Child," why are the narrator's days lonely and sad?
3. What happens at the tables of joy in "Luck"?
4. In "Give Us Our Peace," what kind of army does the narrator call for at the end of the poem?

◆ Critical Thinking

1. (a) In "Pictures to the Wall," to whom do you think the narrator is speaking? (b) How would you describe the theme of this poem? **[Interpret]**
2. In "Luck," what do you think the narrator means by contrasting love and heaven? **[Infer]**
3. Why do you think Hughes chose to use the metaphor of an army in "Give Us Our Peace"? **[Speculate]**

COMPARE LITERARY WORKS

4. Compare the moods of "Pictures to the Wall," "Miss Blues'es Child," and "Luck." **[Connect]**

Introduction to "Montage of a Dream Deferred"

Langston Hughes's "Montage of a Dream Deferred" is a series of poems that together embody the characteristics of jazz described in this introduction. The five poems that follow come from the "Montage."

In terms of current Afro-American popular music and the sources from which it has progressed—jazz, ragtime, swing, blues, boogie-woogie, and be-bop—this poem on contemporary Harlem, like be-bop, is marked by conflicting changes, sudden nuances, sharp and impudent interjections, broken rhythms, and passages sometimes in the manner of the jam session, sometimes the popular song, punctuated by the riffs, runs, breaks, and disc-tortions of the music of a community in transition.

Tell Me

Why should it be *my* loneliness,
Why should it be *my* song,
Why should it be *my* dream
    deferred
5   overlong?

Langston Hughes

Dream Boogie

Good morning, daddy!
Ain't you heard
The boogie-woogie rumble
Of a dream deferred?

5   Listen closely:
You'll hear their feet
Beating out and beating out a—

You think
It's a happy beat?

10   Listen to it closely:
Ain't you heard
something underneath
like a—

What did I say?

15   Sure,
I'm happy!
Take it away!

Hey, pop!
Re-bop!
20   *Mop!*

Y-e-a-h!

Juke Box Love Song

I could take the Harlem night
and wrap around you,
Take the neon lights and make a crown,
Take the Lenox Avenue busses,
5   Taxis, subways,
And for your love song tone their rumble down.
Take Harlem's heartbeat,
Make a drumbeat,
Put it on a record, let it whirl,
10   And while we listen to it play,
Dance with you till day—
Dance with you, my sweet brown Harlem girl.

Boogie: 1 a.m.

Good evening, daddy!
I know you've heard
The boogie-woogie rumble
Of a dream deferred
5   Trilling the treble
And twining the bass
Into midnight ruffles
Of cat-gut lace.

Langston Hughes

Good Morning

Good morning, daddy!
I was born here, he said,
watched Harlem grow
until colored folks spread
5   from river to river
across the middle of Manhattan
out of Penn Station
dark tenth of a nation,
planes from Puerto Rico,
10   and holds of boats, chico,
up from Cuba Haiti Jamaica,
in buses marked New York
from Georgia Florida Louisiana
to Harlem Brooklyn the Bronx
15   but most of all to Harlem
dusky sash across Manhattan
I've seen them come dark
   wondering
   wide-eyed
20   dreaming
out of Penn Station—
but the trains are late.
The gates open—
      Yet there're bars
25   at each gate.
         What happens
         to a dream deferred?

Daddy, ain't you heard?

☑ Check Your Comprehension

1. To what does Hughes attribute "the riffs, runs, breaks, and distortions" of "Montage of a Dream Deferred"?

2. In your own words, describe the central message of "Tell Me."

3. In the poem "Juke Box Love Song," what noises does the narrator say he could make into a love song?

4. What are the sounds of "a dream deferred" in "Boogie: 1 a.m."?

5. In "Good Morning," how does the narrator describe the people as they come out of Penn Station?

◆ Critical Thinking

1. In the introduction, "Montage of a Dream Deferred," written in 1951, why might Hughes call Harlem a "community in transition"? **[Infer]**

2. What "conflicting changes," "sudden nuances," and "sharp and impudent interjections" can you find in "Dream Boogie"? **[Analyze]**

3. In "Good Morning," what do you think the narrator means by "The gates open—Yet there're bars at each gate"? **[Interpret]**

COMPARE LITERARY WORKS

4. How is the mood of "Juke Box Love Song" different from "Tell Me" and "Good Morning"? **[Distinguish]**

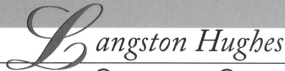

Langston Hughes

Comparing and Connecting the Author's Works

◆ Literary Focus: Rhythm

Rhythm in spoken and written language is an arrangement of beats. A poet creates a beat by combining stressed and unstressed syllables. For example, in the opening lines of his poem "The Tiger," William Blake (1757–1827) repeatedly alternates stressed and unstressed syllables.

　　ˊ ˘ ˘ ˊ ˘ 　 ˊ
Tiger, tiger, burning bright

　　ˊ ˘ ˘ ˊ ˘ ˊ ˘ 　 ˊ
In the forests of the night,

This creates a regular rhythmical pattern. Traditional poetry often follows a rhythmical pattern, which is also called the meter of the poem.

Most of Hughes's poems do not employ a predictable pattern. Consider these lines from "Pictures to the Wall."

　　˘ ˘ ˊ ˘ ˘ ˘ ˊ ˊ 　 ˊ
Shall I tell you of my old, old dreams

　　ˊ ˘ ˘ ˊ ˘ 　 ˊ ˘
Lost at the earth's strange turnings,

The unpredictable arrangement of stressed and unstressed syllables creates an irregular rhythm. Poetry that does not have a regular rhythmical pattern, or meter, is called free verse.

1. Reread the free verse poem "Dream Boogie" or "Pictures to the Wall." What kind of tone does the poem convey? How does this compare to a poem written with a regular rhythmical pattern?
2. Why do you think Hughes chose to write in free verse?

◆ Drawing Conclusions About Hughes's Work

Certain motifs, or themes, recur in Hughes's writing. He frequently stated

that he was trying to capture the essence of popular music. In the biography on pages 162–163, you have also read how Hughes was influenced by his life in Harlem. Another favorite Hughes technique is the use of language that mimics conversation.

The following chart shows how the use of these three motifs—references to music, the city, and informal speech—can be traced in his poem "Juke Box Love Song." Create a similar chart to trace these elements in "Dream Boogie," "Boogie: 1 a.m.," and "Good Morning." Summarize your findings in writing and share them with the class.

Motif	Examples
Music	Juke Box; love song; drumbeat; record
The City	Harlem night; neon lights; taxis; subways
Speech	I could take; you; tone their rumble down; till

◆ Idea Bank

Writing

1. **Essay** One section of Hughes's poetry collection *Montage of a Dream Deferred* is called "Lenox Avenue Mural." Write a short essay that describes how a group of poems can be similar and different to a mural.
2. **Autobiographical Letter** Hughes lived in several small towns before moving to Harlem. Write a letter as if you are the poet corresponding with a friend in such a town who has never been to New York City. Describe the city and your feelings about life there.

3. **Compare and Contrast** Write an essay that compares two of Hughes's poems. Before you begin, create a Venn diagram like the following one to help you organize your thoughts. Place similarities—such as common forms, images, or moods—in the space where the circles overlap. Place differences in the outer regions of the two circles.

Speaking and Listening

4. **Debate** Hughes wrote that "good art transcends land, race, and nationality." Conduct a debate in which two teams argue whether or not Hughes's own poetry achieves this standard. Be sure to use the poems themselves as support for your defense. **[Group Activity]**

5. **Musical Influences** Listen to examples of the instrumental and vocal music that was so meaningful to Hughes: blues, jazz, be-bop, spirituals, and boogie-woogie. Compare the rhythms, moods, and lyrics from one musical form to another. **[Group Activity; Music Link]**

Researching and Representing

6. **Visual Arts** Explore the achievements of the visual artists of the Harlem Renaissance, including sculptors Selma Burke, Sargent Johnson, Augusta Savage, Richmond Barthe, and Elizabeth Prophet, and painters Aaron Douglas, Henry Tanner, Laura Wheeler Waring, William H. Johnson, and Hale Woodruff. Put together a collection of your favorite works. Accompany each selection with a brief explanation of why you chose it. Share your findings with the class. **[Art Link]**

◆ Further Reading, Listening, and Viewing

• Langston Hughes: *The Dream Keeper* (South Carolina Educational TV Network, 1988) Video relating the life and career of Hughes through photos, readings and comments

• Langston Hughes, editor: *A Pictorial History of African Americans* (1956; revised 1995)

• *Against the Odds: The Artists of the Harlem Renaissance* (PBS Home Video)

• *Langston Hughes Reads* (Harper Audio/Caedmon) Audiocassette

• *Langston Hughes: Rhythms of the World* (Smithsonian Folkways Recording) Audio CD

On the Web:

http://www.phschool.com/atschool/literature
Go to the student edition of *The American Experience*. Proceed to Unit 5. Then, click Hot Links to find Web sites featuring Langston Hughes.

$\mathcal{J}$ulia Alvarez In Depth

> "This is why writing matters. It clarifies and intensifies; it reduces our sense of isolation and connects us to each other."
> —*Julia Alvarez, "Writing Matters"*

JULIA ALVAREZ, like many other writers, explores the question of identity. For the essayist, poet, and novelist, this question has always been complicated by her bicultural roots. Born in the United States, raised in the Dominican Republic, and then resident in the United States since the age of ten, Alvarez has spent much of her life moving between two countries and two languages.

Dominican Republic Julia Alvarez was born on March 27, 1950, in New York City, where her father was in this country studying medicine. Soon afterwards, her parents were eager to return to the Dominican Republic. The news from the island was that the oppressive regime headed by Rafael Trujillo was changing for the better. The Alvarez family returned just months after Julia was born. They had not been back long before it was clear that Trujillo's promises of reform were empty. The government continued to rely on secret police, torture, and assassinations to cling to power.

The warmth and love she felt from her extended family mark Julia Alvarez's memories of her childhood in the Dominican Republic. Life there was a parade of sisters, grandparents, cousins, aunts, and uncles. Soon after her tenth birthday, however, Alvarez was pulled from this loving cocoon. Rumors had reached Trujillo of plots against his life. Because Dr. Alvarez was active in the Dominican underground, he was immediately suspected. The family escaped to the United States and settled in New York City.

United States As a young girl in the Dominican Republic, Alvarez had felt comparatively American. Once she was back in the United States, however, she was quickly made aware of her foreignness. Children in school called her names and teased her about her inadequate English. Alvarez found a refuge in reading and writing.

Writing and Teaching After graduating from high school, Alvarez studied at Middlebury College in Vermont and then enrolled in a creative writing program at Syracuse University. After earning her master's degree, she taught writing at various schools and colleges. Some of her poems appeared in small magazines and journals. She first won wide acclaim with *How the García Girls Lost Their Accents*, a series of fifteen interwoven stories that focus on four sisters from the Dominican Republic adjusting to life in the United States.

Alvarez based her next novel, *In the Time of the Butterflies* (1994), on the true story of the Mirabal sisters, who were murdered by Trujillo's agents in 1960 for opposing the regime. This book was a finalist for the National Book Critics' Award in fiction.

Recent Work In her next novel, *¡Yo!* (1997), Alvarez returned to the story of the four sisters in *How the García Girls Lost Their Accents*. This work's favorable reception strengthened Alvarez's reputation as an emerging voice in contemporary literature. This reputation has been further enhanced by the recent publication of another collection of poetry, *The Other Side/El Otro Lado* (1995), and a collection of essays, *Something to Declare* (1998). Alvarez's success has made it possible for her to concentrate solely on her writing. She lives in Middlebury, Vermont, with her husband Bill Eichner and is currently at work on a new novel.

◆ The Dominican Diaspora

The Dominican Republic shares (with Haiti) the large island of Hispaniola in the West Indies. According to some estimates, almost 15 percent of the Dominican population lives outside the Dominican Republic. This scattering of the Dominican people is referred to as the "Dominican Diaspora." Most of the emigrants settle in the United States. They come in search of work, which is hard to find in their native land, where the unemployment rate often reaches 30 percent.

Many Dominican exiles have settled within sight of the George Washington Bridge in a New York City neighborhood called Washington Heights. As with many other ethnic groups in United States history, new Dominican arrivals have been met by family members and friends who have come before them. These close associations help the new settlers in their transition from one country to another. They may have left home, but the island is never far from the thoughts of most "Dom-Yorks."

Although Alvarez and her family left the Dominican Republic for New York,

they are somewhat atypical of the Dominican Diaspora. The Alvarez family fled the country for political rather than economic reasons, and, although the family was not wealthy, they were members of the Dominican professional class. Unlike more recent Dominican immigrants, the Alvarez family settled in a section of New York where there were few other Dominicans. Despite these differences, Alvarez, as one of only a few published Dominican authors writing in English, has been able to reach a wide audience with stories that were at one time little known outside Dominican communities.

◆ Literary Works

Novels Alvarez is best known for her novels, which draw upon her own bicultural identity as a Dominican woman in the United States.

How the García Girls Lost Their Accents (1991)
In the Time of the Butterflies (1994)
¡Yo! (1997)

Poetry Alvarez's poetry uses concise images and compressed language to explore many of the same issues she probes in her fiction: family, identity, culture, and language.

Homecoming (1984)
The Other Side/El Otro Lado (1995)

Nonfiction In her collection of essays, Alvarez explores topics from opera to writing to gardening.

Something to Declare (1998)

TIMELINE

Alvarez's Life		World Events	
1950	Alvarez born in New York; family leaves the United States for the Dominican Republic	1950	Harry S. Truman is president of the United States; Rafael Trujillo celebrates his twentieth year as president of the Dominican Republic
1960	Alvarez family returns to the United States		
1964	Alvarez leaves home in New York for boarding school in Boston	1955	Flannery O'Connor, *A Good Man Is Hard to Find* (short stories)
1967	Graduates from secondary school	1960	United States breaks diplomatic relations with Dominican Republic; Mirabal sisters are killed by government death squads
1971	Receives B.A. degree from Middlebury College in Vermont		
1975	Receives M.F.A. degree from Syracuse University	1961	Trujillo assassinated; death of Ernest Hemingway
1975–78	Teaches writing in a grammar school, convent, prison, and home for the elderly in Kentucky, Delaware, and North Carolina	1962	Cuban missile crisis
		1963	President John F. Kennedy assassinated
1984	*Homecoming* (poetry) published	1965	President Lyndon B. Johnson sends troops to intervene in Dominican civil war
1985–88	Assistant Professor of English at Middlebury College		
1986	On trip to Dominican Republic, begins research on Mirabal sisters	1966	Joaquín Balaguer sworn in as president of the Dominican Republic
1989	Marries Bill Eichner		
1991	*How the Garcia Girls Lost Their Accents* (novel) published	1969	Apollo 11 moon landing
		1974	Watergate scandal forces resignation of President Richard Nixon
1992	Meets Dedé Mirabal, the surviving Mirabal sister	1976	Maxine Hong Kingston, *The Woman Warrior*; United States celebrates bicentennial
1994	*In the Time of the Butterflies* published		
1995	The *Other Side/El Otro Lado* (poetry) published	1978	President Jimmy Carter sends U.S. Navy to Dominican Republic
1997	*¡Yo!* (novel) published	1985	Sandra Cisneros, *The House on MangoStreet*
1998	*Something to Declare* (essays) published	1993	Esmeralda Santiago, *When I Was Puerto Rican*
		1994	Edwidge Danticat, *Breath, Eyes, Memory*
		1996	Leonel Fernández, who grew up in New York City, elected president of the Dominican Republic

Julia Alvarez

Snow

from How the García Girls Lost Their Accents

Yolanda

Our first year in New York we rented a small apartment with a Catholic school nearby, taught by the Sisters of Charity, hefty women in long black gowns and bonnets that made them look peculiar, like dolls in mourning. I liked them a lot, especially my grandmotherly fourth grade teacher, Sister Zoe. I had a lovely name, she said, and she had me teach the whole class how to pronounce it. *Yo-lan-da.* As the only immigrant in my class, I was put in a special seat in the first row by the window, apart from the other children so that Sister Zoe could tutor me without disturbing them. Slowly, she enunciated the new words I was to repeat: *laundromat, corn flakes, subway, snow.*

Soon I picked up enough English to understand holocaust was in the air. Sister Zoe explained to a wide-eyed classroom what was happening in Cuba. Russian missiles were being assembled, trained supposedly on New York City. President Kennedy, looking worried too, was on the television at home, explaining we might have to go to war against the Communists. At school, we had air-raid drills: an ominous bell would go off and we'd file into the hall, fall to the floor, cover our heads with our coats, and imagine our hair falling out, the bones in our arms going soft. At home, Mami and my sisters and I said a rosary for world peace. I heard new vocabulary: *nuclear bomb, radioactive fallout, bomb shelter.* Sister Zoe explained how it would happen. She drew a picture of a mushroom on the blackboard and dotted a flurry of chalkmarks for the dusty fallout that would kill us all.

The months grew cold, November, December. It was dark when I got up in the morning, frosty when I followed my breath to school. One morning as I sat at my desk daydreaming out the window, I saw dots in the air like the ones Sister Zoe had drawn— random at first, then lots and lots. I shrieked, "Bomb! Bomb!" Sister Zoe jerked around, her full black skirt ballooning as she hurried to my side. A few girls began to cry.

But then Sister Zoe's shocked look faded. "Why, Yolanda dear, that's snow!" She laughed. "Snow."

"Snow," I repeated. I looked out the window warily. All my life I had heard about the white crystals that fell out of American skies in the winter. From my desk I watched the fine powder dust the sidewalk and parked cars below. Each flake was different, Sister Zoe had said, like a person, irreplaceable and beautiful.

Julia Alvarez

Papi Working

The long day spent listening
to homesick hearts,
the tick tock of the clock—
the way Americans mark time,
5   long hours, long days.
Often they came only to hear him
say *nada*[1] in their mother tongue.
I found nothing wrong.
To dole out *jarabe*[2] for the children's coughs,
10   convince the *doña*[3] to stay off that leg.

In his white *saco*[4] Mami ironed out,
smoothing the tired wrinkles
till he was young again,
he spent his days, long days
15   tending to the ills of immigrants,
his own heart heavy with what was gone,
this new country like a pill
that slowly kills but keeps you
from worse deaths.
20   *What was to be done?*

They came to hear him say
nada in their mother tongue.

---

1. **nada** (nä´ *th*a): Nothing.
2. **jarabe** (hä rä´ bā): Syrup.
3. **doña** (dōn´ yä): Lady (title used before a woman's Christian name).
4. **saco** (sä´ kō):   Coat.

Storm Windows

She climbed toward the sky
when we did windows,
while I stood by, her helper,
doing the humdrum groundwork,
5   carrying her sloppy buckets
back and forth to the spigot,
hosing the glasses down
under her supervision
up there on a ladder
10   she had forbidden me.

I wanted to mount that ladder,
rung by rung, look down
into the gaping mouths of buckets,
the part in her greying hair.
15   I wanted to rise, polishing into each pane
another section of the sky.
Then give a kick, unbuckling
her hands clasped about my ankles,
and sail up, beyond her reach,
20   her house, her grounds, her mothering.

Julia Alvarez

Writing Matters

One of the questions that always comes up during question-and-answer periods is about the writing life. The more sophisticated, practiced questioners usually ask me, "Can you tell us something about your process as a writer?"

In part, this is the curiosity we all have about each other's "processes," to use the terminology of my experienced questioner. We need to tell, and we also want to know (don't we?) the secret heart of each other's life. Perhaps that is why we love good novels and poems— because we can enter, without shame or without encountering defensiveness or embarrassment, the intimate lives of other people.

But the other part of my questioner's curiosity about the writing life has to do with a sense we all have that if we can only get a hold of the secret ingredients of the writing process, we will become better writers. We will have an easier time of it if we only find that magic pencil or know at which hour to start and at which hour to quit and what to sip that might help us come up with the next word in a sentence.

I always tell my questioners the truth: Listen, there are no magic solutions to the hard work of writing. There is no place to put the writing desk that will draw more words out of you. I had a friend who claimed that an east-west alignment was the best one for writing. The writing would then flow and be more in tune with the positive energies. The north-south alignment would cause blocks as well as bad dreams if your bed was also thus aligned.

See, I tell my, questioners, isn't this silly?'

But even as I say so, I know I am talking out of both sides of my mouth. I admit that after getting my friend's tip, I lined up my writing desk (and my bed) in the east-west configuration. It wasn't that I thought my writing or my dream life would improve, but I am so impressionable that I was afraid that I'd be thinking and worrying about my alignment instead of my line breaks. And such fretting would affect my writing adversely. Even as recently as this very day, I walk into my study first thing in the morning, and I fill up my bowl of clear water and place it on my desk. And though no one told me to do this, I somehow I feel this is the right way to start a writing day.

Of course, that fresh bowl of water sits on my desk on good *and* bad writing days. I know these little ceremonies will not change the kind of day before me. My daily writing rituals are small ways in which I contain my dread and affirm my joy and celebrate the mystery and excitement of the calling to be a writer.

For me, the writing life doesn't just happen when I sit at the writing desk. It is a life lived with a centering principle, and mine is this: that I will pay close attention to this world I find myself in. "My heart keeps open house," was the way the poet Theodore Roethke put it in a poem. And rendering in language what one sees through the opened windows and doors of that house is a way of bearing witness to the mystery of what it is to be alive in this world.

This is all very high-minded and inspirational, my questioner puts in, but what about when we are alone at our writing desks, feeling wretchedly anxious, wondering if there is anything in us worth putting down?

Let me take you through the trials and tribulations of a typical writing day. It might help as you also set out onto that blank page, encounter one adventure or mishap after another, and wonder—do other writers go through this?

The answer is probably yes.

Not much has happened at six-twenty or so in the morning when I enter my writing room above the garage. I like it this way. The mind is free of household details, worries, commitments, voices, problems to solve.

My mood entering the room depends on what happened with my writing the day before. If the previous day was a good one, I look forward to the new writing day. If I was stuck or uninspired, I feel apprehensive. In short, I can't agree more with Hemingway's advice that a writer should always end his writing day knowing where he is headed next. It makes it easier to come back to work.

The first thing I do in my study every morning is read poetry (Jane Kenyon, George Herbert, Rita Dove, Robert Frost, Elizabeth Bishop, Rhina Espaillat, Jane Shore, Emily Dickinson ...). This is the first music I hear, the most essential. Interestingly, I like to follow the reading of poetry with some prose, as if, having been to the heights I need to come back down to earth.

I consider this early-morning reading a combination of pleasure-reading time when I read the works and authors I most love and finger-exercise reading time, when I am tuning my own voice to the music of the English language as played by its best writers.

I read my favorite writers to remind me of the quality of writing I am aiming for.

Now it's time to set out: Pencil poised, I read through the hard copy that I ran off at the end of yesterday's writing day. I used to write everything out by longhand, and when I was reasonably sure I had a final draft, I'd type it up on my old Selectric. But now, I usually write all my prose drafts right out on the computer, though I need to write out my poems in longhand, to make each word by hand.

This is also true of certain passages of prose and certainly true for times when I am stuck in a novel or story. Writing by hand relieves some of the pressure of seeing something tentative flashed before me on the screen with that authority that print gives to writing. "This is just for me," I tell myself, as I scratch out a draft in pencil. Often, these scribblings turn into little bridges, tendrils that take me safely to the other side of silence. When I'm finally on my way, I head back to the computer.

But even my hard copies look as if they've been written by hand. As I revise, I begin to hear the way I want a passage to sound. About the third or fourth draft, if I'm lucky, I start to see the shape of what I am writing, the way an essay will go, a character will react, a poem unfold.

Sometimes if Bill and I go on a long car trip, I'll read him what I am working on. This is a wonderful opportunity to "hear" what I've written. The process of reading my work to someone else does tear apart that beauteous coating of self-love in which my own creation comes enveloped. I start to hear what I've written as it would sound to somebody else.

When I'm done with proofing the hard copy of the story or chapter or poem, I take a little break. This is one of the pleasures of working at home. I can take these refreshing breathers from the intensity of the writing: go iron a shirt or clean out a drawer or wrap up my sister's birthday present.

After my break, I take a deep breath. What I now do is transcribe all my handwritten revisions on to my computer, before I launch out into the empty space of the next section of the story or essay or the chapter in a novel. This is probably the most intense time of the writing day. I am on my way, but I don't know exactly where it is I am going. But that's why I'm writing: to find out.

On the good days an excitement builds up as I push off into the language, and sentence seems to follow sentence. I catch myself smiling or laughing out loud or sometimes even weeping as I move through a scene or a stanza. Certainly writing seems to integrate parts of me that are usually at odds. As I write, I feel unaccountably whole: I disappear! That is the irony of this self-absorbed profession: The goal finally is to vanish. On bad days, on the other hand, I don't disappear. Instead, I'm stuck with the blank screen before me. I take more and more breaks. I wander out on the deck and look longingly south toward the little spire of the Congregational church and wish another life for myself. Oh, dear, what have I done with my life?

I have chosen it, that's what I've done. So I take several deep breaths and go back upstairs and sit myself down and work on the passage that will not come. As Flannery O'Connor attested: "Every morning between 9 and 12, I go to my room and sit before a piece of paper. Many times, I just sit for three hours with no ideas coming to me. But I know one thing: If an idea does come between 9 and 12, I am there ready for it." The amazing thing for me is that years later, reading the story or novel or poem, I can't tell the passages that were easy to write, the ones that came forth like 'greased lightning" from those other passages that made me want to give up writing and take up another life.

On occasion, when all else fails, I take the rest of the day "off." I finish reading the poet or novelist with whom I began the day or I complain to my journal or I look through a picture book of shoes one of my characters might wear. But all the while I am feeling profound self doubt—as if I were one of those cartoon characters who runs off a cliff, and suddenly looks down only to discover there's no ground beneath her feet!

At the end of the writing day (about two-thirty or three in the afternoon), I leave the room over the garage. I put on my running clothes, and I go for a run. In part, this exercise does make me feel better. But one of the best perks of running has been that it allows me to follow Hemingway's advice. I don't always know where I am headed in my writing at the end of the work day, but after I run, I usually have one or two good ideas. Running helps me work out glitches in my writing and gives me all kinds of unexpected insights.

☑ Check Your Comprehension

1. (a) In "Snow," what does Sister Zoe explain to the class about events in Cuba? (b) What does Yolanda mistake snow for?
2. How does Papi spend his "long days" in "Papi Working"?
3. Describe in your own words the situation represented in "Storm Windows."
4. According to Alvarez in "Writing Matters," what is one reason that we love good novels and poems?
5. (a) What is the first thing Alvarez does every morning in her writing room above the garage? (b) Why does she do this?
6. Why does Alvarez sometimes enjoy writing by hand, rather than drafting her manuscripts on the computer?
7. To what advice by the novelist Ernest Hemingway does Alvarez refer in her essay?

◆ Critical Thinking

INTERPRET

1. What does "Snow" suggest about Yolanda's adjustment to life in the United States? [Infer]

2. (a) In "Papi Working," what are many of the people who come to see Papi suffering from? (b) In your opinion, what is the central theme of the poem? [Interpret]
3. A symbol is an object, person, image, place, or event that stands for or represents something else. What do you think the ladder may symbolize in "Storm Windows"? [Interpret]
4. (a) Explain the play on words in the title of Alvarez's essay, "Writing Matters." (b) What is Alvarez's purpose in her essay? [Interpret]
5. What is your opinion of the way Alvarez spends her writing day? Do you think that any part of her routine would serve as a helpful model for you when you write? Explain your answer. [Evaluate]

COMPARE LITERARY WORKS

6. In reading "Papi Working" and "Storm Windows," what impression do you get of the speaker's mother and of her relationship with the speaker? Support your answer with references to the poems. [Connect]

◆ Literary Focus: Reflective Essay

Julia Alvarez's "Writing Matters" is an example of a **reflective essay**. In this type of essay, the writer explores the meaning of his or her personal experiences or observations. The writer also tells his or her feelings about events.

Reflective essays are usually informal and autobiographical. Good reflective essays such as "Writing Matters" leave readers with the feeling of having conducted a dialogue or listened in on a conversation with the writer. In "Writing Matters," Julia Alvarez's voice is clear and strong.

Main Features of a Reflective Essay

• Explores the meaning of a writer's personal experiences

• Reveals the writer's values and aspects of his or her personality

• Uses an informal, conversational style

1. Review the essay "Writing Matters." As you read, make a list of elements in the essay that contribute to its informal tone.

2. What link does Alvarez make between her personal experience and her insights into writing in general?

◆ Drawing Conclusions About Alvarez's Work

In "Writing Matters" and in other works, Julia Alvarez has stated some of her goals and aims as a writer. Following is a chart with quotations from Alvarez concerning her writing. On a separate piece of paper, copy this chart, and then fill in the blank boxes with quotations or passages from Alvarez's fiction or poetry that you feel illustrate her stated goals.

Then write a summary of your findings in which you evaluate whether Alvarez has been able to achieve her literary goals.

◆ Idea Bank

Writing

1. **Postcard** In "Snow," Yolanda recalls an event that happened to her as a child. In a postcard message, retell the story as Yolanda might have done soon after the event happened. Assume that Yolanda addresses her postcard to a friend living in the Dominican Republic.

2. **Compare and Contrast** In a brief essay, compare and contrast your own writing process to that of Alvarez, as she describes it in "Writing Matters." Use a chart such as the one below to organize your main ideas.

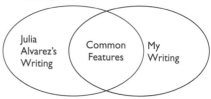

3. **Poem** Write a poem about what you would miss most if you had to move to a foreign country for a year or two. Before you begin writing, think about familiar things that you see, hear, feel, taste, and touch in your everyday life now. Consider how these sensory experiences would change if you lived in another country.

Speaking and Listening

4. **Poetry Reading** Practice reading "Papi Working" and "Storm Windows" aloud. If necessary, ask a Spanish-speaking classmate or teacher to help you with the meaning and pronunciation of the Spanish words. In your oral interpretation, focus on two of the following elements: pitch, volume, pace, rhythm, and emphasis. When you have polished your interpretation, present your reading to a small audience. **[Performing Arts Link]**

5. **Radio Broadcast** Take the part of a meteorologist and create a radio broadcast in which you give a scientific explanation of snow. Assume that your listeners, like Yolanda in Alvarez's "Snow," have never seen snow before. **[Science Link]**

Researching and Representing

6. **Multimedia Presentation** With a small group, explore the history, land-scape, economy, and culture of the Dominican Republic. Develop a multi-media presentation to report your findings. Incorporate photographs, musical recordings, video clips, and objects typical of the Dominican Republic in your report. **[Group Activity; Social Studies Link]**

◆ Further Reading, Listening, and Viewing

- "Julia Alvarez" in *Contemporary Literary Criticism 93* (1996). The article provides extensive biographical information and critical comments on the author's work

- Esmeralda Santiago: *When I Was Puerto Rican* (1993). Santiago's work explores many of the same themes touched upon by Alvarez

- *Merengue Mania!* (1999). Merengue has been described as the national music of the Dominican Republic

- *Americanos: Latino Life in the United States* (1999). This book accompanies the traveling Smithsonian exhibition on Latino life

On the Web:

http://www.phschool.com/atschool/literature
Go to the student edition of *The American Experience*. Proceed to Unit 6. Then, click Hot Links to find Web sites featuring Julia Alvarez.

$\mathcal{A}$my Tan In Depth

"I think I've been fascinated by that theme of separation of yourself into two different nations. It's almost a sense of yourself that's been left in another country."

—*Amy Tan*

AMY TAN did not begin to write fiction until she was in her thirties. Her first novel, *The Joy Luck Club,* was an immediate bestseller, praised by critics and translated into seventeen languages. Tan's next two novels, *The Kitchen God's Wife* and *The Hundred Secret Senses* were also bestsellers.

Tan combines stories of Chinese American family life with tales of life in China, focusing on mother-daughter relationships. The theme of Americanized daughters estranged from their immigrant mothers, their traditions and heritage, is central to her books. Like her characters, Tan did not appreciate her Chinese heritage. In an interview in *MacLean's* magazine, she said, "Somehow I'd been born into the wrong family, that I went down the wrong chute and ended up in a Chinese family."

Family Background Amy Tan's parents were born in China. Her father, John Tan, was an electrical engineer and a Baptist minister. Her mother, Daisy Tan, was born in Shanghai to a wealthy family. They met in China in the dangerous decade of the 1940's. Battles were fought on all fronts: World War II in the first half of the decade, and in the second half of the decade, the fight for control of China between the Japanese, the Chinese Nationalist government, and Communist rebels.

John Tan worked for the United States Information Service during World War II which made it relatively easy for him to leave China for the United States when the war ended. Daisy was not so fortunate; she was imprisoned. She escaped in 1949 on the last boat to leave Shanghai before the Communist takeover. Daisy and John Tan were married shortly after Daisy's arrival in the United States.

The Tan marriage produced three children: Peter, born in 1950; Amy, in 1952; and John, Jr., in 1954. The family moved several times, settling down in Santa Clara, California.

Two Deaths and a Secret Tragedy struck in 1967, when Tan's father and brother Peter both died of brain tumors within a year of each other. Daisy Tan then moved to Switzerland, where they settled in Montreaux.

It was after the death of her husband and son that Daisy revealed to Amy her heartbreaking secret. She had three daughters from her first marriage in China. Daisy Tan long before had given up hope of ever seeing her daughters again, since there was little communication between China and the United States. Amy Tan was stunned at the news that she had three half-sisters in China. She feared that her mother might have loved these three "perfect Chinese" sisters better than herself.

College and Marriage After Tan graduated from high school in Montreaux, she returned to the U.S. and attended Linfield College in Oregon. At first, she studied premed to please her mother. However, science held little interest for Tan, and she transferred to San Jose State University in California, where she changed her major to English and linguistics.

Tan graduated in 1973. A year later, she earned a master's degree and married Louis DeMattei.

First Jobs and First Fiction Tan's first job was as a language development consultant for disabled children. Later she directed a project for children who were developmentally disabled. Eventually, Tan left that work and inched closer to a writing career. With a partner she formed a company specializing in writing speeches for businessmen. Not liking the management side of the business, Tan struck out on her own and prospered as a freelance business writer. Dissatisfaction set in again though, and to stem her boredom, Tan began writing fiction. Her first short story, "Endgame," was published in 1986.

Daisy Tan's bout with a serious illness that same year may have provided the catalyst for Tan's evolution as a novelist. "If I die, what will you remember?" Daisy implored. Tan decided that if her mother recovered she would take her to China to see her long, lost daughters. The trip allowed Tan a new perspective on her mother, and she found inspiration to finish a book of stories she had given her agent before she left.

The book, *The Joy Luck Club,* was published in 1989, and Tan dedicated it to her mother. The inscription reads "You once asked me what I would remember. This, and much more."

Tan's next book, *The Kitchen God's Wife,* was published in 1991. This was followed by two children's books, *The Moon Lady* and *The Chinese Siamese Cat.* In 1995, she published *The Hundred Secret Senses.*

◆ Post-War China

In China during World War II, battles raged all around. The Chinese Nationalist government fought not only the Japanese, who had taken over much of the country, but also Chinese Communists. The Communists won support among the rural Chinese by seizing land from wealthy landlords and dividing it among the poor farmers. In the struggle, many thousands of landlords and educated Chinese were executed.

When World War II ended, full-scale civil war erupted in China. The Communists forced the Nationalists out of China and in 1949 established a new government, The People's Republic of China. Chinese immigrants who came to the United States had very little contact with relatives or friends who remained in China. Formal relations between the U.S. and China did not resume until President Richard Nixon's visit in 1972. After that Americans could visit China legally.

◆ Literary Works

Her Novels Tan's first novel, *The Joy Luck Club* (1989), weaves together the stories of four Chinese women immigrants and their four American daughters. Her two other novels also tell the stories of Chinese immigrants and their children.

The Kitchen God's Wife (1991)

The Hundred Secret Senses (1995)

Tan has also written two books for children.

The Moon Lady (1992)

The Chinese Siamese Cat (1994)

TIMELINE

Tan's Life		World Events	
1952	Amy Tan is born on February 19 in Oakland, California	1950	Korean War begins
1960	"What the Library Means to Me," published in (Santa Clara, CA) *The Press Democrat*	1952	Ernest Hemingway publishes *The Old Man and the Sea*
		1955	Dr. Jonas Salk announces the first successful polio vaccine
1967	Tan's sixteen-year-old brother dies of a brain tumor	1957	USSR launches Sputnik
1968	Tan's father dies of a brain tumor	1960	Harper Lee publishes *To Kill a Mockingbird*
1969	Graduates from high school in Switzerland	1962	Watson and Crick win the Nobel Prize for their work on DNA
1973	Receives B.A. from San Jose State University	1963	U.S. President John F. Kennedy is assassinated
1974	Receives M.A. from San Jose State University; marries Louis B. DeMattei, an attorney	1964	The Beatles' "I Want to Hold Your Hand" tops charts
1976–81	Works as language development consultant for disabled children	1966	The Cultural Revolution begins in China
1981–83	Forms a company that specializes in writing speeches for business-men	1972	President Richard Nixon visits China
1983	Becomes a freelance business-writer	1986	The space shuttle *Challenger* explodes
1986	First short story, "Endgame," is published	1989	Chinese troops crush a pro-democracy rally in Tiananmen Square
1987	Visits China with mother; meets half-sisters	1990	East and West Berlin are formally united
1989	*The Joy Luck Club* is published	1991	The World Wide Web appears on the Internet
1991	*The Kitchen God's Wife* is published	1992	Bill Clinton is elected president
1992	*The Moon Lady,* a children's book, is published	1997	China gains control of Hong Kong
1993	*The Joy Luck Club,* a movie, is issued	1999	Nearly 150 million people use the Internet each week
1994	*The Chinese Siamese Cat,* a children's book, is published		
1995	*The Hundred Secret Senses* is published		

Young Girl's Wish

from The Hundred Secret Senses

Chinese American Olivia and her husband, Simon, visit China with Kwan Li, Olivia's step-sister who spent her childhood in China before emigrating to the United States. The following excerpt occurs after the three arrive in China.

My first morning in China, I awake in a dark hotel room in Guilin and see a figure leaning over my bed, staring at me with the concentrated look of a killer. I'm about to scream, when I hear Kwan saying in Chinese, "Sleeping on your side—so *this* is the reason your posture is so bad. From now on, you must sleep on your back. Also do exercises."

She snaps on the light and proceeds to demonstrate, hands on hips, twisting at the waist like a sixties PE teacher. I wonder how long she's stood by my bed, waiting for me to waken so she can present her latest bit of unsolicited advice. Her bed is already made.

I look at my watch and say in a grumpy voice, "Kwan, it's only five in the morning."

"This is China. Everyone else is up. Only you're asleep."

"Not anymore."

We've been in China less than eight hours, and already she's taking control of my life. We're on her terrain, we have to go by her rules, speak her language. She's in Chinese heaven.

Snatching my blankets, she laughs. "Libby-ah, hurry and get up. I want to go see my village and surprise everyone. I want to watch Big Ma's mouth fall open and hear her words of surprise: 'Hey, I thought I chased you away. Why are you back?'"

Kwan pushes open the window. We're staying at the Guilin Sheraton, which faces the Li River. Outside it's still dark. I can hear the *trnnng! trnnng!* of what sounds like a noisy pachinko parlor. I go to the window and look down. Peddlers on tricycle carts are ringing their bells, greeting one another as they haul their baskets of grain, melons, and turnips to market. The boulevard is bristling with the shadows of bicycles and cars, workers and schoolchildren—the whole world chirping and honking, shouting and laughing, as though it were the middle of the day. On the handlebar of a bicycle dangle the gigantic heads of four pigs, roped through the nostrils, their white snouts curled in death grins.

"Look." Kwan points down the street to a set of stalls lit by low-watt bulbs. "We can buy breakfast there, cheap and good.

Better than paying nine dollars each for hotel food—and for what? Doughnut, orange juice, bacon, who wants it?"

I recall the admonition in our guidebooks to steer clear of food sold by street vendors. "Nine dollars, that's not much," I reason.

"Wah! You can't think this way anymore. Now you're in China. Nine dollars is lots of money here, one week's salary."

"Yeah, but cheap food might come with food poisoning."

Kwan gestures to the street. "You look. All those people there, do they have food poisoning? If you want to take pictures of Chinese food, you have to taste real Chinese food. The flavors soak into your tongue, go into your stomach. The stomach is where your true feelings are. And if you take photos, these true feelings from your stomach can come out, so that everyone can taste the food just by looking at your pictures."

Kwan is right. Who am I to begrudge carrying home a few parasites? I slip some warm clothes on and go into the hallway to knock on Simon's door. He answers immediately, fully dressed. "I couldn't sleep," he admits.

In five minutes, the three of us are on the sidewalk. We pass dozens of food stalls, some equipped with portable propane burners, others with makeshift cooking grills. In front of the stalls, customers squat in semicircles, dining on noodles and dumplings. My body is jittery with exhaustion and excitement. Kwan chooses a vendor who is slapping what look like floury pancakes onto the sides of a blazing- hot oil drum. "Give me three," she says in Chinese. The vendor pries the cooked pan- cakes off with his blackened bare fingers, and Simon and I yelp as we toss the hot pancakes up and down like circus jugglers.

"How much?" Kwan opens her change purse.

"Six yuan," the pancake vendor tells her.

I calculate the cost is a little more than a dollar, dirt cheap. By Kwan's estimation, this is tantamount to extortion. "Wah!" She points to another customer. "You charged him only fifty fen a pancake."

"Of course! He's a local worker. You three are tourists."

"What are you saying! I'm also local."

"You? " The vendor snorts and gives her a cynical once-over. "From where, then?"

"Changmian."

His eyebrows rise in suspicion. "Really, now! Who do you know in Changmian?"

Kwan rattles off some names.

The vendor slaps his thigh. "Wu Ze-min? You know Wu Ze-min?"

"Of course. As children, we lived across the lane from each

other. How is he? I haven't seen him in over thirty years."

"His daughter married my son."

"Nonsense!"

The man laughs. "It's true. Two years ago. My wife and mother opposed the match—just because the girl was from Changmian. But they have old countryside ideas, they still believe Changmian is cursed. Not me, I'm not superstitious, not anymore. And now a baby's been born, last spring, a girl, but I don't mind."

"Hard to believe Wu Ze-min's a grandfather. How is he?"

"Lost his wife, this was maybe twenty years ago, when they were sent to the cowsheds for counterrevolutionary thinking. They smashed his hands, but not his mind. Later he married another woman, Yang Ling-fang."

"That's not possible! She was the little sister of an old school-mate of mine. I can't believe it! I still see her in my mind as a tender young girl."

"Not so tender anymore. She's got *jiaoban* skin, tough as leather, been through plenty of hardships, let me tell you."

Kwan and the vendor continue to gossip while Simon and I eat our pancakes, which are steaming in the morning chill. They taste like a cross between focaccia and a green-onion omelet. At the end of our meal, Kwan and the vendor act like old friends, she promising to send greetings to family and comrades, he advising her on how to hire a driver at a good price.

"All right, older brother," Kwan says, "how much do I owe you?"

"Six yuan."

"Wah! Still six yuan? Too much, too much. I'll give you two, no more than that."

"Make it three, then."

Kwan grunts, settles up, and we leave. When we're half a block away, I whisper to Simon, "That man said Changmian is cursed."

Kwan overhears me. "Tst! That's just a story, a thousand years old. Only stupid people still think Changmian is a bad-luck place to live."

I translate for Simon, then ask, "What kind of bad luck?"

"You don't want to know."

I am about to insist she tell me, when Simon points to my first photo opportunity—an open-air market overflowing with wicker baskets of thick-skinned pomelos,[1] dried beans, cassia tea, chilies. I pull out my Nikon and am soon busy shooting, while Simon jots down notes.

"Plumes of acrid breakfast smoke mingled with the morning

---

1. **pomelo:** A thick-skinned grapefruit.

mist," he says aloud. "Hey, Oilvia, can you do a shot from this direction? Get the turtles, the turtles would be great."

I inhale deeply and imagine that I'm filling my lungs with the very air that inspired my ancestors, whoever they might have been. Because we arrived late the night before, we haven't yet seen the Guilin landscape, its fabled karst peaks, its magical limestone caves, and all the other sites listed in our guidebook as the reasons this is known in China as "the most beautiful place on earth." I have discounted much of the hype and am prepared to focus my lens on the more prosaic and monochromatic aspects of communist life.

No matter which way we go, the streets are chock-full of brightly dressed locals and bloated Westerners in jogging suits, as many people as one might see in San Francisco after a 49ers Super Bowl victory. And all around us is the hubbub of a free-market economy. There they are, in abundance: the barterers of knickknacks; the hawkers of lucky lottery tickets, stock market coupons, T-shirts, watches, and purses with bootlegged designer logos. And there are the requisite souvenirs for tourists —Mao buttons, the Eighteen Lohan carved on a walnut, plastic Buddhas in both Tibetan-thin and roly-poly models. It's as though China has traded its culture and traditions for the worst attributes of capitalism: rip-offs, disposable goods, and the mass-market frenzy to buy what everyone in the world has and doesn't need.

Simon sidles up to me. "It's fascinating and depressing at the same time." And then he adds, "But I'm really glad to be here." I wonder if he's also referring to being with me.

Looking up toward cloud level, we can still see the amazing peaks, which resemble prehistoric shark's teeth, the clichéd subject of every Chinese calendar and scroll painting. But tucked in the gums of these ancient stone formations is the blight of high-rises, their stucco exteriors grimy with industrial pollution, their signboards splashed with garish red and gilt characters. Between these are lower buildings from an earlier era, all of them painted a proletarian toothpaste-green. And here and there is the rubble of prewar houses and impromptu garbage dumps. The whole scene gives Guilin the look and stench of a pretty face marred by tawdry lipstick, gapped teeth, and an advanced case of periodontal disease.

"Boy, oh boy," whispers Simon. "If Guilin is China's most beautiful city, I can't wait to see what the cursed village of Changmian looks like."

We catch up with Kwan. "Everything is entirely different, no longer the same." Her voice seems tinged with nostalgia. She must be sad to see how horribly Guilin has changed over the past thirty years. But then Kwan says in a proud and marveling voice: "So much progress, everything is so much better."

A couple of blocks farther on, we come upon a part of town that screams with more photo opportunities: the bird market. Hanging from tree limbs are hundreds of decorative cages containing singing finches, and exotic birds with gorgeous plumage, punk crests, and fanlike tails. On the ground are cages of huge birds, perhaps eagles or hawks, magnificent, with menacing talons and beaks. There are also the ordinary fowl, chickens and ducks, destined for the stew pot. A picture of them, set against a background of beautiful and better-fated birds, might make a nice visual for the magazine article.

I've shot only half another roll at the bird market, when I see a man hissing at me. "Sssss!" He sternly motions me to come over. What is he, the secret police? Is it illegal to take pictures here? If he threatens to take my camera away, how much should I offer as a bribe?

The man solemnly reaches underneath a table and brings out a cage. "You like," he says in English. Facing me is a snowy-white owl with milk-chocolate highlights. It looks like a fat Siamese cat with wings. The owl blinks its golden eyes and I fall in love.

"Hey, Simon, Kwan, come here. Look at this."

"One hundred dollar, U.S.," the man says. "Very cheap."

Simon shakes his head and says in a weird combination of pantomime and broken English: "Take bird on plane, not possible, customs official will say stop, not allowed, must pay big fine—"

"How much?" the man asks brusquely. "You say. I give you morning price, best price."

"There's no use bargaining." Kwan tells the man in Chinese. "We're tourists, we can't bring birds back to the United States, no matter how cheap."

"Aaah, who's talking about bringing it back?" the man replies in rapid Chinese. "Buy it today, then take it to that restaurant across the street, over there. For a small price, they can cook it tonight for your dinner."

"Omigod!" I turn to Simon. "He's selling this owl as food!"

"That's disgusting. Tell him he's a goon."

"You tell him!"

"I can't speak Chinese."

The man must think I am urging my husband to buy me an owl for dinner. He zeroes in on me for a closing sales pitch. "You're very lucky I even have *one*. The cat-eagle is rare, very rare," he brags. "Took me three weeks to catch it."

"I don't believe this," I tell Simon. "I'm going to be sick."

Then I hear Kwan saying. "A cat-eagle is not that rare, just hard to catch. Besides, I hear the flavor is ordinary."

"To be honest," says the man, "It's not as pungent as say, a pangolin. But you eat a cat-eagle to give you strength and ambition, not to be fussy over taste. Also, it's good for improving your eyesight. One of my customers was nearly blind. After he ate a cat-eagle, he could see his wife for the first time in nearly twenty years."

Kwan laughs heartily. "Yes, yes, I've heard this about cat-eagles. It's a good story." She pulls out her change purse and holds up a hundred-yuan note.

"Kwan, what are you doing?" I cry. "We are *not* going to eat this owl!"

The man waves away the hundred yuan. "Only American money," he says firmly. "One hundred *American* dollars."

Kwan pulls out an American ten-dollar bill.

"Kwan!" I shout.

The man shakes his head, refusing the ten. Kwan shrugs, then starts to walk away. The man shouts to her to give him fifty, then. She comes back and holds out a ten and a five, and says, "That's my last offer."

"This is insane!" Simon mutters.

The man sighs, then relinquishes the cage with the sad-eyed owl, complaining the whole time: "What a shame, so little money for so much work. Look at my hands, three weeks of climbing and cutting down bushes to catch this bird."

As we walk away, I grab Kwan's free arm and say heatedly: "There's no way I'm going to let you eat this owl. I don't care if we are in China."

"Shh! Shh! You'll scare him." Kwan pulls the cage out of my reach. She gives me a maddening smile, then walks over to a concrete wall overlooking the river and sets the cage on top. She meows to the owl. "Oh, little friend, you want to go to Changmian? You want to climb with me to the top of the mountain, let my little sister watch you fly away?" The owl twists his head and blinks.

I almost cry with joy and guilt. Why do I think such bad things about Kwan? I sheepishly tell Simon about my mistake and Kwan's generosity. Kwan brushes off my attempt to apologize.

"I'm going back to the bird market," says Simon, "to take some notes on the more exotic ones they're selling for food. Want to come?"

I shake my head, content to admire the owl Kwan has saved.

"I'll be back in ten or fifteen minutes."

Simon strides off, and I notice how American his swagger looks, especially here on foreign soil. He walks in his own rhythm; he doesn't conform to the crowd.

"See that?" I hear Kwan say. "Over there." She's pointing to a cone-shaped peak off in the distance. "Just outside my village stands a sharp-headed mountain, taller than that one even. We call it Young Girl's Wish, after a slave girl who ran away to the top of it, then flew off with a phoenix who was her lover. Later, she turned into a phoenix, and together, she and her lover went to live in an immortal white pine forest."

Kwan looks at me. "It's a story, just superstition."

I'm amused that she thinks she has to explain.

Kwan continues: "Yet all the girls in our village believed in that tale, not because they were stupid but because they wanted to hope for a better life. We thought that if we climbed to the top and made a wish, it might come true. So we raised little hatchlings and put them in cages we had woven ourselves. When the birds were ready to fly, we climbed to the top of Young Girl's Wish and let them go. The birds would then fly to where the phoenixes lived and tell them our wishes."

Kwan sniffs. "Big Ma told me the peak was named Young Girl's Wish because a crazy girl climbed to the top. But when she tried to fly, she fell all the way down and lodged herself so firmly into the earth she became a boulder. Big Ma said that's why you can see so many boulders at the bottom of that peak—they're all the stupid girls who followed her kind of crazy thinking, wishing for hopeless things."

I laugh. Kwan stares at me fiercely, as if I were Big Ma. "You can't stop young girls from wishing. No! Everyone must dream. We dream to give ourselves hope. To stop dreaming—well, that's like saying you can never change your fate. Isn't that true?"

"I suppose."

"So now you guess what I wished for."

"I don't know. What?"

"Come on, you guess."

"A handsome husband."

"No."

"A car."

She shakes her head.

"A jackpot."

Kwan laughs and slaps my arm. "You guessed wrong! Okay, I'll tell you." She looks toward the mountain peaks. "Before I left for America, I raised three birds, not just one, so I could make three wishes at the top of the peak. I told myself, if these three wishes come true, my life is complete, I can die happy. My first wish: to have a sister I could love with all my heart, only that, and I would ask for nothing more from her. My second wish: to return to China with my sister. My third wish"—Kwan's voice now quavers—"for Big Ma to see this and say she was sorry she sent me away."

This is the first time Kwan's ever shown me how deeply she can resent someone who's treated her wrong. "I opened the cage," she continues, "and let my three birds go free." She flings out her hand in demonstration. "But one of them beat its wings uselessly, drifting in half-circles, before it fell like a stone all the way to the bottom. Now you see, two of my wishes have already happened: I have you, and together we are in China. Last night I realized my third wish would never come true. Big Ma will never tell me she is sorry."

She holds up the cage with the owl. "But now I have a beautiful cat-eagle that can carry with him my new wish. When he flies away, all my old sadnesses will go with him. Then both of us will be free."

Simon comes bounding back. "Olivia, you won't believe the things people here consider food."

We head to the hotel, in search of a car that will take one local, two tourists, and a cat-eagle to Changmian village.

☑ Check Your Comprehension

1. Why does Kwan insist they eat real Chinese food?

2. What is the purpose of Kwan's conversation with the pancake vendor?

3. (a) How do Olivia and Simon react to what they see of Guilin? (b) How does Kwan respond?

4. What are some of the superstitious beliefs and stories in the chapter? How are they used?

5. Why do you think Olivia is convinced that Kwan intends to dine on the cat-eagle?

6. What three wishes did Kwan make on the mountain peak before leaving China?

◆ Critical Thinking

INTERPRET

1. Why does Olivia say that Kwan is in "Chinese heaven"? **[Analyze]**

2. Tan paints a vivid picture of Guilin. How does this Chinese city compare to a contemporary American city? To a frontier town? **[Compare and Contrast]**

3. Kwan says that she was granted the wish of a sister to love with all her heart. Does Olivia return her sister's wholehearted love? Give evidence to support your answer. **[Infer]**

4. In the beginning of the chapter, Kwan is eager to return to her village and see Big Ma. By the end of the chapter, Kwan's mood has changed. Explain. **[Interpret]**

Joan Chatfield-Taylor

Interview with Amy Tan

Dressed in narrow black pants and a bright red sweater, Tan took time out from working on her second novel one recent morning to talk to Cosmopolitan Magazine *about her writing, and growing up Chinese in America.*

Joan Chatfield-Taylor: Is the Chinese-American experience different from the usual generation gap between mothers and daughters?

Amy Tan: There's a tendency to confuse the mother-daughter relationship with the cultural context. When I was growing up, I blamed everything on the fact that my mother was Chinese while I thought of myself as totally American.

Joan Chatfield-Taylor: Your parents wanted you to be a neurosurgeon by profession, a concert pianist by hobby. When you changed colleges to follow your Italian–American boyfriend and switched from premed to English, your mother didn't speak to you for six months. Wasn't this a pretty extreme response?

Amy Tan: Immigrant parents come to America with the idea that they're going to lose ground, economically and socially, but that their children will eventually benefit from what they've done. My mother felt that in spite of all the opportunities I was given, I'd picked the bottom of the pile professionally. Chinese parents express their love by guiding their children in the right direction, and I'd ignored my parents' wisdom.

Joan Chatfield-Taylor: The boyfriend you followed, Louis DeMattei, now a tax attorney, became your husband fifteen years ago. What's special about an Italian-Chinese marriage?

Amy Tan: We have a lot of humorous arguments about whether ravioli is a version of the Chinese dumpling or the reverse. And we always notice that in London, New York, and San Francisco, Chinatown and Little Italy are right next to each other. Sometimes people ask Lou if I've become more American, but he says he's become more Chinese. His caring feelings for my mother are genuine. He was the first to suggest we buy her a place to live.

Joan Chatfield-Taylor: Your stories of life in China seem incredibly exotic. Are they true?

Amy Tan: Only fragments are true. I took images from my mother's stories and painted a bigger picture. My mother has a natural narrative voice. She can talk for three hours straight. When she comes over, I videotape her and just sit and listen.

Joan Chatfield-Taylor: In 1987, she took you to China to meet your half sisters. How did that trip affect you and the book?

Amy Tan: First of all, I didn't take notes there, because I wanted to experience China as a person meeting her sisters for the first time, not as a writer. There was an instant feeling of connectedness, a sense that China was my motherland, America my fatherland. With my sisters, there was instant intimacy—which included instant criticism. They pointed out that I looked tired, for instance.

There was also immediate sibling rivalry. My sisters and I began arguing about who looked most like my mother. We realized that we had inherited certain gestures, facial expressions, our sense of humor, what makes us angry, from my mother. I felt so much closer to my mother.

Joan Chatfield-Taylor: What was it like to watch the recent events in China on television?

Amy Tan: The first thing I would like to emphasize—because these events are so sensitive—is that my feelings are strictly personal. My relatives represent all sides of the situation. My uncle is a high Communist official, and my sister is a member of the Communist party, which is a very small elite in China. I also have relatives who are students and professors. The media was so one-dimensional, the evil villains versus the noble student heroes. But this wasn't a football game, it was my family!

Joan Chatfield-Taylor: Are you worried about your relatives?

Amy Tan: Well, I think they're safe. I feel more of a sadness, because I'm not sure I can be as open. People have pointed out to me that I'm not an ordinary person now, and my uncle is not an ordinary person, so I'm very careful when I write to my relatives.

Joan Chatfield-Taylor: Has success changed your life?

Amy Tan: I wish I could say it was all wonderful. Fame? It feels as if there's another person who has your name. There's a lot more pressure. If I agreed to do everything I'm asked, I would never have time to write another word. If I were an actress, I would love it, but the loss of privacy as a writer is overwhelming.

On the other hand, I wouldn't have been able to have dinner with people like Isabel Allende before. It's every writer's dream to be with the authors you admire. To be considered a peer is still incredible to me. I really haven't adjusted to it yet. But my social life is not hanging out in cafés with other authors. Lou and I still have the same close friends we've always had.

Joan Chatfield-Taylor: What are your work habits?

Amy Tan: I used to write nonstop from 9:00 A.M. to 7:00 P.M., with a break for lunch. On Tuesdays, I went to my writers' group and read what I had written. It was very routine, but now my life is a bit scattered. I'm going to have to disconnect my phone and lock myself away.

Joan Chatfield-Taylor: Do you have advice to offer aspiring novelists?

Amy Tan: You have to develop a discipline, and you have to learn that you can't always wait for inspiration. Also, I think young writers try to imitate the people they admire, and that's dangerous. No matter how well you imitate Tama Janowitz or Jay McInerney, it doesn't work. You have to find your own voice.

Joan Chatfield-Taylor: The voice you chose is a very simple and straightforward one.

Amy Tan: I wanted to have a very accessible voice, because I was writing these stories for my mother. She's a very intelligent woman, but I wanted a kind of English she wouldn't have to struggle with.

Joan Chatfield-Taylor: Did you ever think you would be able to make your living from fiction?

Amy Tan: I dreamed of writing fiction, but my dream was a kind of retirement dream, an old lady dividing her time between gardening and writing.

Joan Chatfield-Taylor: How does your mother feel about your success?

Amy Tan: The day the book was number four on *The New York Times* Best-Seller list, I showed the list to my mother. She looked at it, laid her finger across the line, and asked, "Who's number three? And two? And one?" She's very proud, but none of this impresses her too much, and she doesn't think that I should be impressed either. But she was also saying, "I think you should be number one."

☑ Check Your Comprehension

1. According to Amy Tan, how do Chinese parents express their love for their children?
2. When Tan went to China, did she find it a strange, exotic place, or did it feel familiar?
3. Tan's reaction to political and social turmoil in China is complicated. Explain why.
4. What kind of work habits does Tan recommend for young writers?

◆ Critical Thinking

Interpret

1. Amy Tan says that she thought of herself as completely American while growing up. In what ways do you think her attitude changed later? **[Infer]**
2. Daisy Tan had hoped that her daughter Amy would choose a career other than writing. Why? **[Analyze]**

COMPARE LITERARY WORKS

3. Amy Tan says that she aims to write in an accessible voice. Do you think she succeeded in "Young Girl's Wish"? Cite a prose work by another author to illustrate your answer.

Amy Tan

Comparing and Connecting the Author's Works

◆ Literary Focus: Point of View

"Young Girl's Wish" is told from the *first-person point of view*. That means that a character in the story, in this case Olivia, tells what is happening, or *narrates* the story. Olivia is the "I" or first-person narrator of the story. She is able to relate and comment on only what she knows or thinks she knows. Sometimes Olivia misinterprets what she sees.

By using the first-person voice, Tan is able to portray Olivia fully, relating her thoughts and feelings. Another common point of view is the *third person*. In the third person, a narrator outside the story tells what happens. In one form of the third-person point of view, an all-knowing third-person narrator describes the thoughts and feelings of all the characters.

Tan has said,

"My literature is not in the third person as traditional Chinese literature is; it's in the first person. That's very American."

1. Turn to the first page of "Young Girl's Wish." Find the discussion between Olivia and Kwan about the price of breakfast in the hotel. Explain what Kwan means when she tells Olivia "You can't think this way anymore. Now you're in China."

2. At the end of the selection, Olivia misinterprets Kwan's intentions for the owl. Find at least two other instances in which Olivia underestimates Kwan.

3. Rewrite the first or last paragraph of "Young Girl's Wish" from the third-person point of view with an all-knowing narrator.

◆ Drawing Conclusions about Tan's Work

A critic has said that Amy Tan's novels describe the "sense of living in two worlds—their values, language systems, and histories a universe apart." Find examples of the different ways Olivia and Kwan respond to their experiences in Guilin. The chart on this page lists three experiences. Copy the chart and compare Olivia's reactions to those of her half-sister.

	Olivia	Kwan
price of breakfast		
ugly modern buildings		
owl for sale		

◆ Idea Bank

Writing

1. **Interview** Write at least three questions you would ask Amy Tan if you were to interview her for your school's newspaper.

2. **Descriptive Writing** Reread Tan's description of the open-air market. Look for words that appeal to each of the five senses. Write a description of a trip to a grocery store using similarly vivid words.

3. **Critical Essay** Tan has said, "Within stories you always get a sense, in a direct or indirect way, of the society that shaped the stories." Decide which society, Chinese or American, most shaped "Young Girl's Wish." Explain your answer in a brief essay.

Speaking and Listening

4. **Expressive Reading** Practice reading Amy Tan's advice for aspiring novelists until you can read it smoothly. Find a paragraph from "Young Girl's Wish" that you think exemplifies Tan's voice. Practice reading it, as well. Make a tape recording of your reading of both quotations.
   [Performing Arts Link]

5. **Interviewing** Using a tape recorder, interview another student about his or her plans for the future. Follow up each of your partner's responses with questions that elicit more information. Transcribe and edit the interview. **[Career Link]**

Researching and Representing

6. **Sketch or Paint the Mountains of Guilin** Guilin is a real city in China, while Changmian village is fictional. The mountains and rivers of Guilin have inspired Chinese artists for many centuries. Find pictures of Guilin in travel guides or illustrated books about China. Sketch or paint your own picture of the mountains and rivers. **[Art Link]**

◆ Further Reading, Listening, and Viewing

- Mickey Pearlman and Katherine Usher Henderson: *A Voice of One's Own* (1990). In-depth interviews with contemporary women writers, including Amy Tan

- *David Cohen: A Day in the Life of China* (1989). China as seen by ninety of the world's best photographers

- E. D. Huntley: *Amy Tan* (1996). Critical study of three Tan novels

- Amy Tan: *The Moon Lady* (1992). Story for children originating in her novel *The Joy Luck Club*

On the Web:

http://www.phschool.com/atschool/literature
Go to the student edition of *The American Experience*. Click on Unit 6. Then click Hot Links to the find the Web sites featuring Amy Tan.

Henry Holt & Company
From "The Tuft of Flowers," "The Runaway," "The Death of the Hired Man," "For Once, Then, Something," "The Sound of Trees," "A Brook in the City," "Fragmentary Blue," "Misgiving, " "Nothing Gold Can Stay," "Two Tramps in Mud Time," "Take Something Like a Star" from *The Poetry of Robert Frost*, edited by Edward Connery Lathem. Copyright 1923, 1936, 1944, 1951, © 1958, 1962 by Robert Frost. © 1964, 1967, 1977 by Lesley Frost Ballantine. Copyright 116, 1923, 1930, 1934, 1949, © 1969 by Henry Holt and Company, LLC. Reprinted by permission of Henry Holt and Company, LLC.

Alfred A. Knopf, Inc.
"Laughers," "Juke Box Love Song," "Pictures to the Wall," "Tell Me," "Luck," "Boogie: 1 a.m.," "Montage of a Dream Deferred," "Good Morning," "Dream Boogie," "Miss Blues'es Child" and "Give Us Our Peace" from *Collected Poems* by Langston Hughes. Copyright © 1994 by the Estate of Langston Hughes. Reprinted by permission of Alfred A. Knopf, Inc.

Charles Neider
"An Encounter with an Interviewer" from *The Complete Humorous Sketches and Tales of Mark Twain,* edited and with an introduction by Charles Neider. Copyright © 1961, 1985 by Charles Neider. Reprinted by permission of Charles Neider.

Paris Review
Excerpts from *Paris Review* Interview with Richard Poirier from *Writers at Work: The Paris Review Interviews, Second Series* (New York: The Viking Press, 1963), edited by George Plimpton, 11–34.

G. P. Putnam's Sons
"Young Girl's Wish" from *The Hundred Secret Senses* by Amy Tan. Copyright © 1995 by Amy Tan.

University of Nebraska Press
"The Sentimentality of William Tavener" reprinted from *Willa Cather's Collected Short Fiction 1892–1912*, edited by Virginia Faulkner by permission of the University of Nebraska Press. Copyright © 1965, 1970 by the University of Nebraska Press. Copyright © renewed 1993, 1998 by the University of Nebraska Press.

University of North Carolina Press
"To The Right Honourable William, Earl of Dartmouth, His Majesty's Principal Secretary Of State For North America, &C.," "On Imagination," and "To S. M., A Young *African* Painter, On Seeing His Works" from *The Poems of Phillis Wheatley*, edited and with an introduction by Julian D. Mason, Jr. Copyright © 1966 by the University of North Carolina Press, renewed 1989. Used by permission of the publisher.

University of Tennessee Press
Excerpts from *The Autobiography* by Benjamin Franklin as seen here from Benjamin Franklin: Writings. Reprinted by permission.

Yale University Press
"Prepatory Meditations: The Prologue," "God's Determinations: The Preface," and "Upon A Spider Catching A Fly" from *The Poems of Edward Taylor,* edited by Donald E. Stanford. Copyright © 1960 by Yale University Press, Inc. Reprinted by permission of Yale University Press.

Note: Every effort has been made to locate the copyright owner of material reprinted in this book. Omissions brought to our attention will be corrected in subsequent editions.

Photo Credits

• • • •